C000163896

The US Constitution: After 2

EUROPEAN CONTRIBUTIONS TO AMERICAN STUDIES

This series is published for the Netherlands American Studies Association - N.A.S.A., and the European Association for American Studies - E.A.A.S.

General Editor
Rob Kroes, Amerika Instituut, Jodenbreestraat 9
1011 NG Amsterdam, The Netherlands

* These volumes have been produced for the European Association
of American Studies (E.A.A.S.)

Copies can be ordered from the publisher
Free University Press, De Boelelaan 1105, 1081 HV Amsterdam, The Netherlands

The US Constitution: After 200 Years

edited by
Rob Kroes
Eduard van de Bilt

with contributions from
Tony Badger
William Boelhower
Allen F. Davis
Albert E. Kersten
Ralph Ketcham
Richard King
Rob Kroes
Janet S. Lindgren
Jack Pole
Eduard Van de Bilt
Bart Van Poelgeest
Garry Wills

Free University Press
Amsterdam 1988

CIP-GEGEVENS KONINKLIJKE BIBLIOTHEEK, DEN HAAG

US

The US Constitution: after 200 years / ed. by Rob Kroes, Eduard van de Bilt ; with contributions from Tony Badger ... [et al.]. - Amsterdam : Free University Press. - (European Contributions to American Studies ; 15)
Uitg. ter gelegenheid van de viering van de 200e verjaardag van de Grondwet van Amerika.
ISBN 90-6256-712-6 geb.
ISBN 90-6256-711-8 pbk.
SISO am.n.-vs 393.9 UDC 342.4 (73) "1787/1987" NUGI 654
Trefw.: grondwet ; Verenigde Staten van Amerika ; geschiedenis ; 1787-1987.

Free University Press is an imprint of:
VU Boekhandel/Uitgeverij b.v.
De Boelelaan 1105
1081 HV Amsterdam
The Netherlands

Lay-out: Ansy Jensen
Cover design: C. Koevoets

isbn 90-6256-711-8 ppb
isbn 90-6256-712-6 cloth

nugi 654

© Amerika Instituut, Amsterdam, 1988
All rights reserved. No part of this publication may be reproduced, stored in a retrieval system, or transmitted in any form or by any means, mechanically, by photocopying, recording, or otherwise, without the written permission of the author.

CONTENTS

INTRODUCTION:
THE AMERICAN CONSTITUTION AFTER 200 YEARS

If the Founding Fathers can be considered wise, it is because they acknowledged that even their own wisdom was limited. Although they never intended their proposed Constitution to become a plaything of political whimsy, they allowed the American citizens the opportunity to change or amend their precious document. By doing so, the Founding Fathers not only involved Americans in the debate about the laws of the land to a degree they could not have achieved otherwise but also inaugurated the process of amending their constitutional propositions, that is to say the whole process of adapting and reinterpreting the Constitution according to the circumstances of time. They also stimulated more than they could have done otherwise the creation of Constitutional history.

However hard many of the Fathers narrow-mindedly defended their economic interests - and they did so aggressively, as the notes on the debates in the Constitutional Convention of 1787 show - they also wished to discuss and be discussed, and exhibited an open-mindedness that, in more than one way, is still with us today. The heritage of 1787 consists not merely of a political system that defines the roles and prerogatives of balanced and balancing powers such as Congress, the Presidency, and the Supreme Court, or State and Federal authorities, but also of an awareness of the limitations of others and, more importantly, of oneself. Historians may try to depict the people behind the American Constitution as conservatives who tried to domesticate and limit progressive forces represented by the Declaration of Independence or those political powers urging for democratic reforms. But they can do so only at the cost of suppressing several of the Founding Fathers' ideas that remain important for us even today. Although the Fathers intended to impose structure and authority upon American society and took it upon themselves, as true parents, to rule in their children's name, they also offered a certain amount of independence and responsibility to their offspring.

To focus on the limitations as well as on the greatness of the people who created the American Constitution is the task the Founding Fathers themselves bequeathed to their progeny. As the most sophisticated politicians among them understood well, conflict and consensus, conservative and progressive tendencies, freedom and constraint, are part of every human endeavour - of Constitution building as well as the writing of history. In order to do justice to the American Constitution, therefore, historians have to deal with all of these aspects. That the history of the Constitution, as recent historical studies suggest, is characterised by quarrels over its interpretation and attempts radically to alter its meaning, can come as no surprise: many of the Founding Fathers intended the Constitution to be not a paper barrier against change or an end to political discussion but a living document around which a lively debate had to ensue in order to keep it alive.

A living document, then, alive and kicking after two hundred years. It offers the observer, American and non-American alike, the opportunity to look at it at various points in time, to trace its changing features, and its changing reach. But more than that, not only can we range across time, observing constitutional thought and action in the United States, we can also range across space, tracing the constitution's impact elsewhere as a source of inspiration, or comparing it to the constitutional experience and tradition of different nations at different places.

As the reader will see, such considerations have inspired the order of presentations in this volume. The first chapters take up the intellectual history of constitutional thought in the United States in the early period of independent statehood. As Jack Pole argues, there were many echoes then, of earlier traditions, of earlier thought, reverberating among those that conceived the Constitution. Yet, later on, as following chapters demonstrate, the US Constitution has become a source of reverberation in its own right, most forcefully so within the United States, of course, but also noticeable elsewhere. Therefore, our final chapters will take a comparative view, looking at US Constitutional history through the eyes of foreigners, be they immigrants, as in William Boelhower's chapter, or nationals from the Netherlands or other European countries, as in the last three chapters.

Whatever moves one plans, though, in order to sneak up on a subject as strangely elusive as the US Constitution, it is bound to jump away and change face before one has caught it. Irrespective of the viewpoint or eyesight of the observer, the US Constitution, seen as a living document, can only be a moving target. No book of essays, no amount of scholarly approaches could hope (or should hope, for that matter) to make it "freeze".

The editors

1. THE ANCIENT WORLD IN THE NEW REPUBLIC: THE FOUNDERS' USE OF HISTORY

J.R. Pole

Christian theology has always contemplated a world infused with the Real Presence of the Holy Spirit. But the political scientists of the eighteenth century, whose intellectual heritage was more directly derived from the secular thinking of the Renaissance and the Enlightenment, inhabited a world infused with an entirely different spirit. One of its aspects, as Professor Pocock has persuasively argued, was that time, and its manner of operating on human affairs, had been reduced from theological to a secular dimension.[1] This transformation did not render time a less formidable adversary. Far from it. From the history of the ancient republics to the plays and sonnets of Shakespeare, time was the avowed enemy of human aspirations. But it did mean that human beings could find within themselves, within the scope and context of their own lives, some justification for the effort to control and mitigate time's effects on human fortunes. This in turn offered them, and required of them, a different standpoint from which to make the effort to understand the process of time.

Their world of knowledge, no longer brooded over by the Holy Spirit, was infused instead with a sense of the immediacy of human experience. For many of the *philosophes*, including the new political economists, political science contemplated history as though it occupied space rather than time. History, one might almost say, was a map rather than a process, as it appears to us. On that map the reader could observe, laid out before him, the records of the republics of antiquity, both in their internal governments and in their various forms of association, and at the same instant he could see the record of the Hanseatic League, the so-called German Empire, the republic of the Netherlands, and the highly unstable monarchy of modern Poland and as much more as the eye could discern in the books of history and law, all spread before him in an array all the more fascinating because it was instantaneous.

We may take as a point of departure an observation, also by Pocock, that it is a cardinal principle of modernity in historical explanation that "generations are equidistant from eternity".[2] I am not sure whether this is the same as saying that all generations are present at the same time, but that would not necessarily be a modern

1

outlook, for it is very much the impression that one can easily acquire from the records of the American debates on the newly drafted Constitution of 1787. I am, again, not quite sure whether this could have been expected to mean that the scholar-statesmen of that generation would have felt inclined after a day spent supervising their estates, inspecting, weeding and selecting their tobacco crops, and keeping their account books, to bathe, put on their finest clothes, and keep company with the philosophers of antiquity on an equal footing, for which there was such an excellent Renaissance precedent.[3] Thomas Jefferson certainly enjoyed the books, but would have been more likely to have preferred his carpet slippers for the occasion. What this does mean, however, is that the late eighteenth-century Americans, to an extent that would not have been possible to contemplate in the seventeenth century, or the earlier eighteenth century either, were deeply imbued with a style of secular thought that accepted the truth of certain profound and pervasive generalities about human nature, but that had adapted that knowledge to remove politics from the realm of providence as effectively as Machiavelli had removed it from the wheel of Fortune. Men, assuredly, (even if created equal) were not all alike; but in all times and ages they did act from certain similar propensities. The fate of the Achaean League was direct evidence for the probable fate of the American Confederation; the tendency for large crowds to behave less rationally than individuals or small groups, and in consequence to be swayed by the bad counsel of ambitious and unscrupulous men, resulting in self-inflicted wounds on the state and even to the loss of their liberties, was the same everywhere and at all times. If every Athenian citizen had been a Socrates, said Madison, every Athenian assembly would still have been a mob.[4]

These assumptions about the universal similarities of human nature were accompanied and made all the more valid by other assumptions which are so prevalent that they can easily be missed. They may be called assumptions about the similarity of historical contexts. There was no sense of difficulty about assimilating the situation of the Greek republics of two thousand years earlier with that of the American republics of the seventeen-eighties; the sense in which I have suggested that space prevailed over time was also a sense in which historical situations which offered essentially similar choices of action could be expected to show similar consequences from the actions chosen; all historical circumstances were thus comparable with all others. So pervasive was this attitude, possibly scientific but certainly not in the modern sense historical, that in all the literature of the constitutional debates I have found only one explicit dissent from it. In a debate in the Constitutional Convention in which he was apparently growing tired of the classical learning displayed by the leading nationalists, Charles Pinckney of South Carolina was driven to declare not only that the people of this country - America - were different from the inhabitants of any State they were acquainted with in the modern world, but their *political situation* differed from either that of the people of Greece or Rome "or any other State we are acquainted with among the Ancients". He asked whether any orders such as those introduced by Solon were to be found in the United States. "Can the military habits and manners of Sparta be assimilated to our habits and manners. - are the distinction of patrician and plebeian known among us? - can the helvetic or belgic confederacies, or can the unwieldy, unmeaning body called the Germanic Empire can they be said to possess either the perfection or a situation like ours. - I apprehend not - they are perfectly different, either in distinctions of rank, their constitutions their manners or their policy." He went on to make his own main point, that no general government could "effectively exist" unless the states retained their local rights.[5] But this speech, modern from our point of view, was singular among Pinckney's contemporaries, and elicited no reply. There was no debate *on* the usability of the past. Almost everyone would have accepted viscount Bolingbroke's dictum that "history is philosophy teaching by examples".

An irony about this use of the past by the Founders lay concealed in the fact that they could have derived a similar warning to Pinckney's from Montesquieu, on whom they so heavily depended for other parts of the argument. Writing some half a century earlier, Montesquieu had expressed just the same scepticism about applying lessons drawn from distant time and dissimilar circumstances to the needs of the present.[6]

The lessons to be drawn from antiquity - and the point to be made for present benefit - were commonly expressed in pseudonyms. The most famous of the period, Publius, undoubtedly chosen by Alexander Hamilton, referred to that Publius Valerius who was supposed to have restored the Roman Republic after the fall of Tarquin. As Douglass Adair has shown, all of Hamilton's classical pseudonyms were carefully chosen to make the particular case in point in the cause he was promoting; when, a few years later, he attacked the Whiskey rebels under the name of Tully, Cicero's eighteenth century nickname, he expected his readers to recall Cicero's attack on the Cataline conspiracy; in 1784, Phocion, an Athenian general who never let himself be swayed by personal animosities, had pleaded for clemency towards the tories of New York. All this information, incidentally, seems to have been derived from Plutarch, who was also James Madison's principal source for ancient history.[7]

It was wholly in keeping with this style that Anti-Federalists adopted pseudonyms associated with heroic resistance to tyranny. Brutus, in an earlier incarnation than that in which he published a long series of letters against the Constitution, had delivered Caesar's death blow; (very few risked claiming the name of Cassius - Americans knew their Shakespeare too well for that). Agrippa, the name implausibly adopted by James Winthrop, a former librarian of Harvard College, was one of the conspirators who murdered Caesar - not a major one, perhaps implying some personal diffidence on the author's part. (He may well have been using the pseudonym to convey that he was not a public figure and did not intend to become one.) But even as early as the time of the Townshend acts, one American pamphleteer had perceived the appeal that lay in making a milder claim - a claim, one may say, conspicuous for its humility, that of being a Farmer in Pennsylvania. But the humility of the claim would not have concealed one important aspect of the author's identity, not to be missed in contemporary Pennsylvania, that he connected his life with the land, not with commerce. This style of nomenclature now reappeared rather more conspicuously as farmers hammered the draft Constitution with the soil clinging to their boots. Much the most daring pseudonym of the period was that claimed by Melancton Smith, who simply styled himself "A Plebeian".[8] It was a move that adroitly combined the formal allusion to antiquity with the intensely modern claim to speak as a representative of the lower orders - something that no Federalist would ever have done. The claim, of course, was false, since Smith was a substantial New York merchant. What he could claim was to understand the problems of the poor and to articulate their fears, as he had eloquently done in the New York ratifying convention.

Anti-Federalists made very much less use of classical examples than their opponents. When they did so it was often to invoke some heroic name or to utter the warning implied by that of a heroic-turned-tyrant, rather than to call forth a detailed historical parallel from which the policy needs of their own day could be expounded. When one looks at the two sets of writings with this comparison in mind, the difference is so striking that one has to conclude that the style reflects a difference of substance. Anti-Federalists may in some cases have been less well acquainted with classical literature, but that can hardly be said of Harvard's librarian or of several others whose allusions and literary qualities showed them to be of the same educational class as their Federalist opponents. The reasonable inference to draw from this difference in the presentation of self relates rather to the intended audience than to the educational

4

qualifications of the writers. Publius was susceptible to the criticism that he was writing over the heads of a large number of his fellow-citizens; how many of the farmers, artisans and journeymen of New York and of the other states reached by *The Federalist Papers* were really likely to be engrossed by the history of the Achaean and Amphyctionic leagues? Anti-Federalists would talk to them in the plain language of popular experience, with just a handful of references to ancient times and ancient names to give a touch of class to the argument.

Patrick Henry, speaking in the Virginia ratifying convention, reminded the members of occasions when the peoples of Greece and Rome had lost their liberties through their own carelessness and the ambitions of a few demagogues.[9] Corruption and combination, Melancton Smith warned the New York delegates, had been the chief cause of the destruction of ancient confederacies of Grecian republics, and the new Constitution was so designed as to let in the same kinds of danger.[10] Greek republics, said Brutus, taking up one of the most important of all Anti-Federalist themes, were small; so was that of the Romans. But when they extended their conquests over large territories they changed from being free states to the most tyrannical the world had ever known.[11] It was a weak argument, since no one had proposed that the small states should come into the Union as conquered provinces or without the protections of law and representation. But it was a shot in the general argument that republican government was impossible over large territories.

Almost as much can be learnt from what the Anti-Federalists did not say. For their analysis of society did not differ in essentials from that of their opponents. They knew there were rich and poor, at any rate richer and poorer; no one writing in the period was more revealing of these differences and of their social and political implications than Melancton Smith, who returned in the New York convention to the theme that "the great" had no sympathy with the poor and would tend to engross the power conferred by the Constitution. The same point was made by a Massachusetts farmer, Amos Singletary, who attacked the lawyers and monied men who intended to get into Congress and run the new Constitution. Then they would swallow up "all us little people" just as the great leviathan had swallowed Jonah.[12] (A study of ratification speeches throughout the states would reveal that almost all biblical references came from Anti-Federalists). Federalist rhetoric is secular, historical and political.

But, returning to what Anti-Federalists did not say there was one notable classical precedent that the Anti-Federalists left untouched. For the most striking example in antiquity of efforts to

5

prevent the growth of dangerous inequalities of wealth and power between citizens were those agrarian laws which were said to have been laid down by some founders of early republics, and of which there was an authentic historical record in the case of the Gracchi. The silence of the Anti-Federalists on this theme is all the more remarkable when one considers that James Harrington had incorporated an agrarian law, so fundamental that he turned an adjective into a noun and called it "the Agrarian", into the stabilising structure of his *Oceana* (1656).[13] Harrington stood at the source of the Anglo-American Commonwealth tradition, and one member of the Massachusetts constitutional convention of 1779-80 had gone so far as to suggest that the name of the Commonwealth should be changed from Massachusetts-Bay to Oceana.[14]

Professor Pocock has suggested an explantion of this omission by arguing that Americans, Anti-Federalists presumably no less than their more opportunistic rivals, expected the West to play the part of an Agrarian law in their republic. They may very well have done; they may have been contented with a more or less silent assumption that the West would somehow take care of the problem without requiring the formulation of specific policy. It could be relied on to do so, after all, long after their lifetimes, and people are not generally disposed to make strict rules for the distant future. Settlers in Kentucky had already resolved in 1785 on sound republican terms that the acquisition of more land than a man needed to seat himself and his family on was "a Greevance".[15] And it was such a cardinal thesis of republican doctrine that great inequalities of wealth caused envy, social dissent and civil war that one might have expected at least some complaint about the omission of an agrarian law along the lines of the frequent attacks on the omission of a bill of rights. Land engrossment was already taking place in Tennessee of the kind that appeared to justify conventional republican fears. Land speculation was one of America's favourite futuristic activities. Why, then, was it not on issue in the constitutional debates? The danger was obvious; but so were the opportunities; and perhaps the unstaunched gap in pure republican doctrine lay there. We have to look not to these debates so much as to the Ordinance of 1787 for the major attempt to carry republican doctrine into the West. But that great charter, which has been called the first federal action on a bill of rights, applied only to the Ohio Valley, and left the south west untouched.[16] At the least we have to say that Anti-Federalists had very little to add.

They also had little to add about the other cardinal republican theme of virtue. What Anti-Federalists feared was not so much loss of virtue as loss of power. Before Americans had divided between

6

Federalists and Anti-Federalists they had absorbed from Montesquieu the doctrine that each form of government had its necessary prevailing spirit and that the spirit of democracy was virtue. There was nothing abstract about this. Montesquieu's work contained so much information about the ancient world that Americans could have got all they needed from it, as most of them probably did; no lesson could have come down more clearly than that democracy was inherently fragile. In its purer forms, democracy lacked the structural safeguards needed for protection against mob passions, especially when manipulated by rabble-rousers. For the survival of democracy a virtuous populace was essential, but virtue could never be expected to survive on its own merits without the support of political institutions. Anti-Federalists believed implicitly that the great advantage of the state governments was that they already incorporated the necessary institutional safeguards. while the peoples were virtuous enough. The need for this elaborate structure of superior power, towering over the states, was far from obvious to them.

Virtue was a rather more anxious theme with the Federalists, who had to depend, in part at least, on representation and bicameralism to provide the necessary screen between the mass of the people and the makers of the laws.

The issue brought out one of Publius's more favourable observations on human nature. "As there is a degree of depravity in mankind which requires a degree of circumspection and Distrust", said Madison in *Federalist* 56,

> so there are other qualities in human, which justify a certain portion of esteem and confidence. Republican government presupposes the existence of these qualities in a higher degree than any other form. Were the pictures which have been drawn by the political jealousy of some among us, faithful likenesses of the human character, the inference would be that there is not sufficient virtue among men for self government; and that nothing less than the chains of despotism can restrain them from devouring and destroying one another.

Republican government, then, "presupposes" these qualities; but the other side of this particular coin, the required corollary, should have been that republican government inculcates and sustains them. Republican government should itself serve as the principal school of republican citizens. But the history of republics, so often alluded to in these debates, did not seem to lend much support to this view; and it was for this reason that institutions were required at all levels to act as safeguards against abuses of the opportunities which free

7

government itself offers to the ambitious and the unscrupulous. Madison made this crucial point in a familiar passage of *Federalist* 51: "Ambition must by made to counter-act ambition; the interest of the man must be connected to the constitutional rights of the place". The institutions must in turn themselves depend for their strength on their power to serve self-interest - self-interest locked, as Hume had explained, into the service of the general interest.[17]

The doctrine of the separation of powers had already reached a highly articulate form in America in the Declaration of Rights attached to the Massachusetts Constitution of 1780. But the precise form in which it emerged in the United States Constitution could not have been predicted from any earlier manifestations, or from the theory as derived from the British Constitution or from Montesquieu - still less from Polybius, who was never mentioned in this connection. (The one reference to him in *Federalist* 63 is in connection with a different principle, limiting the power of the separate branches of the legislature, by way of assuring Americans, from the example of Carthage, that the senate would not engross the legislative power.) To understand the extreme form of separation reached in the Constitution one has to begin at the latest with the reign of James II and the Act of Settlement following the Glorious Revolution. Montesquieu's interpretation of the British Constitution is one of the more problematic aspects of his work. Whether Americans were influenced more by his account than by their own knowledge of British government is a question deserving more attention than it has received. In any case the doctrine could have materialised in a variety of forms, and the ultimate American form was a reflexion of American needs in the light of American experience.

Montesquieu, so well aware of the dangers besetting the republic, had insisted on the importance of republican education. It is a curious fact that this particular support of the system, already provided for in the Northwest Ordinance, was completely omitted from the argument. The Constitution says nothing about it, and it was left to Thomas Jefferson in Virginia and a later generation of American statesmen in Washington, to propound the benefits of public education; public education meant taxation, which would never be popular, and the cause was left to languish, until Jefferson's great design for the University of Virginia was finally realised in his lifetime by a later generation of Virginians.

The Federalists were keenly aware of the moral issues in politics, however. Madison argued in *Federalist* 44 that "the pestilent effects of paper money" had constituted a loss, sustained by Americans, on "the industry and morals of the people" and, significantly, on "the character of Republican Government". Publius admits in

Federalist 62 that representatives sometimes forget their obligations to their constituents and prove unfaithful to their trust. Republican government was less subject than others to this misfortune; but here the institutions came to the rescue, for the Senate "interposes as a salutary check on the government".

The frequent and often seemingly indiscriminate use of the past, whether near or distant, to point a moral or to adorn an argument, often makes it difficult to be sure in what sense the past is really being employed. The question that so often arises in the reader's mind is whether a citation from the history of the ancient world, or a quotation from "the celebrated Montesquieu", is invoked as a fundamental building block without whose presence the structure would actually be a different building; or whether it is invoked on the other hand as an adornment or even a makeweight in the course of an argument whose conclusions were already arrived at and would have been exactly the same if the writer or speaker had never heard of Rome or never read Montesquieu.

As a step towards the solution of this problem, I want now to suggest a simple distinction between two types of argument. I will call the first "exemplary" and the second "rhetorical". I think these names explain themselves. The exemplary type uses the past, and the works of philosophers and civil lawyers, as elements in the basic structure of the information about the world which forms the actual experience of mankind - and more particularly, of the makers of the American Constitution. Obviously this experience includes their education; that it draws so little on their religion is one of the features of the period we are dealing with. But it is very certain that education is selective. Federalists knew and frequently insisted that the ancient republics were unstable and liable to dissolution; they dwelt hardly at all on their powers of duration, on their glories and their schools. And it is also vital to recognise that this exemplary element in their arguments was even more fundamentally formed by their own political experience in state government and the Articles of Confederation.

The second type, which I call rhetorical, is distinguished from the first not by the materials it uses but by its purpose, which is to persuade. Different rhetorical invocations will often be used for different audiences; instances of corruption, tyranny, war and destruction will be piled on top of one another with little regard for time or circumstance. There can be no doubt that the ancient republics played a very powerful rhetorical role in the course of the constitutional argument and that it is often difficult to distinguish the rhetorical from the exemplary.

This confusion is part of the problem. I have no desire to make

9

exaggerated claims for the typology I have drawn. The problem is familiar in principle, and many historians have probably used some such distinction. We must begin by appreciating that *all* exemplary material is essentially available for rhetorical deployment. Thus information which makes its appearance, for example, in the debates of the Convention, when men are anxiously trying to satisfy themselves as to what is likely to happen if certain powers are given to the government, or certain institutions are established, will be called forth again, perfectly legitimately, as part of the rhetoric of persuasion when these arrangements are presented to the public. A man who has been persuaded by examples will be entitled to use those examples to persuade others. In this sense, the question as to whether a reference is exemplary or rhetorical might seem to be a mere function of whether you are speaking or listening. But although the distinction may be imperfect, and at times difficult to discern, it is a distinction that marks a difference, and one that does, I think, help to clarify the structure of an argument.[18] Let us see if we can use it.

It is well known that one of the most divisive issues of the Convention arose from the small states' fears of being gobbled up by the large states. Madison was concerned to convince the delegates that there was no such danger. In the course of a speech on this subject he referred them to the published *Journals of Congress* for evidence that in the existing Confederation the large states had in fact shown no inclination whatever to form combinations at the expense of their less numerous neighbours; their own recent history proved these fears to be groundless. "Experience", said the scholarly Madison, "taught a contrary lesson. Among individuals of superior eminence and weight in society, rivalships were more frequent than coalitions. Carthage and Rome tore each other to pieces instead of uniting to devour the weaker nations of the Earth." He went on to argue that the contentions, not the coalitions, of Sparta, Athens and Thebes "proved fatal to the members of the Amphyctionic Confederacy". And then very characteristically he passed straight to the eighteenth century to point out that France and Austria had been rivals as long as they remained the greatest powers of Europe.[19] In a speech that drew on "the heroic period of Ancient Greece, the feudal licentiousness of the middle ages of Europe" and "the existing condition of the American savages", passed to Plutarch's Life of Themistocles, and then drew in evidence the records of the German and Dutch confederations, he argued that the weak had always suffered at the hands of the strong. It was not, perhaps, a very difficult case to make, but it led to an unexpected dénouement: the solution was for the small states to promote the form of government which would

10

approximate them to counties. The individual members of such localities would then have nothing to fear because they would in effect stand in the same relation to the general government as their neighbours from what had been the larger and more powerful states.

"In a word", he concluded, "the two extremes before us are a perfect separation and a perfect incorporation, of the thirteen States. In the first they would be independent nations subject to no law, but the law of nations. In the last, they would be mere counties of one entire republic, subject to one common law. In the first case the smaller states would have everything to fear from the larger. In the last they would have nothing to fear ..."

This assimilation of all experience, remote and recent, into a single historical map, makes these citations a case of the exemplary mode of argument. If, on the other hand, the common stock of knowledge, available to all educated persons, had actually provided very different information, such as would have justified the fears of oppression of the weak even *in a united republic*, then the argument would have had to proceed on different situation might have yielded a different constitution. The style that I have called exemplary is thus by no means merely nominal. When Madison in *Federalist* 45 reassures the states that they "will retain a very extensive portion of active sovereignty" and goes on to observe that the federal head of the Achæan League probably had "a degree and species of power giving it considerable likeness to the government formed by the Convention", he is using rhetoric; elsewhere, in *Federalist* 18, he is willing to cite the weaknesses of the same League. When Butler, Madison and Bedford tell the Convention that like Solon, they must give the people a constitution they will receive - or approve - they are using the rhetorical style.[20] A striking example of the contrast occurs when in *Federalist* 39 Madison goes to great lengths with many examples to explain that the Constitution is "partly national" and "partly federal", with some elements to please the nationalists but with others to reassure the guardians of state rights. It is easy to understand Madison's preference for keeping his notes of the Convention debates so tightly sealed. The rhetorical style as employed by the Madison of *The* Federalist would have been hard to reconcile with the spokesman of consolidation of a few months earlier. But in the Convention his use of history was closer to the rhetorical style.

Both sides in the argument had access to the same sources though some were plainly much more deeply-read than others. Both sides took some of their examples from the internal governments of the ancient world and some from the case histories of earlier forms of confederation. But they extracted different lessons. The Federalist note is struck by Hamilton before Madison has joined the series

(*Federalist* Ten is Madison's first contribution). "It is impossible to read the history of the petty republics of Greece and Italy", he declares at the beginning of Number Nine, "without feeling sensations of horror and disgust at the distractions with which they were continually agitated, and at the rapid succession of revolutions, by which they were kept in a state of perpetual vibration, between the extremes of tyranny and anarchy. If they exhibit occasional calms, these serve only as short-lived contrasts to the furious storms that are to succeed. If now and then intervals of felicity open themselves to the view, we behold them with a mixture of regret arising from the reflexion that the pleasing scenes before us are soon to be overwhelmed by the tempestuous waves of sedition and party-rage. If momentary rays of glory break forth from the gloom, while they dazzle us with a transient and fleeting brilliancy, they at the same time admonish us to lament that the vices of government should pervert the direction and tarnish the lustre of those bright talents and exalted endowments, for which the favoured soils, that produced them, have been so justly celebrated."

This essay is particularly important because it brings the external arrangements of the Confederation to bear on the internal policy of the states. The thrust of the argument is that the American states under the Confederation resemble the ancient republics in all their worst features. There is no secret about Federalist intentions. "The utility of a confederacy, as well as to suppress faction and to guard the internal tranquility of the states, as to increase their external force and security, is in reality not a new idea", Hamilton explains; it had been practiced in different countries and ages and had in fact been advocated by "that great man", Montesquieu. And here Hamilton had the satisfaction of catching the Anti-Federalists in a rhetorical inconsistency, for he pointed out that while they insisted on repeating Montesquieu's opinion that republican government could only be practiced in a contracted territory, they chose to ignore his opinions where they did not fall in with the rest of the Anti-Federalist case. Hamilton is accusing them of using a rhetorical argument where a proper use of exemplary materials would have forced different conclusions. This gave him the opportunity to demolish their favourite position. For if the small territory thesis were valid, then the Anti-Federalists were in difficulties in the existing states of Virginia, Massachusetts, Pennsylvania, New-York, North Carolina and Georgia! No Anti-Federalist, as far as I know, ever effectively replied.

In an essay published on 23 November, 1787, the Anti-Federalist Agrippa tried to deal with some of the more embarrassing evidence about the behaviour from the ancient world by explaining that Greece and Rome were often at war because the Greek and Roman republics considered war the activity most becoming to free men, leaving agriculture, arts and domestic employment to slaves. "Carthage, the great commercial republic of antiquity ... retained her freedom longer than Rome, and was never disturbed by sedition during the long period of her duration." The spirit of commerce was "the great bond of union among citizens". The argument was that the arts of commerce and production flourished under light government but decreased where control was strict.[21] The individual state therefore had nothing to fear from each other in a loose confederation. But Hamilton, unfortunately, had already dealt a devastating series of blows at this benign view of the ancient world in *Federalist* 6, which had appeared a week earlier in New York. Commercial rivalry led to war among commercial nations. "Has commerce hitherto done any thing more than to change the objects of war? Is not the love of wealth as enterprising and as daring a passion as that of power or glory? Have there not been as many wars founded upon commercial motives, since that has become the prevailing system of nations, as were before occasioned by the cupidity of territory or dominion? Has not the spirit of commerce in many instances administered new incentives to the appetite both for the one and for the other?" The ancient world was evidence in the case. "Sparta, Athens, Rome and Carthage were all Republics; two of them, Athens and Carthage, were of the commercial kind. Yet they were as often engaged in wars, offensive and defensive, as the neighbouring Monarchies of the same times. Sparta was little better than a well regulated camp; and Rome was never sated with carnage and conquest." Carthage, he went on, "was the aggressor in the very war that ended in her destruction". And then he passed straight to the histories of Venice and the wars of the Dutch republic, all simultaneously displayed on the great map of history.

In this same essay Hamilton caustically noted that famous leaders including Pericles, had often taken their countries into costly wars for trivial and personal motives. "The celebrated Pericles, in compliance with the resentments of a prostitute, at the expense of much of the blood and treasure of his countrymen, attacked, vanquished and destroyed the city of the Samnians. The same man, stimulated by private pique against the Magarensians, another nation of Greece, or to avoid a prosecution in which he was threatened as an accomplice in a supposed theft of the statuary phidias, or to get rid of the accusations prepared to be brought against him for dissipating the funds of the State in the purchase of popularity, or from a combination of all these causes, was the primitive author of the famous and fatal war, distinguished in the Grecian annals by the name of the *Pelopponesian* war; which, after various vicissitudes,

13

intermissions and renewals, terminated in the ruin of the Athenian commonwealth." Into this series of denounciations of the vices and errors of the most celebrated of ancient republics Hamilton suddenly sprang the name of Daniel Shays, "a desperate debtor" who had plunged Massachusetts into civil war in 1786. There could have been no more cogent example of the theme of the contemporaneity of the past or the relevance of history.

I have quoted Hamilton at some length because these early essays are among the best examples of a theme which can be illustrated from many passages in later essays. The Federalists *do not* rely on the virtues of the early republics as evidence for their own case. The use of example is to point contrasts; the exemplary use of the past is to reject the past. It is particularly significant that all the merits of these republics - and the same was true of course, of the Roman Republic had been inadequate to give them forms of government that could save them from their awful record of internal convulsions and destructive wars. The underlying thrust is clear: the *states* resemble the early republics in their worst features. And this, assuredly, is not mere rhetoric. We would mistake the temper of the times if we underestimated the urgent sense of reality with which Jay, Hamilton and Madison viewed the character of the crisis of their generation as bearing a very close resemblance to those of the ancient republics.

In *Federalist* 18 Madison, with assistance from Hamilton, advanced in detail the negative evidence of the Ampyctionic and Achaean leagues to argue the need for a stronger union on two fronts: both for the sake of maintaining the internal stability of the republics - in this case, of course, the American states - and for security against foreign powers. The former was undone when Philip of Macedon got a seat on the board - a position from which he extended his power over the whole of Greece. I cannot help wondering whether the authors were thinking of a threat uttered earlier, in the Constitutional Convention, by Gunning Bedford of Delaware, that if his state were not satisfied it might form an independent alliance with a foreign power. The warning was severely rebuked and swiftly retracted.[22] But the danger was by no means trivial in principle. Spain occupied enormous reaches of the continent, Britain remained in Canada, while France might one day try to return the her American empire. The danger that if the Americans failed in their efforts to form a stronger union, individual states might make their own alliances, could certainly not be dismissed by prudent men.

On the rare occasions when ancient republics are cited with approval, it is on account of institutions that gave them some stability. Thus in *Federalist* 34 Madison was able to point out that

14

two distinct bodies representing the patricians and the plebeians had subsisted with enough harmony to give the Roman Republic its power of internal endurance; and this system was likened to the proposals under which both the federal government and those of the states would have the power to support themselves by taxation. Madison also cited the examples of Rome and Carthage to argue that when contests occurred between the people and the senates it was the people who prevailed. On these occasions the point of the argument was that the American institutions proposed under the new Constitution replicated these ancient virtues. These were rhetorical arguments. They gave grounds for hope, but did not define the American situation.

An important theme depending on the example of antiquity was argued in the constitutional convention by Charles Pinckney. Defending his state against attacks on slavery, he retorted that if slavery were wrong, it was justified by the example of all the world. Greece, Rome and other ancient states were not the only examples, for slavery was tolerated by France, England and Holland among modern states; in all ages, one half of mankind had ben slaves. To all this John Dickinson replied that if England and France permitted slavery, slaves were at the same time excluded from those kingdoms; as for Greece and Rome, he contended that they were made unhappy by their slaves.[23]

At the heart of all that both the Federalists and their opponents contended for, there lay a different conception of the state and its purposes than any that could be found in the ancient world - or that could be found, I am inclined to think, in the Renaissance, from which they had so much to learn. According to Madison, in *Federalist* 10, differences of faculty gave rise to differences of property: to protect the free exercise of these differences of faculty was one of the principal aims of the state - a justification for its existence. It has been remarked, most recently by John Diggins that the concept of rights, which had inspired the American Revolution, got lost in this constitutional argument and was completely subordinated to the concept of interests.[24] But I think this comment is misplaced. We must assume that all men have rights to the exercise of their faculties in freedom, if they have any rights at all. In a crucial passage of *Federalist* 10 Madison mentions the rights of minorities. That part of the theory was implicit in the whole position, for both Federalists and Anti-Federalists, and when the Anti-Federalists persistently attacked the absence of a bill of rights, they were met with the reply that the rights were already there, protected in several of the state constitutions, and in the specific prohibitions of the federal Constitution. There was no need to deny to the Federal government powers which it had no claim to exercise.

For reasons which we have no time to go into now, the Constitution was founded at a time when the rights and interests of the individual had acquired a primary status in America.[25] The Founders of the American Republic owed soe debts to the civic principles of the Italian Renaissance, but their preoccupation with rights was not among them. Renaissance political thought exhibited no interest in rights; Machiavelli neiter advised the Prince to respect human rights nor to ignore them: they did not exist. It was for reasons of civil stability, not for justice or fairness, that Renaissance thinkers emphasised the value of equality; and they did not mean equality in the distribution of property. In contemplating the American Founders in the light of their knowledge and use of the past it is just as important to recognise what was new in their thoughts as what was old. They could use antiquity for a knowledge of human behaviour, of men's eternal propensities and enduring weaknesses. The record that interested them was a record of action. These debates, with all their learning, betrayed only the scantiest interest in ancient philosophy. Aristotle appears not at all in *The Federalist*; Socrates and Plato once each, and merely for illustration.

The record of historical behaviour was what interested these thinkers, and that record did indeed furnish them with example and food enough for thought. For their intellectual obligation to history was paradoxically both specific and ambiguous. They had to devise a means to reverse the inexorable workings of time. Their aim was to construct a commonwealth out of the materials of their own political institutions and their own experience, which would resist the forces of conflict, corruption, war and decay.

It was an important intellectual step in this direction to recognise not only that change was inevitable, but that its effects could be accommodated by an amendable constitution. The idea of an organic constitution, constantly reinterpreted in relationship to the changing needs and aspirations of the society it served, was probably not fully grasped in 1788, but came into action as soon as the Constitution's life began. It was then that Americans could begin to appreciate that their debt to the past was that of learning to leave it behind. And this, in its turn, as it translated experience into theory, may be thought of as a not inconsiderable step in the course of thinking which changed the historical map into a historical process.

REFERENCES

1. J.G.A. Pocock, *The Machiavellian Moment*, Princeton, 1975, pp. 3-9, 43-7; 541.

2. *Ibid.*, p. 54.

3. Machiavelli to Francesco Vettori, 10 December 1513, in Roberto Ridolfi, *Life of Niccolo Machiavelli*, tr. Cecil Grayson, London, 1963, pp. 151-2. The letter may also be found on the table mats in the restaurant in the village of Sant' Andrea in Perusina, where Machiavelli was living at the time.

4. John Jay, Alexander Hamilton and James Madison, *The Federalist*, ed. Jacob E. Cooke, Middletown, Conn., 1961, p. 374 (*Fed. 55*). This, incidentally, is the *only* reference to Socrates in *The Federalist*.

5. Max Farrand, ed., *Records of the Federal Convention*, New Haven, 1937, pp. iv, 36. The sense of universals portrayed here was characteristic of the age, and pervades the political essays of Hume, but the Americans had occasion to *apply* it.

6. Charles de Secondat, baron de Montesquieu, *De l'Esprit des Lois*, ed. G. Truc, Paris, 1961, book XXX, ch. 14.

7. Douglass Adair, *Fame and the Founding Fathers*, ed. Trevor Colbourn, Williamsburg, 1974, pp. 272-85.

8. By a Plebeian, (Melancton Smith), *An Address to the People of the State of New-York ...*, N.Y. State, 1788. Evans 21465.

9. Cecelia M. Kenyon, ed., *The Antifederalists*, Indianapolis, 1966, p. 241.

10. *Ibid.*, pp. 386-7.

11. Herbert J. Storing, ed., *The Anti-Federalist: Writings by the Opponents of the Constitution*, selected by Murray Day, from *The Complete Anti-Federalist*, Chicago, 1985, p. 113.

12. Kenyon, *op. cit.*, Introduction, p.1. (L)

13. James Harrington, *Works*, ed. J. Toland, London, 1700: *Oceana*, p. 42; *Prerogative of Popular Government*, pp. 234-91.

14. Oscar and Mary Handlin, *The Popular Sources of Political Authority Documents on the Massachusetts Constitution of 1780*, Cambridge, Mass, 1966, p. 26.

15. J.R. Pole, ed., *The Revolution in America 1754-1788*, London, 1970, pp. 379-82.

16. *Ibid.*, pp. 382-8; Robert Allen Rutland, *The Birth of the Bill of Rights, 1776-1791*, Chapel Hill, 1955, pp. 103-5.

17. David Hume, "Of the Origin of Justice and Property"; in Henry D. Aiken, ed., *Hume's Moral and Political Philosophy*, N.Y., 1948, pp. 55-69.

18. In an extremely interesting recent essay, David W. Howe argues that Publius deliberately chose to employ eighteenth century "faculty" psychology - that is, on an analysis which divided the mind into faculties - as a method of persuasion. This strategy emerges from the argument as a prime example of my category of rhetorical as opposed to exemplary argument. If, to the contrary, Howe had maintained that Publius used this method because it was fundamental to the structure of the authors' thought (a difficult proposition to demonstrate of multiple authorship) the argument would have been exemplary.
     Daniel W. Howe, "Eighteenth Century Faculty Psychology and the Rhetoric of the Federalist Papers", *William and Mary Quarterly*, June 1987.

19. Farrand, *op. cit.*, I, p. 448.

20. *Ibid.*, I, pp. 125, 491, 491.

21. Herbert J. Storing, ed., *op. cit.*, pp. 229-30.

22. Farrand, *op. cit.*, I, p. 492.

23. *Ibid.*, II, pp. 371-2.

24. John Patrick Diggins, *The Lost Soul of American Politics*, New York, 1984, p. 61.

25. For a fuller analysis, see J.R. Pole, "The Individualist Foundations of American Constitutionalism" forthcoming in Publications of the Capitol Historical Society, ed. Ronald Hoffman.

2. PUBLIUS DIVIDUUS:
JAMES MADISON AND THE DIVISIONS OF GOVERNMENT

Eduard van de Bilt, University of Amsterdam

The Roman saying "divide et impera" usually has imperialist connotations: originally a term denoting the politics of manipulation by which ancient Rome built its empire, it has come to refer more generally to the Machiavellian strategies used by politicians and warriors in search of conquest and absolute sovereignty. Though clearly interested in political leadership and, as his career shows, himself a master of political manoeuvering, James Madison, however, gives a new meaning to the old saying. With Madison, the phrase "divide et impera" signifies an open-ended political system intended to protect and represent liberty. As Madison himself argued when informing his friend Thomas Jefferson of the results of Philadelphia's Constitutional Convention: "Divide et impera, the reprobated axiom of tyranny, is, under certain qualifications, the only policy by which a republic can be administered on just principles."[1]

If, in a highly un-Madisonian fashion, one would try to define Madison's political theory on the basis of one or two key-words, the term "divisions" almost immediately comes to mind as one of the most appropriate concepts with which to delineate Madison's ideas. Ironically, for someone who is considered a nationalist in 1787, someone who thinks in terms of unity and wholeness, Madison has a remarkable preference for divisions, conflicting tendencies, and oppositions. Despite his comments in, for instance, *Federalist 10*, where he laments conflicts created by rival parties, Madison seems to thrive on dividing people and institutions. He appears to accept divisions not only as a basic aspect of human beings and society, as a negative element that no political thinker or practicing politician can deny when trying to create or implement a government, but also as something positive on which to ground politics. While attacking existing political divisions, at the same time Madison makes divisions the "foundation" of his political philosophy. Ambivalent about the impact of divisions, Madison nevertheless relies on divisiveness to create philosophical and political stability.

Madison seems to do so deliberately. A master of logic, not surprisingly he applies the idea of divisions even to his own position as a political theoretician and lawgiver. One cannot deny, I think, that the Publius who writes *The Federalist Papers* is, to some extent, a split personality. However much John Jay, Alexander Hamilton, and Madison deliberated about their political philosophies and their contributions to the collection of essays, there remain differences between them. More importantly, James Madison himself acknowledges that the Janus face characteristic of all human beings is also part of his heritage: he explicitly mentions and willingly accepts the tensions within his own position, as some of his contributions to *The Federalist Papers* indicate.

That these divisions within divisions complicate the historians' search for the "real" Madison must be clear. And yet, paradoxically, the emphasis on divisions perhaps also enables us to give Madison a new identity as a political thinker, an identity that has important consequences for Madison's position within the history of political thought.

The Madison who emerges here, however, remains tentative, if only because of the scant sources I rely on to sketch his position. Madison's thought is the more complex because one cannot take some of his most important writings literally. While *The Federalist Papers* are clearly Madison's greatest contribution to political thought, too many scholars fail to appreciate their complexity. Whereas historians, political scientists, and philosophers still quarrel about the influence on Madison's (or Hamilton's) work of thinkers such as Hume, Locke, and Montesquieu, other important questions are hardly even raised, let alone properly addressed and answered. Slowly, scholars have become aware that they cannot completely consider the arguments that Madison and Hamilton put forth in *The Federalist Papers* as representing their real convictions. Because they first and foremost participate in the struggle over ratification of the Constitutional Convention's proposals, the papers contain more rhetorical and propagandistic elements than some historians or political scientists have been willing to admit. As such, as part of a propagandistic and highly rhetorical effort to persuade people to accept the proposed American Constitution, *The Federalist Papers* cannot be simply taken at face value. To some extent, Madison and Hamilton create arguments and propound interpretations that mask their "real" intentions and ideas. While *The Federalist Papers* do not give *the* correct interpretation of the American Constitution, they can only partly be used to show the men behind the masks. As Madison's *Notes of Debates in the Federal Convention of 1787* and his correspondence indicate, under the name of Publius both Madison and Hamilton defend proposals with which they are not entirely (or not at all) satisfied. As a result, the argument about Madison's position and ideas I suggest here can only be tentative: it is a preliminary sketch resulting from my first serious engagement in the study of Madison's work and inviting further debate.

i

In *Federalist 55*, Madison emphasises the complexity of human nature: "As there is a degree of depravity which requires a certain degree of circumspection and distrust, so there are other qualities in human nature which justify a certain portion of esteem and confidence."[2] Elsewhere in *The Federalist Papers* Madison remarks: "There is in every breast a sensibility to marks of honor, of favor, of esteem, and of confidence, which, apart from all considerations of interests, is some pledge for grateful and benevolent returns. Ingratitude is a common topic of declamation against human nature; and it must be confessed that instances of it are but too frequent and flagrant, both in public and in private life. But the universal and extreme indignation which it inspires is itself a proof of the energy and prevalence of the contrary sentiment" (351-352).In Madison's view, nothing is simply one thing. Human nature cannot be defined monolithically or reductively, but consists of "contrary sentiments", forces that in a remarkable interrelationship compete with one another and maintain at most an uneasy equilibrium. We are all at once sinners and saints, or, to be more precise, a peculiar mixture of contradictory passions, opinions, and interests. Moreover, every voice or force within us contains positive as well as negative features. Nothing is simply or absolutely positive or negative: on the contrary, everything has its positive as well as its negative aspects, depending on the context or framework in which it operates.

As *The Federalist Papers* show, this conflictual framework also pervades politics. In every political institution "a power to advance the public happiness involves a discretion which may be misapplied and abused" (256). Like energy, power is both necessary for a government to function properly and a threat to its existence. Experience enables the authors of *The Federalist Papers* to create and defend their proposals for a written constitution; but it also tells them to leave open the opportunity to change or amend their precious document and not to rely completely on "parchment barriers" (308). Local "jealousy" endangers the position of the federal government but also functions positively in that it thwarts the rise of executive or Congressional tyranny. The American people are also two things at once: on the one hand, the sovereign power that stands for the republican nature of the American political system and that enables Hamilton and Madison to attack states' rights; on the other hand, a biased mob that has to be represented, that is to say,

22

displaced by delegates to ensure the proper functioning of government. While in matters concerning, for example, the division of powers, "the people themselves ... as the grantors of the commission, can alone declare its true meaning, and enforce its observance" (314), continual "recurrence to the people, as a provision in all cases for keeping the several departments of power within their constitutional limits" (314) can clearly be dangerous: "a nation of philosophers is as little to be expected as the philosophical race of kings wished for by Plato" (315). Similarly, attachment to and protection of local government at once stabilises and destabilises national politics. And, as *Federalist 10, 50,* and *51* show, even liberty itself, one of the aims of government, is a highly hybrid phenomenon. Because, according to Madison, liberty and the existence of factions are intimately related, liberty's very growth contains the seeds of its own destruction. Factions can only arise "in" liberty, but once they are there, they immediately pose a threat to liberty. Liberty can be both valuable and destructive; factions evidence liberty but can also destroy it. "Liberty is to faction what air is to fire, an aliment without which it instantly expires. But it could not be a less folly to abolish liberty, which is essential to political life, because it nourishes faction than it would be to wish the annihilation of air, which is essential to animal life, because it imparts to fire its destructive agency" (78). Factions and liberty, destructive politics and the ideal of government are inextricably linked. Foreshadowing the argument made by Alexis de Tocqueville, who claims that the greatest threat to democracy is democracy itself and that one has to "Use Democracy to moderate Democracy," Madison is aware that liberty will destroy liberty unless liberty moderates itself.[3]

The position of Publius, the narrator of *The Federalist Papers,* is equally equivocal. If human beings consist of conflicting tendencies, or, to put it differently, a plurality of voices, the Madisonian part of Publius shares this fate. Throughout their essays, Hamilton and Madison assume a scientific posture as a ploy of persuasion: Publius implicitly poses as a physician to convince his readers of his credentials. Induced to believe that Publius disdains rhetorical strategies and, in contrast to his opponents, is strictly rational, readers are easily persuaded to see the nation's political problems and anti-federalism as diseases for which Publius offers a cure. This strategy inspires Hamilton to attack his opponents' rhetoric by making use of rhetoric.[4] More intellectually honest and self-reflective than Hamilton, Madison, however, admits that the new political science he attempts to apply to America's political problems is not entirely scientific. While *Federalist 37* is a rhetorical exercise in humbleness and thus part of the rhetorical struggle over ratification of the

Constitutional Convention's proposals, it also indicates the problematic nature of the political scientist's position. Madison points to the issues of prejudices, "the imperfection of the eye" (228), and such problems as "the medium through which the conceptions of men are conveyed to each other" (229), such as, for instance, language, to contest his own position. In Madison's view, even natural scientists should be careful not to be overly optimistic about the scientific nature of their research. But "[w]hen we pass from the works of nature, in which all the delineations are perfectly accurate and appear to be otherwise only from the imperfection of the eye which surveys them, to the institutions of man, in which the obscurity arises as well from the object itself as from the organ by which it is contemplated, we must perceive the necessity of moderating still further our expectations and hopes from the efforts of human sagacity" (228). No political thinker has solved, for instance, the problem of properly defining and discriminating the boundaries between the legislative, executive, and judicial powers, or "between the authority of the general and that of the State governments" (227). Furthermore, language creates problems of its own:

> The use of words is to express ideas. Perspicuity, therefore, requires not only that the ideas should be distinctly formed, but that they should be expressed by words distinctly and exclusively appropriate to them. But no language is so copious as to supply words and phrases for every complex idea, or so correct as not to include many equivocally denoting different ideas. Hence it must happen that however accurately objects may be discriminated in themselves, and however accurately the discrimination may be considered, the definition of them may be rendered inaccurate by the inaccuracy of the terms in which it is delivered. And this unavoidable inaccuracy must be greater or less, according to the complexity and novelty of the objects defined. When the Almighty himself condescends to address mankind in their own language, his meaning, luminous as it must be, is rendered dim and doubtful by the cloudy medium through which it is communicated (229).

According to Madison, the eagerness of human beings to divide themselves into factions is only one of the difficulties the Founding Fathers of the American Constitution had to face: while this eagerness is one of the clearest signs of the divisiveness inherent in everything human, truth, interpretation, and meaning are also too often "divided" or equivocal. Human beings "are but men and ought not to assume an infallibility in rejudging the fallible opinions of

24

others" (226).

ii

If human beings are motivated by more than one driving force, these forces have to be taken into account. If one and the same tendency can have different effects or consequences, all of these have to be taken seriously. If nothing or no one is simply one thing but consists of several voices that maintain a conflictual or dialogical relationship, this relationship should not go unheeded. Madison's "Representative Men", predecessors in the field of constitution-building such as Plutarch's Solon and Lycurgus, became famous because they adjusted their political systems to the circumstances and nature of their fellow-citizens; yet they also ended up ostracising themselves or committing suicide hoping thus to induce the people to accept their proposals and convince them that they themselves, the law-givers, were not interested in gaining power. Faced with the same problem, Madison luckily found a solution less fatal to himself and equally profitable to his fellow-citizens: he created a system that offered no individual or group, not even its founder, the opportunity of attaining uncontrolled power, because he made the system internally divided. The solution Madison applies to the problem of factions is only the most obvious and famous example of his reliance on the idea of divisions: the policy of containing divisions by dividing society even further can be found on all levels of Madison's political theories.

By perpetuating divisions, Madison's political philosophy tries to keep them within limits. If, as Madison argues in *Federalist 51*, in general "government itself [is] but the greatest of all reflections on human nature" (322), his own "blueprint" of government is no exception to the rule. Madison's political ideas reflect human nature but they do so in more than one way: while reflecting the divisiveness inherent in everything human, Madison's political theories also try to keep the divisions within boundaries. The "policy of supplying, by opposite and rival interests, the defect of better motives, might be traced" not only "through the whole system of human affairs, private as well as public" (322), but also through Madison's own political philosophy.

The executive, legislative, and judicial powers, as well as the Federal government and the individual states, are engaged in a continual power struggle or balancing act that offers none of the authorities involved the opportunity to gain complete or absolute powers. While remaining independent, the executive, legislative, and judicial powers continuously intrude upon one another's political realm only to find that similar as well as dissimilar ideas, attitudes, or interests create a balance between them. The "encroaching spirit of power" (308), present in all of them, is turned into a successful because partly self-defeating tool of government. Jealousy and rivalry too have not only negative influences but also are creative "solutions" to the problem of political turmoil. If a society harbours democratic as well as aristocratic tendencies, why should one not allow these forces to engage and thus control one another? While executive and administrative power is needed to direct society and implement policies, this power also needs protection against itself in order not to become excessive. In Madison, all authority is questioned. Although Madison abhorred "the evil of imperia in imperio," he nevertheless took care not to give any power, whether the executive or the people, absolute sovereignty.[5] In theory, there should be only one sovereign in politics; in practice, however, its power in Madison's scheme was limited. The people, who come closest to being America's absolute sovereign, turn out to be no sovereign at all. Among other things, indirect elections severely limit their influence. Furthermore, the very concept of "the people" appears to some extent an empty rhetorical construct, intended to circumvent or contain the political leverage of the individual states. And what applies to the people, also applies to possible substitutes in the struggle over or definition of political supremacy: their sovereignty is divided or, at least to a certain extent, hollowed out by adversary forces. Accepting the divisive and divided nature of human existence, Madison makes a virtue of a vice. He involves individuals, groups of people, passions, opinions, and interests in a power-play, a dialogue of voices that sustain or correct each other or cancel each other out. In order to create political stability Madison relies on the interaction of forces: politics is turned into a relational network a field of tension between contending forces that are equally important and are allowed an equal amount of freedom.

Jeremy Bentham could not have created a more efficient Panopticon than Madison's system of surveillance. Madison, however, surpasses Bentham the more because he refuses to let Bentham's supervisor remain outside of the system of checks, balances, divisions, and suspicions. Thus, interested as he is in allowing everything and everyone involved in politics to participate in its realm, Madison is perhaps the political thinker who comes closest to developing an open, non-dogmatic and self-critical political philosophy, a philosophy without a centre or anchor to ground the theory and without an absolute sovereign to control the political realm. He creates a system in which "governments will control each other, at the same time that each will be controlled by itself" (323).

If, however, Madison intends politics to be a play or a dialogue between contending voices, he is not an advocate of free play. Madison is only in a limited sense a "relativist". While eager to let any idea, instinct, attitude, or interest play its role, he does after all establish a hierarchy of values in his political philosophy and create a framework within which political ideas or actions ought to be enclosed. Although he creates a system that is based on distrust, a system that distrusts itself, a play of forces in continual tension with one another, he himself is too balanced a thinker not to create a few parameters that keep this struggle or dialogue within certain boundaries. In Madison, the interrelated elements of hope and fear, optimism and pessimism, and the anxiety about anarchism or despotism are combined with the notions of liberty, republicanism, justice, and the public good to create a political system that contains clear-cut values directing society and its developments. Madison's *Federalist Papers* are not the work of an unpractical theoretician who dreams about utopian communities, but carry the stamp of a highly pragmatic politician and philosopher who is aware of the world's complexity and intent upon dealing with the negative as well as the positive features of human beings and questions of power. While every interest or opinion is allowed or even forced to be part of politics, Madison does not want any opinion or interest to become excessive. In order to achieve this, he explicitly and unequivocally states the values to which political powers and their citizens should subscribe. Madison redefines politics: he wants governments and their citizens to rely in their political ideas and attitudes not so much on absolutes as on an intricate awareness of limits and excesses, the boundaries of which are indicated by Madison's "positive" ideals. A few concepts or ideals, however vaguely defined, are, of course, necessary to lead rulers and the ruled. But Madison never permits his idealism to lose touch with reality. To give one example of Madison's "realist" views in the words he himself used (again in the letter to Jefferson): even if "a complete [sic] supremacy some where is not necessary in every Society, a controlling [sic] power at least is so, by which the general authority may be defended against encroachments of the subordinate authorities, and by which the latter may be restrained from encroachments on each other."[6] Such notions as "liberty" and "the public good" ideally set the boundaries for political behaviour; but within these boundaries freedom reigns.

Furthermore, although his political theory is an invitation to participate in a political dialogue with the fewest possible absolutes, Madison appears to find in the very idea of politics and government the stability or centre he refuses to locate elsewhere. In contrast to, for instance, the later analyst of the American political scene Henry Adams, Madison, apparently persuaded by his own medical metaphors, considers politics and government as a possible antidote against the diseases that plague humankind. It seems as if the divisions that are so typical of human beings and society can only be involved in a proper dialogue on the level of politics and government. When properly applied to politics and government, the problem of divisions is its own solution; the cause of the disease turns out to be also its remedy. Politics and government are healing devices: they attract, reflect, and deflect the different voices and keep them in a structured but ongoing play. It is as if politics merely has to "copy" the divisions inherent in human nature to keep these conflicting tendencies within boundaries, a form of wishful thinking that sometimes betrays the medical man in the philosopher/politician Madison.

iii

If this interpretation of Madison's *Federalist Papers* is plausible, a few recommendations are justified.

To try and pin Madison down on contradictions is a highly complex affair. Madison's greatness consists precisely in his playful handling of contrary tendencies within human beings, in his attempt to create a non-dogmatic, internally dialogised theory and form of government, and in his awareness that society needs values giving direction to it yet offering freedom within "restraints." Madison tries to change the debate about politics from a search for centres of powers to a discussion about the interplay between limits and excess. Instead of trying to locate the source of power that can uphold the political system of a society, Madison attempts to show that every instinct, interest, or idea has a role to play in politics - often even more than one - and that politics consequently consists in the balancing act that allows these elements to act themselves out without doing damage to the structure of society.

Also, more than Walter Lippmann, who, because of his *Preface to Politics*, is often considered the first political thinker to apply Freud's ideas to politics, Madison is the Dr. Freud of government, not just a political homeopath who believes that the cause of a disease can be a remedy, but also a political psychoanalyst, who accepts the dark sides of human nature and lets them work themselves out by bringing them out into the open.

Madison is as modern, in this respect, as such later political thinkers or politicians as the little magician of Kinderhook, Martin van Buren, or John Stuart Mill. In comparison with later theorists

28

who seek an absolute centre for their political theories in parties, in the individual, in the Supreme Court, or in narrow definitions of liberty and the public good, Madison is perhaps the least absolutist political philosopher. As the theorist of liberty defined in terms of an open-ended, internal dialogue, in terms of self-reflectivity and self-criticism, Madison deserves a place in political thought and every political science seminar next to figures like John Stuart Mill and Karl Marx.

REFERENCES

1. James Madison to Thomas Jefferson, 24 October 1787; *The Papers of James Madison*, 10, ed. Robert A. Rutland (Chicago: University of Chicago Press, 1977), p. 214.

2. .*The Federalist Papers*, ed. Clinton Rossiter (New York: Mentor, 1961), 346; all page references in the text are to this edition.

3. Quoted in James T. Schleifer, *The Making of Tocqueville's Democracy in America* (Chapel Hill: University of North Carolina Press, 1980), p. 184.

4. Despite recent works such as Albert Furtwangler's *The Authority of Publius* (Ithaca: Cornell University Press, 1984) a rhetorical reading of *The Federalist Papers* remains an interesting but difficult task that may lead to new interpretations of the essays. The essays Jay, Hamilton, and Madison wrote are not just logical expositions of the Constitutional Convention's proposals but are part of a propaganda struggle that is highly rhetorical. A literary reading of *The Federalist Papers* that focuses on rhetorical constructs, for instance the use of the concept "the people", probably undermines some of the "traditional" interpretations of Hamilton, Madison, and the Constitution itself. Despite obvious differences between the two, Madison is not absolutely opposed to Hamilton in his reliance on rhetorical devices. One of the more interesting moments of *The Federalist Papers*, for instance, occurs when Madison employs the voice of "an advocate for the Southern interests" (340) when trying to deal with the issue of slavery and the Constitution (see *Federalist 54*).

5. Madison to Jefferson, 24 October 1787; *The Papers of James Madison*, 10, p. 209.

6.   *Ibid.*, pp. 209-210.

3. THE CONSTITUTION AND THE MODERN PRESIDENCY ORIGINAL INTENT AND CURRENT NEEDS

Ralph Ketcham

When Aristotle wrote that "man is a political animal", he meant that part of human nature, an essential, ennobling part, was to have a concern for the public good, to have an opportunity to discuss and help resolve public matters, and to have pride in the quality of the shared life of the community - that is, to be a *citizen* of the *polis*. Without such participation, such fulfillment of that part of our nature which welcomes and enjoys effective public life, we simply under-value and under-nourish some of our humanness.

It is precisely this deep sense of publicness that is an often under-emphasised part of the outlook of the founders of the American republic. As they learned Latin and Greek, they absorbed the rich ideals of leadership and public life in the writings of Homer, Cicero, Virgil, Livy, Plutarch, and others. Then, their first systematic study of politics was very likely cast in the then conventional, Aristotelian framework: governments were by one, the few, or the many, and in each category there were good and bad forms. Kings could be tyrants or, in the eighteenth century designation, "benevolent despots", the few could be oligarchs or aristocrats, while rule by the many could be turbulent and corrupt mob rule (what Aristotle termed "democracy"), or good government under a constitutional polity. The key in any case was not the number who ruled, but the quality of government that resulted; whether, in Aristotle's terms, governments are good, ruling "with a view to the common interest", or "perversions", ruling "with a view to the private interest".[1]

This understanding of the political had an important, and often overlooked or misconstrued influence on the ideas of leadership - and citizenship - of those who drafted the Constitution of 1787. The debates both during and after the Federal Convention reveal the essentially qualitative emphasis of all concerned. That is, those drafting the constitution expected their work to be judged according to the *quality* of government it would provide: would it "establish Justice, insure domestic Tranquility, provide for the common defence, promote the general Welfare, ... secure the Blessings of Liberty" and altogether "form a more perfect Union"? Note the nouns emphasising the essentials: Justice, Tranquility, Welfare, Liberty, Union - all qualities of the society, vital to the people, and to be sustained by government - as Aristotle had taught. With these agreed-upon goals, or "goods", the problem becomes one of framing a government - processes, institutions, and so on - that will be effectual to those ends.

What Americans were agreed on in 1787-1788, then, was the Aristotelian emphasis that government should be an active agent for pursuit of the public good (Justice, etc.) as well as the Lockean emphasis that government should derive from the consent of the governed. But the purpose was prior to the *procedure*. Majority rule would have to be so organised as to retain the *substantial* value of nourishing the public good. Put oppositely, the democratic process would deserve repudiation if it proved hostile to that good. The constant awareness by the revolutionary generation of their responsibility in "trying" government by consent, whether they would enhance or diminish its standing in the world, meant that they would have to "make it work", cause it to result in "the good life", reflect what Hume called "public spirit". Otherwise it would not merit praise or even survival.

During the long dispute with Britain leading up to Independence, attention had focussed on the legislature. Drawing on the ancient English practice of the people's voice in government being confined to one branch of the legislature (the House of Commons), and on the colonial experience of the lower house being the place of effective assertion of local interests against imperial power, Americans in 1776 tended to think government by consent consisted largely of a fully empowered, responsive legislature. Somehow the "superior" and "inferior" offices - the executives who administer the law and the citizens who elect the legislators - were less attended to.

As disillusionment with legislative performance heightened during the 1780s, though, attention naturally shifted to executive power as a check or stimulant, and to the *quality* (qualifications) of those who chose the legislators. That is, what were the uses of leadership and of citizenship in a self-governing polity? Might each need to be improved or exalted in order to contend with the palpable deficiencies of, as Madison put it in Federalist No. 48, "the legislative department ... drawing all power into its impetuous vortex?"

Though these concerns, even fears, drove some critics back toward such antidemocratic devises as hereditary office-holding and more stringent limitations on suffrage, a much more creative, and in the end more influential reaction turned to "republican solutions": how could executive energy be both derived from the people and enlisted on behalf of good (as opposed to tyrannical) government, and how could the "discretion of the people" be improved so they would choose better (more able, wiser) officials? The two directions were

32

linked, moreover, because in order for the executive power to be both a substantial check on and a qualitative supplement to the flawed legislature, and remain within the republican principle, it too would require derivation from and dependence on a *qualified* electorate.

Debate in the Federal Convention revealed the close connection between the construction of the executive power and assumptions about the capacity of the people for self-government. James Wilson early asserted two vital propositions: that "the executive consist of a single person", and that he be elected by the people. To Wilson the executive could be as thoroughly republican an officer as a legislator. "Prejudices against the Executive", he told the Federal Convention, "resulted from a misapplication of the adage that the parliament was the palladium of liberty." That may have been true "where the Executive was really formidable" and was independent of the people as in Great Britain, Wilson explained, but in a republic where the executive power was both limited and derived from the people, the situation was entirely different.[2]

Governor Morris further helped the Convention move away from legislative pre-occupation by observing that since "the Legislature will continually seek to aggrandize themselves, ... one great object of the Executive is to control the Legislature." Harking back to Roman and Tudor examples, Morris pointed out that "the Executive Magistrate should be the guardian of the people, even of the lower classes, against Legislative tyranny, against the Great and the wealthy who in the course of things will necessarily compose the Legislative body."[3]

Wilson also insisted that the stability and justice of republican government required that it rest, like a pyramid, on the broad base of the people themselves. Good government, he said, had to be both "efficient and free ... But ... to render government efficient, power must be given liberally; to render it free as well as efficient, those powers must be drawn from the people, as directly and as immediately as possible." This proposition was a commonplace among American Whigs of the revolutionary era in discussing *legislative* power, but Wilson moved boldly to apply it as well to the executive: "he who is to execute the laws will be as much the choice, as much the servant and, therefore, as much the friend of the people as he who makes them." In fact, Wilson found the grant of power to the executive necessary for "efficient" government safe and justifiable *only* if the executive was held in direct responsibility to the people. This "chain of connection", as he put it, would keep the executive attuned to "the interests of the whole", generally less susceptible to the blandishments of special interests than notoriously faction-ridden legislatures.[4]

33

American theories of a powerful "president of all the people", and the practices of such a presidency under Jackson, the two Roosevelts, and Lyndon Johnson, have all simply worked out the implications of Wilson's argument. Thus, though the scope and structure of the contemporary presidency could not have been envisioned by the Founders, led by Wilson especially, they fashioned an office consistent in spirit with its development in the hands of its most notable twentieth century incumbents.

The opposition to popular election of the president revealed, though, how the question of executive leadership was tied to that of the competence of the electorate. In opposing direct election, George Mason "conceived it would be as unnatural to refer the choice of a proper character for Chief Magistrate to the people, as it would to refer a trial of colours to a blind man." The size of the country, he thought, would make it impossible for the people to properly "judge of the respective pretensions of the Candidates".

Members of the Federal Convention, that is, generally accepted the idea that citizenship, active participation, in a self-governing society required *qualification*, some grounds for supposing that the voting would be exercised with responsibility to the public good and with reason and a sense of justice. To some members this meant a version of the restriction, familiar in ancient Greece, eighteenth century Britain, and some of the new states, of suffrage to freeholders, on the hallowed principle that those with "a stake in society", those who owned part of it (land), could be expected to vote responsibly and fairly.

Though the Convention rejected all explicit property qualifications for either voting or office-holding and the severe restrictions on office-holding for non-native citizens, the more liberal arguments objected not to the *idea* of voter qualification, but to the foolishness of injustice of the time-honoured restrictions proposed. George Mason stated the republican ideal forthrightly: "The true idea ... was that every man having evidence of attachment to and permanent common interest with the Society ought to share in all rights and privileges." This qualification, he thought, was not restricted to freeholders. Merchants, artisans, and financiers who owned no land and parents of children destined to live in the country might also feel the requisite "permanent attachment".[5] Clearly, members of the Convention did not regard the traditional freehold restriction as entirely consistent with the emerging republican ideology of the new nation - but how could *responsible*, rather than selfish, manipulated, mindless, or factional participation be accentuated? Members were equally united in taking that question seriously.

Benjamin Franklin rejected outright the supposed connection

34

between wealth and public virtue: "Some of the greatest rogues he was ever acquainted with, were the richest rogues". Though the poor were perhaps tempted to dishonesty to overcome poverty, Franklin thought the rich at least as much tempted because "the possession of property increased the desire of more property." The author of *Poor Richard's Almanac* was well aware that the industrious tradesman and the yeoman farmer were at least as likely to develop in their occupations the essential moral qualities of citizenship as was the rich merchant or large landholder - to say nothing of the slave-owner. If this were so, on what just grounds could suffrage and office-holding be conferred on some and denied on others?

Franklin was formulating a theory of citizenship linked to good leadership and good government: If ambitious, industrious people, grateful for the freedom and opportunity afforded by good laws and encouraged in virtue by the nature of their occupations, were given the rights of citizenship, the very exercise of those rights would further help insure that the people would be able to choose good leaders. Franklin, that is, made the critical "wager" required at some stage in every effort to join self-government and good government: that the people were capable of attaining the skill and judgment need to make wise and public-spirited choices - as Franklin put it, much, perhaps everything, depended on "the virtue and public spirit" of the people.[6]

Three ideas, then, lurked in the "considerable pause" that ensued when the Federal Convention first took up the design of the Executive department. First was a time-honoured conviction that purposeful government, led by a powerful, active executive, might be as it always had been, the essential means to a beckoning national prosperity, freedom, and greatness. Second was the dawning awareness that this sort of executive might, in a republic, be not a threat to liberty and the public good but instead be the very instrument of that liberty and good. The principle of government empowered by consent, that is, could transform the often tyrannical executive into, in Wilson's words, "the servant and friend of the people". Finally the members of the Convention saw that the exciting prospects for such benign and constructive power depended, like so much else, on the existence among the people of, in Franklin's words, "virtue and public spirit". The linkage of the ideas, moreover, apparent to and accepted by all members of the Convention, was both simple and crucial: Only a properly qualified citizenry would likely elect a properly qualified executive fit to exercise the broad powers of leadership good government required.

The president in the new constitution, then, *was* vested with "the executive Power" in its full eighteenth-century connotations, and his wide grant of specific powers were such that they became a major target of opponents of the Constitution - but the authority had been conferred, was ratified, and remained in the document for presidents to use - as many have, I would argue legitimately and in the spirit of the framers, for two hundred years. And the electoral college idea, as the Convention debates show clearly, rested not on hostility to government by consent but on earnest intention to protect that principle from two corruptions equally damaging to good government: mindless, demagogic, circus-like campaigns among the people at large, and cabalistic, faction-ridden executive elections in Congress or in state legislatures. The convention *did* accept the essence of the argument of Morris and Wilson that the president could be depended upon to be the vigorous friend of the people if they were given the power to choose him. Finally, in refusing to limit suffrage in the Constitution itself, and in allowing liberal provision for immigrants to become citizens, the Convention attested at least a guarded confidence in the idea that the people - common people, from anywhere in the world - might possess, or come to possess, the "virtue and public spirit" to elect similarly qualified officials, especially in the amply empowered presidency.

The equations linking good government, active leadership, and public-spirited citizenship, moreover, are still relevant in contemporary American politics - or at least an understanding of them can help us identify some of the problems that plague our public life. We have seen, for example, in the years since the New Deal, the growth of what has been called "the imperial presidency". The trend has been toward not only a vast extension of the functions and bureaucracy of the federal government centered in the executive branch, but also the growth of the political dominance and personal power of the president, most notable in the "regimes" of Lyndon Johnson and Richard Nixon. Some of this development can be seen clearly as within the intent of the founders. The country has much enlarged the scope of public or governmental authority in ways that accept an Aristotelian responsibility for "the good life". The New Deal itself, John Kennedy's attention to "the quality of life" in the nation, and the huge enlargements of the National Endowments for the Arts and the Humanities under Johnson and Nixon illustrate the point.

But, though one need not doubt the good intentions of Franklin Roosevelt, Johnson, and other twentieth century presidents, there is nonetheless in their rhetoric and proclamation of large goals something seriously amiss. From the perspective of the founding era the "amissness" is poignantly evident in Roosevelt's often-noted remark that he intended to pursue Jeffersonian ends with Hamiltonian means. He meant by this, of course, that he would seek the democratising,

36

humane goals he found in Jefferson's words and deeds with a Hamiltonian "loose construction" of the constitution. Roosevelt thus regarded his presidency as having discovered more effective means, suited to the twentieth century, to achieve Jefferson's democratic ideals. In doing this, however, Roosevelt assumed and accepted tenets of government and party very different indeed from those implicit in Jefferson's leadership. Perhaps the essence of Roosevelt's idea of party and leadership is evident in what his admirers have often called his mastery of coalition politics. That is, he gathered support from diverse constituencies and groups in the country, and then molded them into a political party that could win elections and put a programme into effect.

Under such an idea, the task of leading changes radically from that envisioned by the founders. Attention shifts, inductively, to the parts, and conceptions of the whole increasingly are aggregations of some kind. The political version of this outlook, first celebrated in the United States in the Jacksonian era, welcomes the growth of interest groups and political parties since they, as Martin Van Buren proclaimed, "rouse the sluggish to exertion, give increased energy to the most active intellect, excite a salutary viligance over our public functionaries, and prevent that apathy which has proved the ruin of Republics."[7] The role of the leader, then, becomes largely that of the broker, perhaps with a substantial idea of his own of direction for public policy (as, e.g. Andrew Jackson and Franklin Roosevelt had), but essentially in need of gathering support from various groups in the nation, which, giving and taking, might arrive at positions suited to the times. In its twentieth-century form this is usually called "conflict-of-interest" politics where an interplay of competitive forces is left to define "truth", in this case seen as whatever action the democratic political process takes. The resultant is thought of as "right" not because of its accord with any objective standard but because of its issuance from the process of open-accessed, competitive interaction.

What slips from view in this understanding of politics and leadership is any notion of a public interest definable either as an objective standard (such as the "law of nature" and "inalienable rights" Jefferson appealed to in the Declaration of Independence), or even as a perspective or standpoint from which to consider public questions - the idea that as a beginning the public interest might consist of being interested in the public, that is, being able and willing to *ask* the question, "what in case x or case y would be for the public good?" Might we discern, this question asks, if we put our minds to it, an answer, a political response, that would be in part beyond partial interests and perspectives and instead achieve the *public* concern and priority characteristic of good government anytime or anywhere? The point would be to discuss particular problems and concerns within the framework of the larger question. All involved, officials and citizens, would be aware of their partialities and perhaps even contribute insights from them, but each would as well have to rise above them in some degree, to consciously, deliberately subordinate the partialities. In fact such an outlook is, quite simply, *the* mark of the responsible citizen as well as the faithful public office holder. Such a qualitative foundation for considering the public business, moreover, was implicit, as we have seen, in what the Constitution expected of citizens and rulers. The framers could not have conceived, I suspect, to say nothing of validated, a "conflict of interest" idea of politics or the brokering style of leadership appropriate to it because both would have violated the deeply ingrained concept of government as the active pursuit of ideal right.

The contrast between these models of leadership stands out most sharply in the presidencies of Lyndon Johnson and Richard Nixon. They accepted enthusiastically the theory and practice of conflict-of-interest politics and, applying them with vigour and effect, each gained for a time an awesome domination of the nation's public life: they were imperial presidents. Each can also be said to have pursued large-sized programs plausibly described as in the public interest: The Great Society and detente with Russia and China. But each also exhibited traits that compromise grievously the idea of civic virtue. Johnson's arm-twisting, devious, bombastic style, and Nixon's willingness to sanction almost anything in pursuit of victory at the polls, both enervated key aspects of responsible citizenship and leadership. The people were cajoled and manipulated or demeaned as they were subjected to appeals to their baser instincts, to "war resolves" extorted from Congress, and to statements (lies) later declared "inoperative" by the president's spokesman. The leaders deceitfully withheld information from the public, used federal agencies to spy on the people, and sanctioned crimes and "dirty tricks" to win elections - all in the name, so it was proclaimed, of defending the national interest and sustaining necessary political ascendancy.

Some such conduct, of course, is common enough in democratic politics, but Johnson and Nixon, we might say, transformed it into a public philosophy that poisoned both leadership and citizenship. At the heart of their pursuit and conduct of the presidency was a candid, deliberate coalition politics that celebrated the assembling of diversities, the accommodating of conflict, and the winning of elections. Instead of keeping uppermost the needs to pursue "ideal right" for the nation, to articulate this honestly and compellingly to the people, and to keep electoral and administrative methods attuned to

38

those propositions, Johnson and Nixon subordinated everything to the requirements of conflict-of-interest politics. Their leadership, though seemingly strong and responsive to the public (remember the landslide victories of 1964 and 1972), actually so corroded the sense of dignity and public honesty that a whole generation of Americans became more alienated from their government than any other in our history.

And it is this alienation, this fundamental relinquishment of the concern and public spirit essential to good citizenship, that reveals most poignantly the fateful liability of a politics that neither asks nor expects more than partisan self-interest. When the people see the president and his advisors bamboozling or pandering to the people, or declaring that, as Attorney General John Mitchell told the Senate Watergate Committee, "compared to what was available on the other side" in the 1972 election, any evasions, cover-ups, or devious methods needed to assure a Nixon victory at the polls were fair enough, then the public discourse has been prostituted. And it is not the dishonest, even illegal, hidden actions - such as are revealed in the Pentagon Papers or on the Nixon tapes - that are most damaging, but rather what the presidents *openly* defended as proper public philosophy.[8] Nixon's repeated defences in news conferences during the summer of the Senate Watergate Hearing (one year before his resignation and before any of the White House tapes had been released) of F.B.I. investigations limited by the need to protect "national security", or "covert operations" for the same purpose, and of the cleverness and zeal of his Committee to Re-elect the President, all display a manipulative contempt for the "discretion of the people". Johnson's virtuoso brokerage of interests both in Congress and throughout the country - a skill of which he was intensely proud - though admirable in some ways, also had the effect of intensifying the conflict-of-interest model of politics.

The imperial presidency of the 1960s and 1970s, then, was not a revival of the active, patriot model implicit in the Constitution, but rather was an odd and incongruous strategem to impose an energetic leadership on pluralistic, conflict-of-interest politics. The Johnson and Nixon White Houses seethed with plans and actions and programmes and politics expressing the President's will to dominion and achievement, but the ethos was partisan and manipulative and brokering rather than intent on "ideal right" - largely because of the view of public life avowed by the leader. Johnson and Nixon, that is, had a concept of leadership suited to a politics that started with an awareness of the diverse parts, then sought policies a majority of these "factions" might support, and finally mobilised these supporters to win elections and pass legislation.

From the perspective of the founding era, though, something is missing. As the debates in the Constitutional Convention reveal, and as the Washington and Jefferson presidencies show in some degree, there can be real, perhaps indispensable benefit in non-partisan leadership. This benefit arises especially from the need in the nation for some focus on the public good. The recurral in the United States of aspiration that the president be a "leader of all the people", that there be some office seeking to look (and stay) beyond partisan strife, and the support some presidents have gained in the country by achieving a relatively non-partisan standing (one thinks especially of Dwight Eisenhower), make the point. However powerful the pressures to involve the presidency in party politics, and however much presidents (and students of the presidency) might celebrate their *necessary* role as *party* leader, there is nonetheless a strong sense of something lost, of a trading off of a vital resource in the nation's public life, when partisanship becomes pervasive.

This is not to suggest that we ought to eliminate political parties, or even that they ought to be weakened or entirely disassociated from the presidency. Up against the excessive influence of "single-issue" special interests, at least, political parties can make large, constructive contributions to public life. One critical dividing line, though, might allow the United States to keep the benefits of strong political parties and regain some of the benefits of a less partisan chief executive. During presidential campaigns it is entirely appropriate, even useful and essential, for the candidates to run on party tickets. This facilitates identification with issues, links the presidential candidate to like-minded office-seekers, provides organisational support, and all together helps the public evaluate the candidate and his/her character and stand on policy questions. It might as well clarify the position of the president-to-be on the enduring issues that tend to divide political parties in democracies. At the same time, however, it might be best for the presidential candidates to hold back from more blatant and divisive campaign partisanship, in anticipation cf the posture that will be assumed in office - indeed, many candidates have done this in some degree, both out of their own respect for the office and an accurate perception that parts of the public, at least, would respond favourably to such an attitude.

This posture would require, though, that once elected, the president desist from overt partisanship. He/she would not, of course, speak at or otherwise aid in party-fund-raising efforts, nor would he/she campaign for or even endorse others running for election. Though the president would seek support for his programmes among members of Congress (and thus likely work especially with members of "his" party) he would not do so in an openly partisan way. The

40

president would not pay particular attention to party membership in appointments to office (and especially not engage in such manifestly partisan acts as appointing wealthy party fund-raisers to ambassadorships), though his ideological affinity to his "party-of-election" would doubtless lead to many of that party being appointed as trusted and effective aides. The idea, then, would be to leave overt partisanship, as much as possible, at the White House door.

The fact that the early presidents tried very hard (with some success) to do this, and that many later ones have spoken and in some measure acted in that mode, suggests both its benefits and its capacity to elicit public support. At the Consitutional Convention the over-riding concern, in devising ways to elect the president and in defining his relation to the other branches, was to protect the office from corruption in its full, classical meaning: the displacement or impairment of the public good by any form of bias, partisanship, or private interest. The electoral college, as an alternative to either direct election, election by state legislatures, or election by Congress, was intended to diminish intrigue, factionalism, and demagogy in the selection of the president. His veto power, right to make appointments, and conduct of foreign affairs were intended both to limit the sway of the supposedly more faction-ridden legislatures and to allow the president to defend himself (and the supposed above-party nature of his office) against other branches and other sources of power. The founders thought it essential that the government as much as possible be attuned to the public good, which by definition meant disempowering factions, or special interests. And the executive was traditionally and overwhelmingly thought to be the branch best positioned to do that. It was further assumed that there would be strong support among the people for such non-partisanship - perhaps of the sort monarchs have often elicited as over against the parochial concerns, self-serving programmes, family biases, and regional baronies that tugged against the national interest.

It is precisely this posture and this prospect for public support, moreover, that may still be essential to the proper and effective conduct of the office of the presidency. Some distancing of the president (at least while in office) from demeaning partisanship might actually *strengthen* him in our constitutional system of government and *increase* his support in the nation. Throughout American history where the president has managed to achieve an above-party posture, at any rate, he has gained large and sometimes irresistible public backing - one thinks of Madison's post-1815 nationalism, Theodore Roosevelt's pure food and conservation campaigns, Franklin Roosevelt's depression leadership, Eisenhower's 1955 "Spirit of Geneva", and even Richard Nixon's rapprochement with China in 1972. In

41

each case the president moved clearly, even dramatically, to a stance or action that transcended narrower concerns and in the process gathered widespread support in the nation. The president in these cases gained that support both because he did manifestly act for the good of all and because the public so perceived him. We can scarcely imagine, in fact, the proper conduct of the nation's business without, at least at some notable junctures, the appearance of this leadership for the public good - nor can we imagine national good health and self-respect without the capacity of the people to understand and respond to such leadership. The suggestions for accentuating the non-partisanship of the presidency, then, seek simply to enlarge the scope for such a posture and for public responsiveness to it.

There would be problematic trade-offs, of course; most impor-tantly the loss of power (the colloquialism "clout" is peculiarly appropriate) the president might suffer by distancing himself from politics. The modern understanding especially has assumed that the president must be the effective, active, enthusiastic leader of his party in order to increase his support in Congress, secure election of officials beholden to him, nurture his party with lucrative offices, and keep it strong for the election of its loyal supporters. All this vital strength comes, the argument goes, only when the president is the avowed and active leader of his party. There is something to this argument, and its trade-off needs to be pondered seriously. What the president might lose by disavowing party while in office, however, he might more than make up by being thus better positioned for credible non-partisanship and better able to benefit from a widespread longing among the people for that kind of leadership. (This argument, in-cidentally, is congenial to the idea of a single, six-year term for the president, to eliminate any bias, or perception of it, induced by re-election politics.)

It seems at least possible, then, that a revitalisation of the non-partisan executive, sought so earnestly in 1787, might two centuries later provide a useful means for strengthening the links between wise leadership, improved citizenship, and good government viewed as axiomatic by the American founders. It is not that we need somehow to return to the particular circumstances and uses of government of the eighteenth century - that would be as undesirable as it would be impossible - but that we need to find the means for our day of moving constructively to validate the still-essential equations that good leadership can encourage proper citizenship, that such citizens can better choose wise leaders, and that both are crucial to good government. Even the most cursory look at the public life of the United States, and of many other modern democratic nations, makes quite clear that good government does not flow automatically from the democratic process and that we stand as much in need of active, public-spirited leadership and improved citizenship as did the fledgling American states after Independence. As Washington explained in his Farewell Address, under "popular governments" there will always be enough "spirit of party" to provide "useful checks upon the Administration of Government and serve to keep alive the spirit of liberty." There was as well, though, a "constant danger of excess" which he hoped the "force of public opinion might mitigate and assuage." It was of "primary importance", then, Washington added, that "public opinion be enlightened", and that government exert itself to that end. Only then could the "baneful effects of the Spirit of Party" be overcome and the nation experience the benefits of good leadership and good government. These qualifications, evoking the wisdom of Aristotle, are as relevant today as they were two millennia or two centuries ago.

REFERENCES

1. *Politics*, Book III, Chapter 7.

2. Max Farrand, ed., *The Records of Federal Convention*, 4 vols., New Haven, CT, 1937, II, 301, August 15, 1787.

3. Debate of July 19, 1787; *Ibid.*, II, pp. 52-54.

4. Speeches of January 1790; quoted in Geoffrey Seed, *James Wilson*, Millwood, NY, 1978, pp. 134-137.

5. Farrand, *Records*, II, p. 56, July 19, 1787.

6. *Ibid.*, II, pp. 203-205, 236-237, August 7, 9, 1787.

7. Quoted in Michael Wallace, "Changing Concepts of Party in the United States: New York, 1815-1828", *American Historical Review*, LXIV, 1968, pp. 487-489.

8. John Mitchell, testimony of July 11, 1973, in *The Watergate Hearings*, New York, NY, 1974, pp. 209-211.

4. THE UNCONSTITUTIONAL PRESIDENCY

Garry Wills, Northwestern University

Like one half of a vaudeville team, Checks is hard put to get employment anymore without his old partner, Balances. You book them as a single act. Together, they almost *are* the Constitution, according to modern explicators. We congratulate ourselves on what, because of interposing Cs and Bs, our government cannot do. We boast of its talent for stalling. The system of checks and balances is a clever device for limiting power, dividing responsibility and inhibiting actions by a single part of the government.

Yet the greatest power in the world - power to destroy that world - is not hedged about with constitutional restrictions. The president has a monopoly on the decision to release nuclear weapons. Neither Congress nor the Supreme Court can retard or scrutinise that power if the president deems their use necessary. The president would be acting under his authority to repel sudden attack employing what Richard Barnet of the institute for Policy Studies calls, with anticipatory officialese, "anticipatory retaliation". The massiveness of presumed external threat precludes the luxury of internal challenge or self-correction. Constitutional machinery will, at that point, be irrelevant.

But, at that point, is not everything but the threat irrelevant? In such a case, all bets would be off. Constitutional niceties would be the least of our concerns when many things besides the Constitution - including the world - might not be working much longer. We cannot judge our everyday government in terms of Doomsday.

Yet the shadow of Doomsday has darkened everyday government. President Roosevelt built and President Truman dropped the first atom bombs by their wartime authority as commander in chief. But the discipline of secrecy adopted in that period of emergency has been extended and normalised, like the office of commander in chief, into our half-war time of global conflict. Keeping our nuclear secrets was a principal concern of the security program Truman initiated in 1947 - a regime in which power was symbolised by graduated "clearances" to progressively "classified" material; in which keeping ordinary citizens from such arcana was a constant self-policing task; in which an attorney general's list created whole categories of "un-American" citizens; and in which the president had a secret army, the CIA, for use as his preventer of nuclear conflicts by preemptive intelligence and subversive feats.

The CIA is an unconstitutional body. It evades the provision, in Article I, that "a regular statement and account of the receipts and expenditures of all public money shall be published from time to time." (From one time to the next time means continually, without a gap, as in the reporting requirement of the president.) Reporting in secret to a few select members of Congress is not "publishing"; and the approximate sums smuggled into the defence budget do not constitute a "regular statement and account" - not the kind, for instance, that the IRS demands of citizens.

Thus the government is not accountable to its citizens, while the citizens have to be accountable to the government a reversal of the order spelled out by the framers of the Constitution. Yet how, in our world, could it be otherwise? We cannot let the public scrutinise things for which it lacks the proper clearance; and telling what the CIA does - by showing how it spent its money - goes against the whole reason for having a CIA, which is to act in the dark. And such actions are required by our quasi-war status.

In time of war, constitutional liberties are regularly suspended or interrupted. Manpower and resources are commandeered for the national need. Censorship is imposed. War having been declared, the office of commander in chief expands with the growing military forces over whom the president exercises that office. With a return to peace, the secrecy of censorship is lifted, resources are returned to private disposal, and the commander in chief has military authority over a dwindling number of citizens still under arms.

Yet that is not what happened after World War II. War measures were partially retained or reactivated - which means that the Constitution was only partially restored. Much of the government's activity would now be beyond the ordinary citizen's scrutiny. Its actions could be justified, not by accountability to an informed public, but only by access to information from which the public (for its own good) must be excluded. Undeclared wars would be waged by the commander in chief, without the consent (or, at times, the knowledge) of Congress. The office of commander in chief became the ordinary diplomatic stance of the president. Loyalty to the commander in chief was treated as a duty of all citizens in peacetime, not simply that of a soldier in war. Continual arming, and guarding of our arms, was a form of deterrent warfare that might become, at any moment, actual warfare. The nation was made up of "minutemen" on standby.

Quasi-soldiers do not often treat their highest officer the way advocates of the Constitution envisioned that citizens would treat the president and other public officials. We hear a good deal about distrust of power and suspicion of officeholders in the arguments for ratification. James Wilson, for instance, the principal figure in Pennsylvania's ratification, answered fears of the single executive by saying the president would be exposed and vulnerable. The single executive's responsibility is not diffused, as it would be in an executive council. His peril is the pledge of our safety, since, in Wilson's words, he is "conspicuously held up to the view and examination of the public ... Our first executive is not obnubilated behind the mysterious obscurity of counselors." He who stands alone will easily fall. The citizens will be quick to punish offences so obvious to their gaze. "The executive power", Wilson said, "is better to be trusted when it has no screen ... The President cannot roll upon any other the weight of his criminality."

Only such arguments could justify the adoption of an executive office so startling in its powers as the Constitution proposed to the nation in 1787. The experience with so many royal governors during the colonial period had made Americans shy away from singular authority. The president of Congress during the Confederation period had only precarious tenure on a position of little leverage in itself. The Articles of Confederation provided that "no person be allowed to serve in the office of president more than one year in any term of three years."

By offering a plan for a president perpetually re-eligible in continuous four-year terms, the Constitution raised the fears of elected monarchy in some, fears of the very plan Hamilton had espoused in the convention. Jefferson wrote from France that no president should be allowed more than one term. James Wilson, who said the president would have a special bond with the people at large, combined the argument for efficiency through concentrated authority with his argument for vulnerability through concentration of responsibility. Any forfeiture of the popular trust would lead directly to impeachment. The president was denied that immunity the Constitution conferred on members of the Senate or House: "For any speech or debate in either House, they shall not be questioned in any other place." The president, Wilson argued, would be questioned for all his words and acts:

"The executive as well as the legislative power ought to be restrained. But there is a remarkable contrast between the proper modes of restraining them. The legislature, in order to be restrained, must be divided. The executive power, in order to be restrained, should be one. Unity in this department is at once a proof and an ingredient of safety and of energy in the operations of government."

Accountability to the public is the essence of the president's office in Wilson's profound argument on its authority and its responsibility. And exposure was the basis of accountability. The president's office was to be photogropic, living on the trust established by openness: "Appointments made and sanctioned in this highly respectable manner will, like a flagrant and beneficial atmosphere, diffuse sweetness."

Yet the modern presidency has become nyctitropic, turning toward the darkness, preferring covert actions, replacing accountability with deniability. The discipline of darkness that surrounds his most awesome power - custody over nuclear weaponry - sheds the reverse of an aura, a penumbra, on any actions that can be associated with "national security". That term, as Egil Krogh admitted at his Watergate sentencing, tends to unstring the knees of citizens, making them fall down in genuflection. When we have given the president the power to blow up the world at his discretion, it seems captious to deny him the right to bomb Cambodia or Libya at will.

In the nyctitropic presidency, secrecy is a source of power as well as its symbol. The wartime justification of secrecy used to run this way: the citizens must be kept in the dark, as a necessary evil, in order to keep the enemy from knowing what one's country is doing and taking action on the basis of that knowledge. The modern presidency takes the old means and makes it the end: The citizens are kept in the dark about what the enemy already knows, lest the citizens take action to stop their own government from doing things they disapprove of. The Cambodians knew they were being bombed by the Nixon administration; the American Congress was deceived on that matter, not the Soviet Politburo. Fidel Castro knew of the assassination plots against him, but we did not - which means that when Castro accepted missiles to put an end to the secret war against him, President Kennedy was lying to the world about the unprovoked placing of missiles, and Krushchev was telling the truth about the provocations that had led to the crisis. The Soviets and the Cubans knew what Kennedy was still hiding from Americans (the existence of Operation Mongoose).

The president as commander in chief is not called to account - indeed, cannot be, without disobedience in the militarised citizenry. Loyalty to him is the measure of "American" strength. Questioning him is weakening the country, which cannot "afford to see another presidency destroyed". Political scientist Aaron Wildavsky has even written: "Another effort to impeach or to force a president to resign, thus reversing the result of the election without recourse to the people, would create a crisis of legitimacy." Impeachment may reverse the result of an election, but it hardly does so without resort to the people. It is a *constitutional* procedure, derived from the people's fundamental compact. Wildavsky must think the Constitution allows only one impeachment try per generation (or, perhaps, one per century).

Leonard Garment, who seems to specialise in protecting government officials from accountability, says that Watergate's evil legacy was a "prosecutorial ethic" in government. Here is the situation he *denounces*: "Watergate marked the beginning of an unprecedented attempt to root out evil and wrongdoing from American politics and to promote virtue and rectitude in the country's public life." We have travelled some distance from the days of the founders when the promotion of political virtue is called an evil outcome. The situations Garment describes sounds like the state James Wilson thought he was setting up. The president, according to Wilson, "should be alike unfettered and unsheltered by counselors. No constitutional stalking horse should be provided for him to conceal his turnings and windings, when they are too dark and too crooked to be exposed to public view."

Impeachment is not a breakdown of the system. When presidents violate the Constitution, impeachment is the system at work. The unhealthy state is one in which presidents are no longer held accountable. An active citizenry demanding that an administration give an account of itself is the one requirement the framers made on the people. They did not expect the public at large to be loyal soldiers, obeying orders without question. In fact, a citizenry unwilling to impeach a president who has broken his oath to uphold the Constitution would be considered a corrupted citizenry by the framers, the one constitutional defect for which there is no cure. As Wilson put that condition: "For a people wanting to themselves, there is indeed no remedy in the political dispensary."

The president is not our "commander in chief" (unless we are *all* in the military forces). That is what George Washington taught us, by such emphasis on his *civil* authority and his *citizen* responsibility as president. He maintained the neutrality policy against great opposition, because he thought the young republic should not form its ethos under war conditions. We see the evil of that in the retention of a war mentality through our whole "postwar" period of the last 40 years. The president's authority to make decisions in the dark, to conduct a continual half-war on the verge of nuclear war, or to let his subordinates do so, is profoundly at odds with a Constitution based on constant scrutiny by, and accountability to, the citizens. The Constitution is being hollowed out by the very means we have adopted to protect "the free world". When the executive branch of the United States imitates the enemies of freedom by mining the harbours of nations with which we are not at war, then lies about that to Congress, then holds itself immune from popular judgement, the opposition to despotims has taken on the forms of despotism.

This is not the kind of executive power the framers envisioned when they proposed with trepidation but with a corresponding determination - to impose limits on all parts of the government *especially* the presidency.

5. THE CONSTITUTION AS AN INSTRUMENT FOR SOCIAL REFORM

Allen F. Davis, Temple University

The founding fathers, by providing a way to amend the constitution, created an instrument to change society and to alter the relationship between the government and the community. But social reformers, who over the years have attempted to use the amendment process, have discovered that those who drafted the constitution created a rather blunt and unwieldy instrument, probably more blunt than they intended.

Article five of the Constitution provides that an amendment must pass both houses of Congress by a two-thirds vote, and then be ratified by the legislatures of three-fourths of the states. An alternative means for amending the Constitution provides for the states to take the initiative, but two-thirds of the states have to agree to call a convention to propose new amendments. Either way, amending the Constitution requires an overwhelming consensus that has to be achieved both nationally and in the states.

Many attempts to amend the Constitution have failed, most recently the Equal Rights Amendment. Since the adoption of Article five about 5000 amendments have been proposed, but only twenty-six have been approved and the first ten, the Bill of Rights, were added almost immediately. The prohibition movement succeeded in winning the passage of the eighteenth amendment in 1919, but the reform consensus quickly disappeared and the measure was overturned fourteen years later with the twenty-first amendment. The difficulty of amending the Constitution caused some reformers, most notably the abolitionists, to call for a more radical approach. "Overthrow this government", the usually conservative Susan B. Anthony cried in 1856, "commit its bloodstained constitution to the flames, blot out every vestige of that guilty bargain of the fathers...."[1]

I would like to examine two efforts by reformers to amend the Constitution rather than to burn it; one that ultimately succeeded, the campaign to win voting rights for women; and one that failed, the attempt to prohibit child labour. Perhaps we can learn something about the amending process, but also something about American society and the nature of reform.

Neither the Declaration of Independence nor the Constitution gave political rights to women. "I can't say that I think you are very generous to the ladies", Abigail Adams wrote to her husband John in

1776, "for Whilst you are proclaiming peace and good will to men, emancipating all nations, you insist upon retaining an absolute power over all wives."[2] But Adams and the other founding fathers had no idea of giving up that absolute power, in fact they thought that the superiority of men was ordained by God and nature. Except on very scattered occasions, and sometimes by accident, women had no right to citizenship in Colonial America, nor did the Revolution grant them that privilege, except for some reason in New Jersey where the constitution of 1776 declared that "all free inhabitants" meeting property and residency requirements could vote. In the 1780s and 90s a number of women took advantage of the loophole, but the law was soon changed. One male political leader thought it a "mockery" and "perfectly disgusting to watch female voters cast their ballots. "It is evident", he announced, "that women generally are neither by nature, nor habit, nor education ... fitted to perform this duty with credit to themselves, or advantage to the public."[3] In 1807 New Jersey changed the law specifically disenfranchising women. Women were not only denied the vote in the new republic but they had few other rights and privileges. In most cases, as in England, single women and widows could make contracts, represent themselves in court and conduct business, but as soon as they were married they forfeited these rights. In some states women began gradually to obtain more rights, but it was the mid-nineteenth century before the first married-women property law was passed that allowed women to retain control of property brought into a marriage. And women were prevented from going to college or entering the professions, could only under the most unusual circumstances sue for divorce, and in many other ways were unequal before the law.[4]

Many women chafed under these restrictions, and beginning in the 1830s women began to take part in reform movements, especially the temperance and abolitionist movements. Women like Sarah and Angelina Grimké shocked men and women alike by making speeches in public. "men and women were created equal", Sarah Grimké argued. "Whatever is right for men to do, is right for women. All I ask of our bretheren is that they will take their feet from off our necks and permit us to stand upright on that ground which God designed us to occupy."[5]

A number of American women went in 1840 to the World Anti-Slavery Convention in London. Elizabeth Cady Stanton, a brilliant writer and speaker as well as a wife and mother, and Lucretia Mott, a Philadelphia Quaker reformer, were angered when they were not allowed in the hall but forced to sit behind a curtain. They vowed to work for women's rights when they returned to America. It took them eight years, but they called a meeting at Seneca Falls, New

York. About 100 women and a few men attended the 1848 meeting. They drafted and read a women's Declaration of Independence. It was a self evident truth that all men and women were created equal, that men had usurped women's freedom and dignity. But where the Declaration charges George III with a series of grievances the women substituted "Man" for the "King". "Man endeavored in everyway he could to destroy women's confidence in her own powers, to lessen her self respect and to make her willing to lead a dependent and abject life." Among other things, the gathering asked for equal rights of education, the right to appear on public platforms, work equality before the law, and the "sacred right to the elective franchise."[6] They would have been dismayed if they had known that it would take seventy-two years before women won that right.

Many women worked hard to promote the abolition of slavery, and after the Civil War, they fought to win citizenship and voting rights for blacks. In fact many women reformers associated themselves with the slaves. "Her bondage, though it differs from the Negro slave", Stanton wrote, "frets and chafes her just the same. She too sighs and groans in her chains, and lives but in the hope of better things to come."[7]

Many women served as nurses or in other capacities during the Civil War and they fully expected that they would win the vote for themselves as well as for the freed slaves. But it soon became obvious that the male politicians did not want to include women in the 13th amendment that gave voting rights to the black man. It was the "Negro's Hour", the men pointed out and urged the women to have patience. "No, no, this is the hour to press women's claims", Stanton replied, "we have stood with the black man in the Constitution over half a century, and it is fitting now that the constitutional door is open that we should enter with him into the political kingdom of equality. Through all these years he has been the only decent co-peer we have had. Enfranchise him, and we are left outside with lunatics, idiots and criminals for another twenty years." But in the 14th amendment the word "male" was inserted into the Constitution for the first time, and it would be much more than fifty years before it was eliminated.[8]

The arguments against woman suffrage (used by both men and women) usually stressed women's special role, even women's superiority. "I do not wish to see the day come when the women of my race in my state shall trail their skirts in the muck and mire of partisan politics", a congressman from Florida announced in 1915. "I prefer to look to the American woman as she always has been, occupying her proud estate as the Queen of the American home, instead of regarding her as a ward politician in the cities. As the mother, the wife, the sister, she exercises a broader and deeper and mightiert influence than she can exercise or hope to on the stump and in the byways of politics in this land."[9] Some of the suffrage advocates used the same argument for women's special role, even for women's superiority, and implied that if given the vote women would vote for all the right causes, temperance for example, which was just what the politicians feared.

The suffrage forces won a few battles, a number of states allowed women to vote in school elections, and in the West women began to achieve more equal treatment. The territory of Wyoming gave full political equality to women in 1869, and when Wyoming became a state in 1890 it became the first to give women the vote. Colorado, Utah, and Idaho followed quickly, but between 1896 an 1910 no additional state granted women the right to vote. It was not that women gave up the struggle, in fact during the period from 1896 to 1910 women made great strides in other areas of American life. They went to college in greater numbers, and they began to enter the professions, indeed some of the pioneers created professions for themselves in social work, administration and scholarship. And the suffrage reformers bombarded the state legislatures with petitions, but why should the politicians support a voteless constituency? "At every political convention all matters of right, of justice, of the eternal verities themselves", one woman decided "are swallowed up in the one important question, 'will it bring party success?' and to this a voteless constituency cannot contribute in the smallest degree, even though it reprint the Ten Commandments, the Sermon on the Mount, the Golden Rule, The Magna Charta, and the Declaration of Independence."[10]

The suffrage reformers were not always united. One group began to argue that votes for middle class women should be supported in order to counteract the danger represented by the influx of so many immigrant men, who could be manipulated by the political bosses. Jane Addams and a few other women defended the political shrewdness and integrity of the new ethnic voters, both men and women. Addams took the traditional role of women as wife, mother, and housekeeper and argued that in an urban industrial age women must become municipal housekeepers, that in order to protect their homes and their families they now must be concerned with clean streets, a pure municipal water supply, and parks and playgrounds. In order to assure the health and safety of their families they needed the vote.[11]

In general the tactics of the National American Woman Suffrage Association (the largest and most important suffrage organisation) was not to use coercion, not to appear radical or to antagonise voters, and to be non-partisan. But after about 1910 they began to change.

They broadened their efforts; instead of just targeting law makers they set out to convert the masses of voters in the hope that the public would put pressure on the state legislatures. But perhaps even more important was the emergence of a younger group of leaders and the impact of the suffrage movement in Europe, especially in England. There are many women worth mentioning, but I will let Carrie Chapman Catt and Alice Paul stand for the new efficiency and militancy.

Carrie Chapman Catt, an efficient administrator and tireless organiser, devised the strategy that finally secured the vote for women. Catt, who grew up in Iowa, joined the Iowa Woman Suffrage Association as a young woman of 28 shortly after her first husband died. Before remarrying she insisted on a legal agreement giving her four months away from her husband to work for the suffrage cause (something unheard of at the time when it was assumed that husband and wife would never be apart). In 1915 she became the president of the National American Woman Suffrage Association. Prospects did not seem too bright in that year. Three additional states had granted women the vote bringing the number to 7, but there were groups like the National Association Opposed to Woman Suffrage, which argued that it was only the radicals who wanted the vote and declared that woman suffrage, socialism and feminism were "three branches of the same Social Revolution". But for the first time in the twentieth century a woman suffrage amendment had been brought to a vote in Congress in 1914. The Senate defeated it 35 to 34 and the House 174 to 204.[12]

Catt and an army of helpers coordinated the state campaigns with her work in Washington. The Washington headquarters sent precise information to the states on ways to put pressure on congressmen in local districts. They maintained a file on each congressman and senator. "There were facts supplied by our members in the states about his personal, political, business and religious affiliations; there were reports of interviews ... there was everything that could be discovered about his stand on woman suffrage...." The careful planning began to produce results, but a group of more militant women led by Alice Paul broke with the NAWSA. Paul, a Quaker from New Jersey had participated in some of the English suffrage battles. She had been arrested and participated in hunger strikes along with Emmeline Pankhurst and the other British suffragettes. Paul and her group picketed the White House, chained themselves to the fence, blocked the streets, and carried banners asking: "Mr. President, How long must women wait for liberty". In the summer of 1917 the government arrested over 200 women protesters and charged them with obstructing the sidewalk. It was just the kind of publicity that

Alice Paul sought and it probably forced Wilson, who was a reluctant supporter of Woman suffrage, to cooperate with the more moderate group. World War I also accelerated the movement for suffrage. Fourteen states petitioned congress in 1917 and twenty-six in 1919. Early in 1919 the House of Representatives passed the suffrage amendment by the required two-third margin and the Senate followed with little debate. Fourteen months later Tennessee became the thirty-sixth state to ratify and at last the women had the vote. We are no longer petitioners", Catt announced in celebration, "We are not wards of the nation but free and equal citizens."[13]

The passage of the nineteenth amendment did not have the far-reaching results that either its opponents or its supporters predicted, but it was ratified because after a long struggle an overwhelming consensus in favour of votes for women had finally been achieved.

Some of the same women who worked hard to promote suffrage also struggled to prohibit child labour. "I do not know why it is that women and children are invariably classed together", one reformer remarked. "I suppose it comes from two reasons: one because of the maternal relation; and second from their common political disabilities."[14] For the progressive reformers who tried to restructure society and to humanise the industrial city in the two decades before World War I, nothing was more troubling than the sight of little children, some as young as eight or nine, working ten or twelve hours a day in a factory. They were horrified by the look of stunted, sullen children. They feared for the future of a country that treated its most precious resource so carelessly. For the generation of reformers who optimistically thought they could restructure society, and who thought that environment was more important then heredity, improving parks and playgrounds, making better homes and schools were all part of their reform agenda, but if children were put to work at an early age then there was no way that their lives could be transformed, and the dream of building a better society would end in failure.

Jane Addams and her co-workers at Hull House tried to give candy to children in their neighbourhood on the west side of Chicago at Christmas time the first year they spent in the neglected and run down section of the city. They were shocked and surprised when the children refused to take the candy; then they learned that these children worked ten hours a day, six days a week in a candy factory. Promoting child labour reform became one of the first crusades undertaken by the settlement residents and they discovered, as other reformers would as well, that one could not solve the problem in the neighbourhood, or in the city. Their campaign led them to the state and then the nation. It led them eventually to seek an amendment to the Constitution.

It was hard to avoid the presence of child labour in a neighbourhood such as the one in which Hull House was located. Some children worked in factories, others helped their families work on garments in their tenement rooms. Still others became newsboys, or shoeshine boys. The Hull House campaign against child labour started, however, when Florence Kelley became a resident in 1891, and Kelley would lead the anti-child labour crusade not only in Chicago, but also in the nation, over the next two decades. Kelley grew up in a prosperous neighbourhood in Philadelphia. After graduating from Cornell University she applied for graduate school, but no American university would accept her because she was a woman. Disappointed but undaunted, she enrolled at the University of Zurich where she was converted to socialism, translated some of Engels's work and fell in love. She married a Polish doctor and had three children, but after they returned to the United States the marriage collapsed. Kelley headed for Illinois where the divorce laws were more lenient than in New York. Hull House became a place to live and a base from which to work. She had written an article about the dangers of child labour before moving to Chicago, but when John Altgeld, the reform governor of Illinois, made her a special investigator for the state she began to document the abuses of child labour with a vengeance. Kelley was a big woman who combined determination with a sense of humour, but she was something like a steam roller when she set out to pursue a goal. On one occasion she could find no lawyer in Chicago willing to take a child labour case against some of the prominent stores and factories in the city. So she went to law school at night, passed the bar exam and took the cases herself.

The Hull House reformers led the fight in Illinois to get a factory act passed that prohibited the employment of children under fourteen, at night, or for more than eight hours during the day. The reformers, led by Kelley, combined their moral outrage with carefully organised statistics to win the day in Springfield, the state capital. But in 1895 the State Supreme Court in Illinois found the eight hour provision unconstitutional. The reformers kept trying to get child labour laws passed, but either the legislature or the courts defeated their efforts. Reformers in Massachusetts, Pennsylvania, and other states had similar experiences. After all, many businessmen argued, it was good for children to work. They usually nostalgically recalled their own rural childhoods and how milking the cows and doing chores around the farm as children taught them discipline and character. Of course employing children at low wages was also very profitable. The reformers on their part, in their zeal to protect the children, often failed to appreciate how important children's wages

56

were in maintaining a marginal existence for many immigrant families, and they probably exaggerated the plight of some groups such as the newsboys.[15]

Frustrated at the local and state level, the child labour reformers organised on the national level. The National Child Labor Committee, formed in 1902, was a joint effort of social reformers like Kelley, who had moved to New York in 1899 to become Secretary of the National Consumer's League, clergymen like Edgar Gardner Murphy of Alabama, who was disturbed by the use of children in the southern textile mills, and assorted other reformers, including a number of socialists. Only in America did socialists work for child labour legislation rather than promoting the ownership of industry by the government.

The members of the National Child Labor Committee publicised the plight of working children. They wrote books and articles, organised exhibits and collected statistics. They even hired photographer Lewis Hine (whose haunting photographs of working children are now considered art) to document the danger and demoralising influence of work on newsboys, textile workers and other child wage earners. Some of the child labour reformers supported a federal child labour bill introduced in Congress in 1907, but others thought that the control of child labour should be a local and state matter. The nation was obviously not ready for this legislation; it went down to an overwhelming defeat. At the reformers' urging, however, President Theodore Roosevelt called a White House Conference on the Care of Dependent Children in 1909, and in 1912 the reformers finally achieved the creation of a Children's Bureau in the Department of Commerce and Labor. Julia Lathrop, a Hull House resident, was appointed as director. The Bureau had no power of enforcement, but it did become a place to gather statistics and promote change.

In 1912 twenty-two states still permitted children under fourteen to work in factories, thirty states still allowed children under sixteen to work more than eight hours a day, and twenty-eight states still let children under sixteen work at night. Even in states like Illinois and Massachusetts where the laws were reasonably strict, newsboys, those that worked in the sweating trades, and many employed in agriculture were not covered by the legislation. After two decades of struggle some of the reformers decided that local and state efforts were not enough.

Finally in 1916 the reformers convinced a reluctant President Woodrow Wilson that he should lend his support to a national child labour law pending in Congress. With the President's endorsement the Keating-Owen Act passed and was signed into law in the fall of 1916. It made illegal interstate commerce in goods produced in factories employing children under fourteen, or children under sixteen for more than eight hours a day or at night. It did not attempt to regulate work of children in the home, the street or in agriculture, but it was the product of the progressive consensus and it did pass. The bill had been opposed by the National Association of Manufacturers, most Southern states and many people using the same old arguments: children needed to work to give them training and improve their character, to help them support their families (especially their widowed mothers) and in addition the law was an abridgement of states rights.

The reformers' victory was short lived, however, because on June 3, 1918, only nine months after the act had taken effect, the Supreme Court ruled 5-4 in *Hammer v. Dagenhurt* that the act was unconstitutional. The majority of the court argued that the child labour law was an unwarranted exercise of the commerce power; the act regulated local labour conditions not interstate commerce. Disappointed, but not admitting defeat, the reformers introduced and passed a similar act, but this time the bill levied a federal tax on manufacturers who used child labour. The Supreme Court again, this time 8-1, declared the law unconstitutional.[16]

After two defeats at the hand of the Supreme Court the reformers, as a last resort, tried to amend the Constitution. Although there was bitter debate, the amendment, which gave Congress the power (but not the obligation) to regulate employment of those up to the age of eighteen, passed both houses by the necessary margin, but getting it ratified was another matter. Times had changed since 1916; much of the progressive consensus had given way to the social and cultural sag of the post war period. The opposition to any restriction on the employment of children had hardened and become somewhat irrational. Much of the opposition also was tied into both the woman suffrage and prohibition amendments. As one man put it, "They have taken our women away from us by a constitutional amendment; they have taken our liquor away from us; and now they want to take our children."[17] *The Manufacturers' Record* charged that the amendment would take "entirely from the parents the right to have their children, sons or daughters, do any work of any kind, so long as they are under 18 years of age", including "driving the cows to pasture, or hoeing the vegetables, or doing any work of that character, even for their own parents. Under the bill the mother would have no right to teach her daughter to do any housework whatsoever, whether it be sweeping the floors or doing the dishes."[18] Even the president of Columbia University, Nicholas Murray Butler, joined the opposition. "So far from protecting childhood", he declared, the Amendment is "a deliberate attempt to put forty-five million of our population under

58

the control of the Congress of the United States.... It might easily be made the entering wedge for a purely Communist attitude of the Government toward the people."[19]

The Communist theme became important as the amendment fell victim to Red Scare tactics. One editor decided: "The proposed amendment is fathered by Socialists, Communists, and Bolshevists. They are active workers in its favor. They look forward to its adoption as giving them the power to nationalize the children of the land and bring about in this country the exact conditions which prevail in Russia."

"If adopted this amendment would be the greatest thing ever done in America in behalf of the activities of Hell. It would make millions of young people under 18 years of age idlers in brain and body, and thus make them the devil's best workshop. It would destroy the initiative and self-reliance of manhood and womanhood of all the coming generation." The Woman Patriot, a vitriolic right wing publication sponsored by a group that had opposed woman suffrage, announced. "This benign-looking amendment drawn and promoted principally by an American socialist leader (Mrs. Florence Kelley, translator of Karl Marx and friend of Frederick Engels, who instructed her how to introduce socialism into the flesh and blood of Americans), is a straight Socialist measure. It is promoted under direct orders from Moscow." Often Florence Kelley bore the brunt of the attack and the critics usually mentioned her Russian-sounding married name even though she had divorced her husband and dropped that name more than thirty years previously.[20]

There were other arguments against the amendment as well, and it probably was a mistake to make the age eighteen, but the amendment ran into difficulty largely because there no longer was a reform consensus that supported it. It failed to be ratified even in states like Massachusetts and New York, which had usually been sympathetic to child labour legislation. By the end of 1925 four states had ratified but ten had rejected the amendment, and the amendment was effectively dead. After the depression hit and the mood of the country had changed a few more states did approve the amendment. By 1933 twenty states had ratified, but the amendment was never approved by the necessary three quarters of the states. The concept of child labour legislation was written into many New Deal bills, especially into the codes approved by the National Industrial Recovery Administration, but that law was declared unconstitutional in 1935. It was not until 1938, with the Fair Labor Standards Act, that a federal law prohibited the employment of children, but the problem of child labour still remains, as witness recent investigations of sweating labour and itinerant farm workers.

What can we conclude about the amendment process? Mary Berry in a recent book on *Why the ERA Failed* decides that amendments get passed only when two conditions prevail simultaneously. First, proponents must show that a constitutional amendment (and *only* a constitutional amendment) can remedy some serious social wrong; and second, there must already exist a broadbased and regionally diverse consensus in the states that such an amendment is desirable.[21] Amending the constitution is a slow, frustrating and difficult process at best. The requirement of ratification by three fourths of the states allows the opposition to an amendment to get organised. To be successful a campaign to support an amendment must be carefully organised and it can't last too many years or the support may well erode. For reformers seeking an amendment is usually the last resort, and the process is often maddening, but probably the founding fathers designed the process intentionally and well. Reform can cut both ways. If the process of amendment were easier the danger of an amendment requiring school prayer, or insisting on the teaching of creationism, or outlawing abortion would be much more immediate. Those who drafted the Constitution 200 years ago in Philadelphia knew what they were doing. They quite intentionally made the amendment process slow and arduous, and a very blunt instrument for social reform.

REFERENCES

1. Quoted in Alma Lutz, "Susan B. Anthony", in Edward T. James, ed., *Notable American Women*, Cambridge: Harvard Univ. Press, 1971, I, p. 53.

2. Abigail Adams to John Adams, March 31, 1776, republished in Alice S. Rossi, ed., *The Feminist Papers*, N.Y.: Bantam, 1974, pp. 10-11.

3. Mary Beth Norton, *Liberty's Daughters: The Revolutionary Experiences of American Women, 1750-1800*, Boston: Little Brown, 1980, pp. 191-93.

4. Marylynn Salmon, *Women and the Law of Property in Early America*, Chapel Hill: Univ. of North Carolina Press, 1986.

5. Gerda Lerner, *The Grimké Sisters from South Carolina*, Boston: Houghton Mifflin, p. 192.

6. Ellen Carol DuBois, *Feminism and Suffrage: The Emergence of an Independent Women's Movement in American, 1848-1869*, Vol. I, Rochester N.Y.: Charles Mann, 1881, p. 860.

7. Elizabeth Cady Stanton, Susan B. Anthony and Matilda Joslyn Gage, eds., *The History of Woman Suffrage, 1848-1861*, Ithaca: Cornell University Press, 1978, p. 23.

8. *Ibid.*, Vol. II, pp. 267-270; DuBois, *Feminism*, pp. 60-61.

9. Aileen S. Kraditor, *The Ideas of the Woman Suffrage Movement, 1890-1920*, New York: Columbia University Press, 1965, p. 26.

10. *Ibid.*, p. 220.

11. Allen F. Davis, *American Heroine: The Life and Legend of Jane Addams*, New York: Oxford University Press, 1973, pp. 186, 87.

12. Kraditor, *The Ideas*, pp. 219-48; Anne F. Scott and Andrew M. Scott, *One Half the People: The Fight for Woman Suffrage*, Philadelphia: J.B. Lippincott, 1975.

13. Kraditor, *The Ideas*, pp. 219-48; Eleanor Flexner, *Century of Struggle: The Woman's Rights Movement in the United States*, revised edition. Cambridge: Harvard Univ. Press, 1975, pp. 286-303.

14. Allen F. Davis, *Spearheads for Reform: The Social Settlements and the Progressive Movement*, New York: Oxford University Press, 1967, p. 133.

15. *Ibid.*, pp. 123-33.

16. Mary Frances Berry, *Why ERA Failed: Politics, Women's Rights and the American Process of the Constitution*, Bloomington: Indiana Press, 1986, pp. 45-55.

17. Quoted in Walter Tratner, *Crusade for the Children: A History of the National Child Labor Committee and Child Labor Reform in America*, Chicago: Quadrangle, 1970, p. 171.

18. *Ibid.*, p. 173.

19. Quoted in Jeremy F. Felt, *Hostages of Fortune: Child Labor Reform in New York State*, Syracuse: Syracuse University Press, 1965, p. 202.

20. Tratner, *Crusade*, pp. 172-175; J. Stanley Lemms, *The Woman Citizen: Social Feminism in the 1920s*, Urbana: University of Illinois Press, 1973, pp. 209-226.

21. Berry, *Why ERA Failed*, pp. 1-3.

6. LOCATING THE CONSTITUTION

Janet S. Lindgren, University at Buffalo

In the United States the constitution is "at hand", a pervasive if elusive part of the atmosphere. This is so true that the question for Michael Kammen's 1986 book, *A Machine That Would Go Of Itself: The Constitution In American Culture*, is not how he found enough detail to fill four hundred closely packed pages (or where he got that marvelous title). Rather the question is how and where he chose to locate the constitution in his thinking, and thus in his research. The same question is there for each of us who sees the constitution as part of the world in which we work.

In this article I want to talk about how and where Americans, and especially American scholars, have located the United States Constitution in their thinking. Underlying this endeavour is my belief that the location of the constitution in our thinking is a matter of choice and that the choice matters. Each of the three arguments through which I work is a variation on that theme.

I start with an argument - with former Chief Justice Burger, about how we think about the constitution and what might be attempted in celebration of its bicentennial. In the process of building this first argument I also mean to make clear my sense of the nature and possibilities of argument.

The second argument moves from the bicentennial to the body of Supreme Court opinions. Normal constitutional scholarship has taken those cases as its domain and is sufficiently established that scholars can worry in it rather than about it. They worry about the legitimacy and the substance of choices made by the justices. A growing body of recent constitutional scholarship in the law schools collectively constitutes an argument for work beyond the cases.

The final argument takes place in the vast open spaces beyond the cases. Scholars working there and concerned with constitutions impose their own order on the issues and the archives. One choice is to maintain the constitution at the centre as the given, selecting material that reflects on it and organising presentations around it. It is a very different experience to work in other than constitutional terms and learn about the constitution in the process. Constitutional scholarship so organised explores constitutional place rather than giving the constitution its place.

An Argument about Celebrating the Constitution

Warren Burger resigned as Chief Justice of the United States Supreme Court to head the National Commission on the Bicentennial of the U.S. Constitution. He knew what he wanted to accomplish:

> Now the ordinary affairs of life, don't bring constitutional questions, so we've all taken (the constitution) for granted too much. Now we are going to try to break through that." (*NYT*, p. 10)

> "Essentially we have defined our objectives as 'a history and civics lesson for all of us.'" (Haberman, p. 33)

> Addressing lawyers he insisted, "... we of the legal profession must take the lead in educating the American people about the Constitution and the principles on which it is based." By that he meant, "we ... must discuss ... with the American people the unique system of separated and divided powers we created to provide internal checks and produce the balance that has given us an ordered liberty unparalleled in history. (*NYSBJ*, p. 58)

The overall effort is to inform. "I like that word better than educate" Burger later decided, "nobody likes to be educated". (*NYT*, p. 10)

> "We hope", Burger says, "to have copies of the Constitution on the checkout counter of every supermarket in the U.S."

> "Would you happen to guess", he asks an interviewer, "how many restaurant placemats would be in this country with the Preamble to the Constitution across the top?" "Several hundred million. *** McDonald's alone uses up toward 10 million a day." (*NYT*, p. 10)

This is enough, in caricature, to capture Burger's - and the National Commission's bicentennial effort. That effort has been to teach what the constitution *is*, to inform a people who don't face constitutional questions in their ordinary lives. It assumes that if the constitution is going to be a living heritage you've got to learn its greatness.

An argument - and that is what I am assembling - requires an "other", another world, a set of alternative assumptions. For that I use my own position, and in fairness I present it in as rough and truncated a version as I did Warren Burger's position:

> The constitution and the judicial decisions that develop it are

part of the atmosphere in the United States. So too, to *start* a list, are religion, family, ethnicity and community. It is in that atmosphere that argument goes on about fundamental choices, made and remade, that constitute United States society. In that sense the constitution shares a place at the heart of everyday life.

Among those others the constitution has some special attributes that can make it a valuable part of the atmosphere in which social argument occurs. (1) It is formally applicable to all citizens. While the formality may mean that resort to it does not come naturally, it may also mean that it is available by default when no other possibilities are forthcoming. (2) It provides both structure and open spaces. (3) It is longstanding yet changing. (4) Given the adversary development of the constitution through litigation, it may help normalise the tension that is built into argument.

We need the others to understand when constitutional presence matters, when it combines, when it is displaced. We lose the others when the constitution is celebrated as a thing in itself. The bicentennial could be - could have been - an occasion to try to nurture involvement and argument, and our understanding of the possibilities for the constitution as part of that.

I am quite serious about this alternative, even though I realise that within the world of official celebratory planning, where the mandate of the Commission was "to educate people and teach people the greatness of that document", my "other" may seem one of Feyerabend's "dream worlds" (p. 32).

Argument requires opposition, an "other". At the same time, it demands connection. The connections are emotional as well as rational. Warren Burger is serious about the constitution. So am I. Both of us have devoted the last year to pursuing our respective constitutional visions (though rather more of you will have heard of his). Common commitment might constitute enough of a connection that he and I could hear one another - or that outsiders could hear us both.

The tension between opposition and connection is the dynamic of argument. The difficulty is sustaining this tension so that understanding can grow, against the human inclination to resolve tension. A sustaining atmosphere for the argument I have sketched could have existed at an early meeting called to draft the mandate of the bicentennial commission. No such atmosphere could have been expected when all state committee chairpersons and executive directors later met to share planning and programme promotion ideas. By then

65

whatever tension there might have been between opposing possibilities had been resolved in favour of "an enormous history lesson on the meaning and functioning of our uniquely successful system of representative democracy." (Habermann, p. 33)

An Argument about the Constitution
as the Choices of Judges

An overwhelming proportion of constitutional scholarship is located within the opinions of the Supreme Court. The opinions of judges are analysed and criticised, the lives of judges and of famous cases are chronicled, and the choice-making of judges is the predominant concern of constitutional theory. Even the current rush of scholarly attention to the work of the founders has been tied to the question of how the judges should interpret the constitution. Those who write within the cases seldom comment on this choice of location. That seems to me the surest measure of what is normal within constitutional scholarship.

Understanding how that came to be the normal location of constitutional scholarship takes us back at least as far as the Supreme Court decision in 1803 that judges, who must apply the law, would determine whether statutes comported with the constitution and thus were "law". The eventual consequence of that decision was an elaborate body of published judicial opinions about the constitution. The resulting body of opinions constituted a constitutional world that was - and is - diverse and complex yet contained, rich with possibilities yet (almost) manageable in magnitude.

The diversity within the judges' opinions is striking. There is diversity within a case because the judge who writes the opinion for the court is very likely to explore and then reexplore the issue. There will be further diversity if other members of the court, agreeing with the official outcome but not the official reasoning, explain their positions - with the same tendency to "back up and do it again". The justices who disagree with the outcome may provide their own dissenting explanations. Nor do they escape the temptation to "play it again". To these add the explanations of the judges of the appellate and trial courts in the federal system or the explanations of the judges of the state courts when the case comes by that route. To the richness of any one case add other cases on the same issue, other cases on parallel issues, and prior decisions on all of these. This remarkable diversity within the cases is multiplied by the diversity of issues across which cases range.

The explosive force of diversity is confined by the style of

66

reasoning dominant within the cases and by the interaction of the judges. Legal reasoning is a process of connecting. Current decisions are made consistent with prior decisions to whatever extent possible. Judges working from very different positions explicitly argue with each other in their opinions, forcing diversity into a conversation.

Diversity is likewise contained by the physical existence of the cases. The entire relevant judicial world is all there within the familiar taupe covers of the West Publishing Company volumes as well as the competing colours of competing companies. All the taupe covers will probably be lined up together in any library that stocks the courts. West Company provided pre-computer order with its "key number" indexing system and integrated volumes. In the computer age LEXIS and WESTLAW provide access to the same richness through customised searches within the case database.

The combination of case diversity and case containment produced, and continues to produce, a dense environment for scholarship. That density, I think, has determined much of the development of constitutional scholarship.

Density is attractive in the first place. There is lots to work with but, if the boundaries hold, some limits on the possibilities. There is enough richness to support difference but close boundaries encourage interaction. And always the world of cases grows denser, and thus more attractive. The judges add increasing numbers of opinions. Scholars attracted to the cases add to the density and thereby increase the attraction for other scholars.

As the density within the domain of cases increases, the gap widens between constitutional scholarship within the cases and that outside. Writers working within the cases build on prior work within the cases. Their writing is increasingly for insiders who know the players and the positions. Working within the cases comes to require an enormous investment of time and energy. Those starting within the cases have decreasing amounts of energy free for reaching outside the cases. Those working outside the cases cannot readily borrow from scholarship within the cases.

Finally, density sharpens substantive concerns that attract still more scholars. Those working within the cases are continually surrounded by judges exercising the power of judicial review, saying "no" to the legislatures. Judicial choice is immediate and clear; the choices of the legislatures are seen by reflection at best. In this setting scholars have become overwhelmingly concerned with the legitimacy of constitutional choices made by judges. The now common perception that the judges were wrong in their nay-saying during the Progressive period and the New Deal reinforces concern with the legitimacy of judicial choice. As more is written about the legitimacy of the judges' choices more scholars are drawn to what increasingly parades as a crisis issue.

It is in the nature of "normal" that it doesn't have to argue. The existence and continuing force of normal scholarship *are* its argument. A growing body of constitutional scholarship in the law schools collectively constitutes an argument for work that reaches beyond - but still includes - the cases. The particular arguments vary in the way they contrast and connect with normal constitutional scholarship.

1) A first group of scholars takes the legitimacy of judicial choice as its central concern but reaches outside the cases for answers. In doing so these scholars share the concern that informs a great deal of normal constitutional scholarship. Scholars who seriously confine their work to the domain of cases must find legitimacy for the choices of the judges within the cases. Generally this has meant drawing legitimacy from the process of judicial decision-making itself. Herbert Wechsler tried it with "neutral principles" in the sixties. John Hart Ely attempted it with a "representation-reinforcing" mode of decision in his 1981 book, *Democracy and Distrust*. Each provoked a whirlwind of writing in response - not about the question, but rather about the proper answer.

By the eighties a larger proportion of those who joined in the fray were inclined to reach beyond the cases to solve this problem posed by the cases. Explorations have ranged from the possibilities of drawing on republican values to ways of finding communities of shared meaning and beyond. Each foray has generated debate over whether the judges have valid recourse to the alternative suggested, or whether its use would simply constitute another judicial imposition that would have to be legitimated.

This work constitutes a striking "other" to constitutional scholarship within the cases. Its writers draw on worlds that are simply unavailable to normal constitutional scholarship. At the same time, this work is closely connected to normal constitutional scholarship - it is, after all, struggling with the same question. The result has been engagement and sometimes bitter attack. Whatever the ultimate fate of this work, it is not its present fate to be ignored.

2) Another group of scholars maintains the conventional focus on cases, but does not treat the opinions of the judges as exercises of power that require legitimation. In fact, Robert Burt took constitutional cases as signalling that there could not be a legitimate exercise of authority.

> (T)he proper purpose of judicial intervention is to signify that the dispute at hand is so deeply divisive as to moot the applicability of basic democratic principles. From this perspective judicial authority cannot depend on unquestionably legitimate authority. (p. 485)

James White saw cases as a "continuing and collective process of conversation and judgment". (p. 264)

This change in perspective changes the questions. Burt wanted to know how courts could "ensure that anyone's claim for inclusion in a communal relation receive sustained, serious attention from all others". (p. 500) In answer he parallelled the teaching of the biblical parables and the teaching of the judges.

> Judicial invocation of the Constitution recurrently uses the same methods as these parables: converting all into needy outsiders by confounding insider and outsider and then offering hope for ultimate protection by mapping a path back inside for everyone. (p. 471)

For White the process of "conversation and judgment" that occurs in cases constitutes a culture of argument. What White wants to know is how that "culture of argument" functions in law. Like Burt, White finds his parallels outside law.

Like scholars who work within the cases, Burt and White are willing to start with cases and continue attending to cases. There the connection ends. What Burt and White see when they look at a case is very different from scholars who see an exercise of judicial authority that must be legitimated. In turn their questions are different and they draw on different bodies of learning. Their tone and style are markedly different. Without much connection their work produces little tension. It may be their fate to be often footnoted but little engaged.

3) A final group of scholars explores the creation of constitutional meaning, but without preferring the contributions of the judges. These writers vary by the breadth of the domain they set. Those closest to case-based scholarship have moved only to include the legislature. Those with the furthest reach move to society at large.

Louis Fisher argued the existence and importance of constitutional interpretation in Congress. He supported his argument with studies of "the debates in 1789 on the President's removal power; the concept of coordinate construction as understood by Thomas Jefferson, Andrew Jackson and Abraham Lincoln; and the judicial doctrines that present the Supreme Court as the 'ultimate interpreter'." (p. 709) Then he moved to contemporary practice and studied the Fair Labor Standards Amendments of 1974, the legislative veto and a section of the Organized Crime Control Act. Fisher concluded that Congress can and does make "significant contributions to the constitutional dialogue". "The Court is neither final nor infallible. Judicial decisions rest undisturbed only to the extent that Congress, the President, and the general public find the decisions convincing, reasonable, and acceptable." (p. 746)

In an earlier article I traced the interaction of New York's courts and its legislature on constitutional issues between 1870 and 1920. I chose that period because of the established perception that during that time the courts effectively cut off legislative participation. I found instead that "(d)uring this period it was the interaction between New York's courts and legislature - not judicial ultimatum - that determined constitutional content, and within that interaction it was the legislature, so often pictured at the mercy of the courts, that tended to dominate." (p. 591)

Both Fisher and I undertook relatively cautious adventures. Although we were not willing to stay within the domain of cases we did not stray beyond the traditionally conceived domain of law. Robert Cover exercised no such caution. He started with communities, for "the Constitution is a widespread, though not universally accepted basis for interpretations; it is a center about which many communities teach, learn, and tell stories." (p. 25) For him the Mennonite community "creates law as fully as does the judge". (p. 28)

> (T)he interpretations offered by judges are not necessarily superior. The Mennonites are not simply advocates, for they are prepared to live and do live by their proclaimed understanding of the Constitution. Moreover, they live within the complex encodings of commitments ... that ground the understanding of the law that they offer. (p. 29)

When Cover is done the most that he will claim for judges is that "(they) are like the rest of us. They interpret and they make law." (p.67) Cover followed the advice with which he concluded: "We ought to stop circumscribing the *nomos*; we ought to invite new worlds." (p. 68)

The tension between opposition and connection is the dynamic of argument. This third cut of work has generated more comment than engagement. The reason for the weakness of the tension, and the resulting absence of argument, varies with the piece.

70

Those of us who add the legislature's involvement to that of the courts complicate the working world enormously. The qualifications, exceptions and variations that are required in our work make it easier to resist the view we bring. So too does the fact that we work without the support of years of case studies. In my work on New York I could only say that a 1947 study of judicial review in Virginia and a 1936 survey of federal legislation supported my conclusions. However strongly I put the case for generalising from New York State at the turn of the century, my sample had to carry a lot of weight. The "other" we provide is suggestive, qualified and by example, against a bulwark of writing about constitutional choice within judicial opinions.

Cover's *nomos* includes the judges of case-based scholarship - and everyone else. His reach is so far beyond those who dominate constitutional inquiry that I think they do not feel pressure from his work. Cover is respected, even revered, but his connection to and his opposition to case-based scholarship are neither immediate enough nor strong enough to have produced much real engagement.

With this third group I finish accounting for a collective argument for constitutional work that reaches beyond - but still includes - the cases. At the same time that it is an argument for a broader reach it is a vivid reminder of the power of settled boundaries. The closer writers stay to work within bounds the greater the engagement and thus the force of their argument. The further writers reach beyond the boundary the less force they exert on it. Continuing the work that Cover exemplifies will require both patience and faith.

An Argument about the Constitution as Constant

Work in the preceding section that argued against case confines was still subtly shaped by those cases. The possibility of engagement with the opposition was enhanced by working on issues to which the court had spoken. Billing as the prestigious "Foreword" to the *Harvard Law Review*'s annual Supreme Court issue required at least some connection to the work of the Supreme Court. Selection for publication would have been facilitated by being recognisable as "a constitutional law piece", especially in these bicentennial years.

Michael Kammen, in *A Machine that Would Go of Itself: The Constitution in American Culture*, didn't argue against constitutional inquiry shaped by the cases and thus he avoided having his own energies and efforts shaped by it. Instead he simply cut off the world of cases, its producers and perpetuators. From the first paragraph he

71

declared his concern was "not (with) lawyers, nor judges, nor professors of constitutional law". (p. xi) That left rather a lot for Kammen, the cultural historian: "the cultural impact of the United States Constitution", "the place of the Constitution in the public consciousness and symbolic life of the American people." (p. xi)

Writers who escape to the vast open spaces beyond the cases must impose their own order on the issues and the archives. In doing so the constitution might be the constant or one of the variables, the organising concept or part of the data. Therein is the argument of this section, an argument between Kammen's work and my own.

Kammen's choice is vividly captured in miniature in a self-portrait at the end of the first appendix. "The Roper Center's Office of Archival Development at the University of Connecticut in Storrs", he explained, "has a computer-accessible archive of thirty-five polling organizations that have been active since the later 1930's."

> By punching in such key words as 'Constitution', 'Bill of Rights', 'Supreme Court', etc., it is possible to obtain lists of pertinent polls in each category. The researcher can then request the tabulated results of particular polls that appear most relevant to the inquiry being pursued. (p. 404)

At the Roper center, and throughout his book, Kammen organised and selected by the Constitution (and its synonyms). It was his constant.

Kammen voted with pages and his considerable reputation for the constitution as the constant, for the constitution as the central organising concept. This is a choice that could easily become established: 1) *A Machine That Would Go Of Itself* provides a descriptive base that will make it easier to work where Kammen has been than where he has not. He provides detailed research directions for those who may wish to follow him. 2) Critics who think Kammen has left much to those who come after nonetheless assume he has set the inquiry: "put(ting) the Constitution into its historical and cultural context, ask(ing) the important questions, and introduc(ing) the themes around which a national discussion can be fruitfully structured", (Andrews). 3) Organisation by the constitution gives shape - familiar shape at that - to research plans. That can be reassuring to the scholar about to invest an enormous amount of time and energy and is attractive to dissertation committees and to funding sources. 4) Organisation by the constitution coincides with constitutional niches that already exist within academia, at least in law, history and political science. 5) Organisation by the constitution is consistent with the mystique and magnetism of the constitution, "the Supreme Law of the Land".

The bicentennial has reinforced the choice to put the constitution at the centre of scholarly efforts. It was not mere chance, I think, that Kammen's book was published on September 17, 1986, one year to the day before the bicentennial of the signing of the Constitution. Bicentennial funding for scholarship was available for several anticipatory years. Numerous symposia, colloquia and conferences have been organised around the constitution, especially in the last year. While the bicentennial has provided momentum for all work connected to the constitution the primary force has been centripetal, toward the constitution at the centre.

With the approach he had chosen Kammen could describe the constitutional "perceptions and misperceptions, uses and abuses, knowledge and ignorance of ordinary Americans". The enormity of that job was eased somewhat by the built-in preference for sources that explicitly use the term "constitution" (or one of its synonyms), as would be more likely in the official and self-congratulatory material with which Kammen admitted being much concerned. It was matched by Kammen's seemingly boundless energy. The descriptive task was enormous - and accomplished. What Kammen could not do was evaluate. He could not explain "the cultural *impact* of the United States Constitution" while cutting off the rest of that culture. Nor could he "describe the *place* of the Constitution in the public consciousness and symbolic life of the American people" without other pieces of that consciousness and symbolic life.

The "other" to *A Machine That Would Go Of Itself* is the book that I still hope to find. A cultural historian could take American culture or some cut of it as the constant and make the constitution a *part* of that. If Kammen had made American public consciousness or symbolic life the constant and *included* the constitution within the cultural parameters he would have had the possibility of saying something about the constitution's place and impact. Doing so would not have been without its risks. Placing the constitution in a full cultural context would have greatly increased the magnitude of an already enormous task. The increase in complexity might have made it difficult to say *anything* about the constitution. If either of these was solved by sampling, the vulnerability of the evaluation would have been greatly increased. One may learn more about the constitution by focussing less upon it - but the risk is learning nothing at all.

For a legal academic (and I suspect for others) "constitutional inquiry" that does not centre on the constitution is distressingly yet invitingly open. That openness forces at least three choices. The first choice is of the questions that will organise the inquiry. Choosing is the easy part for anyone willing to listen to their own recurring questions. For me the questions are about the nature of "social argument" the process by which the choices that constitute a society are found and made. The hard part is suppressing the anxiety that accompanies a choice to leave familiar territory. For some the new territory will be a different - but still recognisable - field of academic inquiry, complete with its traditions, methods, and body of literature. For some there will be no recognisable academic inquiry along the lines of the question chosen. Proceeding into unfamiliar territory of either sort requires audacity, with an equal measure of faith in the correcting powers of the intellectual exchange that should somehow follow if you get it wrong.

Settling on the questions that mark the domain of inquiry opens up the choice of how and where to look for answers within it. Sensible calculation informs the choice, but so does instinct. Robert Darnton set out to investigate "ways of thinking in eighteenth century France" (p. 3), a broad domain by any measure. He described of his choice in making his way through the "incredibly rich" archives of the Old Regime.

> There is no better way, I believe, than to wander through the archives. One can hardly read a letter from the Old Regime without coming up against surprises.... When we cannot get a proverb, or a joke, or a ritual, or a poem, we know we are on to something. By picking at the document where it is most opaque, we may be able to unravel an alien system of meaning. (p. 4)

> ... I have pursued what seemed to be the richest run of documents, following leads wherever they went and quickening my pace as soon as I stumbled on a surprise. Straying from the beaten path may not be much of a methodology, but it creates the possibility of enjoying some unusual views and they can be the most revealing. (p. 6)

In my own work intransigence has played the part of Darnton's opacity and surprise. I have chosen a web of argument about manufacture in homes, in New York City, at the turn of the century. There are perfectly sensible reasons for the choice, but there is also the fact that it was the one issue which absolutely refused to behave for me in an earlier comprehensive study.

Choosing a domain and a way through it probably leads to dense detail and certainly leads to another choice. Having sought complexity and depth by adding to the constitution (rather than simplifying by sorting with it), how does one follow the constitution through the resulting dense and varied material? For me, the solution has been very consciously to impose a working structure on the material while at the same time using the material exposed and uncovered to rethink the structure itself.

I am working from a series of paired research perspectives, with the constitution being moved progressively further and further into the background: first, manufacturers of cigars and the cigar makers International Union, who fought and refought the constitutionality of successive statutes prohibiting the manufacture of cigars in dwellings; then, Florence Kelley, who preached an "everyday citizen's obligation to change the constitution to meet social needs" and the Socialist Cigarmakers Union who sought to reconstitute the social system within which the forms of manufacture would be determined; finally, Italian women home garment workers for whom family ties displaced constitutional constraints and an early constitutional scholar whose "family" was created by constitutional discourse. I match these pairings in turn with the recent work of constitutional scholars in the law schools. I am interested in their perception of their own contribution to social argument, and that is built into their writing.

I do not expect this capsule description of my work to convey more than my determination to impose structure on rich and rowdy material. Carefully imposed structure seems to me essential for tracking a constitution in material that is not chosen to highlight or respect the constitution. The structure I have imposed is as complex as the material it shapes. Above all, this structure is as consciously imposed as it is always tentative.

I have just followed a series of choices faced by writers whose constitutional work does not centre on the constitution. Each choice brings the writer's instincts and understandings to the surface. That makes the writer vulnerable but it also makes the writer's way of thinking accessible. That accessibility is critical because it is a way of thinking that will mark this as a body of work, as something other than pieces of other wholes. As a body of work it will provide an argument against scholarship that continues to limit us to what we can learn with the constitution at the centre.

REFERENCES

James Andrews, "Review: A Machine that Would Go of Itself", *Christian Science Monitor*, September 22, 1986, p. 23.

Warren Burger, "Lawyers and the Framing of the Constitution", *New York State Bar Journal*, January 1987, p. 10.

Warren Burger and Irvin Molotsky, "On Fixing the Constitution and

Spilling Gravy all over the Preamble", *New York Times*, April 16, 1987, p. 10.

Robert Burt, "Constitutional Law and the Teaching of the Parables", *Yale Law Journal*, Vol. 9, 1984, p. 455.

Robert Cover, "Foreword: Nomos and Narrative", *Harvard Law Review*, vol. 97, 1983, p. 4.

Robert Darnton, *The Great Cat Massacre and other Episodes in French Cultural History*, 1984.

John Hart Ely, *Democracy and Distrust: A Theory of Judicial Review*, 1981.

Paul Feyerabend, *Against Method*, 1975.

Louis Fisher, "Constitutional Interpretation by Members of Congress", *North Carolina Law Review*, vol. 63, 1985, p. 707.

Phil Haberman, "Bicentennial Ideas Exchanged at Disney World Planning Session", *Wisconsin Bar Bulletin*, December 1986, p. 33.

Michael Kammen, *A Machine that Would Go of Itself: The Constitution in American Culture*, 1986.

Janet Lindgren, "Beyond Cases: Reconsidering Judicial Review", *Wisconsin Law Review*, 1983, p. 583.

Herbert Wechsler, "Toward Neutral Principle of Constitutional Law", *Harvard Law Review*, vol. 73, 1959, p. 1.

James Boyd White, *When Words Lose Their Meaning: Constitutions and Reconstitutions of Language, Character and Community*, 1984.

7. THE SOUTHERN MANIFESTO: WHITE SOUTHERNERS AND CIVIL RIGHTS, 1956

Tony Badger, The University of Newcastle upon Tyne

Franklin Roosevelt once told socialist leader, Norman Thomas, who was impatient about the lack of New Deal action on behalf of southern blacks and sharecroppers, "I know the South and there is a new generation of leaders in the South and we've got to be patient." Roosevelt had reason to be optimistic. He could look over to Capitol Hill and see young, enthusiastic, pro-New Deal southern politicians: Hugo Black himself; Black's friend and protege Lister Hill, who would succeed him in the Senate; other congressmen from Alabama like John Sparkman, who described himself as a TVA liberal, and Luther Patrick, who courted the support of CIO steel workers in Birmingham; Claude Pepper, elected to the Senate despite supporting minimum wage legislation; and that former administrator for the NYA in Texas, Lyndon Johnson. In his own executive branch, Roosevelt could see formidable administrators like Clark Foreman, Aubrey Williams, and Will Alexander, whose Washington experience had caused them to turn their back on the traditional southern white liberal faith in gradualism and paternalism in race relations.

Together these southern New Dealers were putting together an alternative strategy for modernising the South. Conservative elites in the region sought economic growth through the promise of minimal government regulation and cheap docile labour. Low-wage industry attracted by these inducements would not threaten the existing patterns of dependence and deference in the South. By contrast, southern liberals sought to modernise the South through the creation of mass purchasing power, the extension of political democracy, and the protection of civil liberties of blacks and labour organisers.[1]

After World War II there seemed further cause for optimism. It was as if there was a time-lag in the impact of the New Deal on the South. War-time prosperity meant that southern states, even Mississippi, could at last afford to participate in the welfare programmes that relied on federal matching funds. At the local and state level, politicians were elected who stressed economic rather than racial issues and thereby appealed to a biracial coalition of lower-income whites and the small, but increasing, black electorate. Attacking established economic interests, moderate on the race issue, senators like Estes Kefauver of Tennessee, governors like Sid McMath of

Arkansas, Kerr Scott of North Carolina, Earl Long of Louisiana, and mayors like Delesseps Morrison of New Orleans, appealed to rural and urban white workers, organised labour, women, veterans and blacks.[2]

At the same time, federal spending during the war and after was the catalyst that heralded the regions take off into self-sustained economic growth. Social scientists argued that this economic modernisation would spell the end of traditional race relations in the South. Segregation would be incompatible with the demands and needs of a mobile, educated, labour force in the southern cities. Numan Bartley has recently identified the years 1935-1945 as a crucial turning point in southern history, when a growth-oriented metropolitan elite took over power from the traditional rural, small-town, county-seat elite. Economic self interest, many felt, would impell such community leaders to seek peaceful racial change.[3]

Faith in such responsible and moderate leaders underpinned the Supreme Courts implementation decree in the *Brown* school desegregation cases. The southern justices - Hugo Black, Stanley Reed, and Tom Clark - left their colleagues in no doubt as to the immensity of the change that the Court was asking the southerners to make. The speeches of the lawyers from the South Carolina and Virginia defendants virtually threatened the Court with defiance. The Court's decision to place enforcement of school desegregation in the hands of local federal district courts, who would monitor the plan of local school boards, rested not only on the justices' awareness of the likely local complications, but also on their belief that in the South reasonable moderate leaders would encourage their communities into voluntary compliance with the Court.[4]

The justices' optimism was misplaced. Southern liberal politicians were not the voice of the future. As race became a central issue once more in southern politics, so southern moderates ran for cover, becoming in the words of one Mississippi observer "closet moderates". Candidates vied with each other to see who could most vehemently proclaim their loyalty to segregation. As Birmingham lawyer, Charles Morgan, noted, "what has emerged (in Alabama) is a politics of segmentship in the strategy of outflanking the political enemy on the race issue." The Negro, remarked Frank Smith, "has become the only issue, with top prizes going to those who shout against him the loudest and demonstrate the most convincing hatred for his friends in national politics."[5] As for school desegregation, southern community leaders did not encourage voluntary compliance with the Court. Rather they sanctioned absolute defiance of the Supreme Court - where violence and intimidation directed at black plaintiffs prevented desegregation cases even reaching the federal courts and massive resistance - where the State, the National Guard or mobs closed

78

schools that had been ordered to integrate.[6]

What had gone wrong? It is tempting to believe that southern leaders had no alternative but to bow to the irresistible forces of popular racism. The segregationist pressure groups in the South, like the White Citizens Councils, certainly aimed to create a climate of popular conformity in which no dissent on the racial issue was to be tolerated. Their propaganda relentlessly screamed common themes: the Supreme Court decision was itself unconstitutional; southerners were obligated to defy it; school desegregation was part of a communist conspiracy to destroy the United States; southern blacks were happy; only outside agitators wanted change; school desegregation would lead to the mongrelisation of the white race. At the core of the message was the assumption of black inferiority: their animal and beast-like qualities meant that school desegregation was a threat to the very existence of the white race. Surely southern leaders, especially those courtly and dignified senators, did not really believe the rantings of a Tom Brady, a Willie Rainach or a Leander Perez, the forerunners of the "good ol' boy segregationists" of the 1960s. As South Carolina politician, William Jennings Bryan Dorn, who as a congressman mobilised southern opposition in the House to the Civil Rights Bill in 1956 and 1957, said recently, "we didn't really believe the things we had to say then."[7]

It seems unlikely that southern leaders in the 1950s were cowed by a rampant populace. The structure of southern politics had never before been noted for the knee-jerk responsiveness of its leadership to mass sentiment. On the contrary, as I will try to argue, defiance of the Court appears to have been the chosen preference of southern conservative elites. Similarly, southern moderate politicians may have been scared into submission by the popular racism of their constituents. But, as Lewis Killian noted, southern moderates tended to "surrender to the mob before it even gathers". As Carl Rowan bitterly complained, "apparently a moderate is any white southerner who can prove that he hasn't lynched any crippled old negro grandmother during a prayer-meeting hour." The maintenance of the maximum degree of segregation appears, I would suggest, to be the chosen preference of most southern moderates.[8]

This paper attempts to test these contentions by examining the Southern Manifesto issued in March 1956: a blast of defiance at the Supreme Court calling for resistance to the school desegregation by all lawful means. The Manifesto was signed by all but three senators from the states of the old confederacy, and by all but four southern congressmen outside Texas.

I am trying to answer three questions. First, what were the aims of the southern conservative leaders who formulated the Manifesto? Did they take the Manifesto seriously or were they simply making a rhetorical stand to keep their constituents happy? Second, why did so many southern representatives sign it - including so many self-proclaimed liberal or moderate politicians? Were they coerced as one analysis suggests? Seventy-five per cent of southern congressmen would have preferred not to sign the Manifesto, estimated one of the North Carolina representatives who did not sign. Said one representative, "I had a gun in my belly"; said another, "I am not making strong enough speeches to suit the folks back home." Alternatively were the moderates expressing their personal preference for a status quo in race relations? Third, what were the motives of those who did not sign and what were the political consequences for them? Did their experience suggest that there was a liberal alternative, a road not taken by their more timid colleagues.[9]

I

The Manifesto itself is relatively restrained by the standards of the Citizens Councils. It is also routine and derivative. The draftsmen stated that "we regard the decision of the Supreme Court in the school cases as a clear abuse of judicial power. It climaxes a trend in the federal judiciary to invade the legislative field in derogation of the authority of Congress, and to encroach upon the reserved rights of the states and the people."

The Manifesto then reiterated the defence made in the school cases - that the fourteenth amendment did not mention education; that the twenty-six states who considered the amendment either ratified their existing system of separate schools or established new segregated systems. It then turned to *Plessy* and to *Lum vs Rice* to bolster the established legal principle which had been overturned by a Supreme Court which "with no legal base for such action, undertook to exercise their naked judicial power and substituted their personal political and social ideas for the established law of the land."

The decision, it then continued, was "creating chaos and confusion in the states", and destroying amicable race relations. The changes sought by outside agitators would destroy the system of public education in some of the states. The signers "pledge ourselves to support by any and all lawful means measures calculated to bring about a reversal of this unwarranted decision of the Supreme Court and to prevent the use of force in its implementation.[10]

Who was responsible for drafting this Manifesto and what were their intentions?

It was no surprise that Strom Thurmond should have originated the idea of a manifesto blasting the Supreme Court. As one senate staffer recalled, the senate office of the former Dixicrat presidential candidate spewed out a stream of vicious racist material. In his unsuccessful senate bid in 1950, Thurmond had vied with his opponent as to who could be booed loudest in their debates by the Negro galleries. Although Thurmond had won election in 1954 as a write-in candidate against the hand-picked candidate of the party establishment in South Carolina, his views on race were exactly in tune with every other leading politician in South Carolina. His predecessor in the Senate, Burnet Maybank, had been an enthusiastic New Dealer, but he had also walked out with "Cotton Ed" Smith from the 1936 Democratic Convention when a Negro minister gave the invocation. Thurmond's senate partner, Olin Johnston, had been a moderate New Deal governor, championing the rights of trade unions. But his biographer, Robert Burts, has worked his way steadily through the vast uncatalogued boxes of the Johnston papers in the Caroliniana Library in Columbia, South Carolina, and has found not a single trace of a concession to racial moderation in the whole of Johnston's career. As Howard Quint has shown, public voices calling for compliance with the Supreme Court decision in South Carolina amounted to a dean of education at the University of South Carolina who was fired, five clergymen who were forced by their congregations to leave, and the editors of two weekly small newspapers in Cheraw and Florence, one of whom had to sell up as a result.[11]

Thurmond was not popular amongst his senate colleagues. His idea for a manifesto would have got nowhere, if it had not been taken up by Harry F. Byrd of Virginia who prevailed upon Walter George of Georgia to summon a meeting of the southern senators. Byrd was not under pressure from segregationists, although segregationist support for the League of Defenders pressure group was steadily increasing in the south side black belt of Virginia from the fall of 1955. Byrd at the beginning of 1956 was troubled by two rather different threats.

First, his machine appeared vulnerable to the consequences of economic change. Urban-suburban development in Virginia was producing young politicians who challenged the traditional fiscal conservatism of the Virginia oligarchy. Anti-organisation Democrats mounted two formidable primary challenges to Byrd's candidate for governor and sniped with unprecedented success at the administration in the state legislature. A young liberal Republican also stung the machine with a sizeable vote in the 1954 general election.

Even more disturbing to Byrd was the prospect that Virginia might adopt a policy of token compliance with the school desegregation decision. The Gray Commission, appointed by Governor Stanley,

81

recommended tuition grants for parents who did not wish their children to go to integrated schools, but did envisage local option for some school districts. Byrd, who read the Commission's report on a trip to Europe, was adamant that even a little integration was too much. His organisation vigorously campaigned for a constitutional convention that would pave the way for tuition grants, but he then intended to mandate the state to close any schools that desegregated. Buoyed by James J. Kilpatrick's editorials in the *Richmond News-leader* on the doctrine of Interposition, Byrd took up the idea of the Manifesto as a rallying cry for the South, which would show southerners that they could massively resist the Supreme Court: that token compliance was not inevitable.[12]

When Walter George, the senior southern senator, convened the meeting to consider issuing such a manifesto, he appointed a subcommittee of Richard Russell of Georgia, John Stennis of Mississippi and Sam Ervin, Jr., of North Carolina to draft it. What were their motives?

There are a number of accounts which suggest that the dignified and fastidious Russell, the unofficial leader of the South and the most powerful southern politician in post-war congress, was uneasy and unenthusiastic about the Manifesto. It was widely thought, indeed, that the Manifesto was simply a device to cast his colleague, Walter George, in a favourable light since George had to face a primary challenge from that masterly exploiter of poor-white racism, Herman Talmadge. It is certainly true that George was being challenged by Talmadge, that the old internationalist war horse had little stomach for the Manifesto, and that he refused to make the "one speech giving the Supreme Court hell" which Roy Harris, the segregationist eminence grise in Georgia, argued would ensure his re-election. George did in fact withdraw from his primary battle less than two months after the Manifesto was issued. But it was not the white heat of Talmadge racism that forced him out, it was his failure to drum up any financial support from his usual corporate backers in Georgia, from Coca-Cola, Atlanta bankers and Georgia industrialists. This Georgia financial elite were entirely happy with the prospect of Herman Talmadge in the Senate.[13]

What of Russell himself, Russell "made men think". Everyman according to Russell could earn respect "on the basis of purely personal traits ... effort, attitude, responsibility and achievement ... He rejected absolutely the kind of politics that preaches that the world owes anybody anything." That admiring reminiscence of Russell was penned by Jesse Helms, whom Russell borrowed to run his TV and radio campaign in his presidential bid in 1952.[14]

There is no evidence that Russell wanted to protect Walter

George from the Talmadge forces. If anything he seems to have been happy to see the militant Talmadge replace the more circumspect senior senator. Russell certainly worked closely with Talmadge in the States Rights Council, Georgia's equivalent of the Citizens Councils. And Russell himself was certainly under no pressure from the Talmadge forces: no southern politician in recent times has been as impregnable a position within his own state as Russell was in Georgia in the 1940s and 1950s.

There is also no evidence that Russell wan unenthusiastic about the Manifesto. On the contrary he was proud of his role in drafting it, and the language of the Manifesto is often directly taken from the press statement Russell made on the evening of May 17th 1954 when the first Brown decision was announced. The Manifesto was entirely consistent with Russell's belief that the Court had been steadily moving to erode the rights of the states; that the Court had become the tool of the executive branch of the government, manipulated by the Solicitor General and the Attorney General. Russell was particularly incensed by the amicus curiae briefs of the government in the original Brown case and at the Supreme Court's request to be briefed by the Attorney General on the implementation of Brown. Russell was convinced that the judges were "an assortment of political hacks and college professors" with no judicial experience who had based their decision, forgetting all the law and precedent, "on a book by a Swedish sociologist who said that our constitution is a plot against the common people of the United States."[15]

No man was more committed to the idea of a modernised South than Russell: he worked ceaselessly for industrialisation of the region and a diversification of agriculture. But no man was more committed to the traditional pattern of race relations. In the 1930s and 1940s he viewed anti-lynching legislation and the FEPC as simply part of the Communist Party programme. His staff kept a clipping file on Negro crime in northern cities, violence in the North, of social diseases amongst negroes, and of cases of prominent whites marrying blacks. The last particularly sickened Russell and it was the mongrelisation of the race that he feared above all else.

> I am unalterably opposed to any conduct which will lead to the eventual amalgamation of the races. I have been a student of history for many years and I have never found a case where a people of mixed blood ever developed their civilisation, nor am I aware of any instance when they maintained their achievements when miscegenation was complete.

Russell's solution to the racial problem was his Bill in 1949 to establish a Voluntary Racial Relocation Commission. Funded for $ 4.5 billion over five years, the Commission would make grants to enable blacks to move north and whites to move south, until all the states had roughly the same black-white ratios. His intention was to remove discontented blacks from the South, to foster economic growth in the South by exchanging illiterate blacks for highly skilled whites, but above all to expose the hypocrisy of northern civil rights advocates who came from states with small Negro populations. Russell wanted to tap what he believed was a consensus amongst the mass of northern whites whom he believed were sympathetic to southern attitudes to blacks. In the same way the Manifesto's declaration of southern outrage and determination was designed to make most northerners think twice about supporting federal intervention in the South.[16]

Russell was determined to resist racial change to the bitter end. "If they overwhelm us", he promised, "you will find me in the last ditch." He was concerned however that not all southerners felt the same way. In 1958 he confessed, "I have been somewhat concerned to note that some of our people have been brainwashed until they feel absolutely helpless and seem to quit." When Atlanta businessmen, alarmed at the prospects of the public school closing as mandated under state law in the event of desegregation, moved to institute token compliance with desegregation in 1960, Russell was appalled. "We must stand firm against the efforts to stampede our people to accepting the fatal bait of 'token integration' in our schools." Russell's drafting of the Manifesto, then, was entirely of a piece with his resistance to any change in the traditional pattern of southern race both before 1956 and after.[17]

Of the two other senators who cooperated with Russell in drafting the Manifesto, John Stennis of Mississippi had been elected to the Senate in 1947 in a special election to succeed the notorious Theodore "The Man" Bilbo. Stennis had campaigned as a moderate against the relentless anti-semite, John Rankin. It was, noted Frank Smith, the last time the description moderate was not a term of vile abuse in Mississippi's politics.[18]

Stennis's courtly dignified manners, so very different from the vicious Negrophobia of his colleague James Eastland, should not obscure the fact that Stennis did not dissent in any way from the racial orthodoxy of white Mississippi. The difference between the racism of delta politicians and that of a demagogue like Bilbo was merely one of style, not substance. Bilbo's vicious Negro baiting campaign of 1946, his last, was also the first time that he picked up overwhelming support in the black belt, which had previously hated his aggressive support of New Deal economic programmes. In the 1940s and 1950s, Mississippi had already become a "concentration

84

camp of the mind" as Jessica Mitford described it on the race issue. The dissenters from white supremacy orthodoxy were a mere handful of voices: newspaper editors Hodding Carter, who taped his car bonnet every night so that he could be alerted to a car bomb in the morning, Hazel Brannon Smith, whose Holmes County newspaper was boycotted by the citizens council, PD East whose iconoclastic *Petal Paper* was so idiosyncratic that he lost all his subscribers within Mississippi; the Mississippi Children's Code Commission, a steadfast lone voice against the repeal of the compulsory education law; and the maverick chaplain of the University of Mississippi, Will Campbell. When Campbell played table tennis with a black clergyman in the University's YMCA building, he was reported by the campus police to the dean. Campbell protested in vain to the dean that table tennis was a inherently segregated game which fulfilled the separate but equal doctrine perfectly. The players both had the same sized bats; they were separated by a tightly drawn net; and the ball was white. Such rare dissent from racial conformity was as anathema to John Stennis as it was to every other white Mississippi politician.[19]

Sam Ervin's biographer has suggested that Ervin was uneasy with the Manifesto, that his meetings with Russell were merely perfunctory meetings to approve Russell's drafts, and that his role was simply one of eliminating a few of Russell's more intemperate references to malicious and tyrannical judges. Ervin however had been appointed to the Senate precisely because of his determined opposition to the Supreme Court decision. In 1954 when the senior senator from North Carolina, Clyde Hoey died, the front runner for appointment to the senate seat was lawyer Irving Carlysle who was invited to give the keynote speech at the state Democratic convention. The convention took place three days after the *Brown* decision. Carlysle inserted a paragraph on the need for good citizens to obey the law of the land laid down by the courts. He received a standing ovation, as a friend noted, not for "approval of what you said. They just admire your stinkin' courage." Governor Umstead had no intention of appointing any advocate of positive compliance with the law to the Senate. Instead he appointed Sam Ervin.[20]

As in Virginia so in North Carolina, the political establishment moved from considering token compliance to presenting the electorate with the alternative of either voluntary perpetuation of school segregation or a closing of schools. William Chafe has shown that this shift was not caused by hardening public opinion; on the contrary there was evidence of apathy amongst voters; public opinion polls stressed the relatively small number of bitter-end resisters and a number of cities had announced their willingness to envisage token integration. The decision to opt for resistance reflected the conscious

85

preference of governor Luther Hodges and his mounting belief that the Supreme Court decision could be outflanked. The North Carolina plan was enthusiastically endorsed by Sam Ervin who saw it as a legal means of maintaining voluntary segregation. The Manifesto he helped to draft was entirely consistent with North Carolina's strategy.[21]

I have tried to demonstrate that the drafters of the Manifesto were deadly serious. They were not going through the motions to satisfy sentiment back in their constituencies: those sponsoring the Manifesto were convinced that the southern public was not stirred up enough on the issue of segregation and feared that southerners did not believe that the Supreme Court could be halted. Reference to the lack of interest of those whites abound in Russell's correspondence. As one of the congressmen who took the Manifesto round members of the house wrote, "you and I know there is too much apathy and indifference among the white people ... our situation with regard to the race question is far more serious than the average person realises." The aim of the Manifesto therefore was first to act as a rallying cry to southern whites, not to placate popular sentiment but to stir it up. Second, the Manifesto aimed to coerce white politicians who might be wavering in their determination to resist desegregation, in particular the five or six southern senators who Russell lamented were even prepared to agree with the decision. Third, the aim was to signal to the North the complete and serious nature of the South's determination to resist, in the hope that northern politicians would back off. As statements by Adlai Stevenson and some nervous northern newspaper editors indicated, the Manifesto signed by "distinguished and responsible" leaders of the South gave some northern liberals pause before seeking to enforce the Court decision. Finally, the Manifesto was a warning to the Court. Early drafts of the Manifesto contained a threat implicit in the reminder to the Court, "That the congress is granted authority by the constitution to limit the appellate disjurisdiction of the court." The Manifesto in its final form still served notice on the Court that southerners would not comply in the way the court hoped. In the next couple of years the southerners proposed a variety of anti-court measures designed to soften the will of the Court to enforce its decision. The Court's handling of school desegregation in the next few years suggests that that warning may have been effective.[22]

II

The success of the Manifesto in coercing wavering southerners was immediately demonstrated by the willingness of moderate or

86

liberal southern congressmen to sign the Declaration of Principles. The irony was that conservative leaders believed that southern white public opinion was not sufficiently roused in favour of segregation. Moderate leaders believed the opposite. Public opinion, they feared, was irresistibly committed to the defence of segregation.

Lister Hill was Hugo Black's old friend and his successor as senator from Alabama. He had followed Black's lead on minimum wage legislation, public power, rural electrification, and taxation. He had pioneered the development of federal assistance for hospital building. Yet, as Drew Pearson noted, Hill faced with a re-election struggle in 1956, almost fell over himself in his rush to sign the Manifesto. The senator explained to Judge Richard Rives of the crusading Fifth Circuit Court that he did not want to sign, but that his constituents left him no alternative. Rives sardonically noted that he was glad Hill had been able to rise above principle. Rives was an old friend of Hill and a long-time political ally, but as the Fifth Circuit Court made repeated decisions protecting black rights, so Hill disowned him. Hill and Rives had offices in the same Federal building in Montgomery, yet Hill never talked to Rives after 1956. Similarly Hill cut off all personal or public contact with his mentor and patron, Hugo Black.[23]

The refusal of Hill and his fellow senator, John Sparkman, came at a crucial time in Alabama race relations. The governor of Alabama, "Big Jim" Folsom had made remarkable statements about fair treatment of blacks. In particular, he appointed registrars committed to black voter registration. He privately encouraged Martin Luther King Jr. to push for the complete desegregation of the Montgomery buses rather than the first come first served seating on a segregated basis which the bus boycott leaders originally asked for. Folsom likened a resolution of interposition by the state legislature to a hound dog begging at the moon. Talk of nullification made him ask, "what are you going to do now that the Feds. have the nuclear bomb?" But Folsom looked in vain for support from other Alabama politicians notably the two liberal senators.

In the early months of 1956 Folsom lost control of the race issue in his state politics. In 1954 Folsom had been elected with the largest first primary margin for years. In 1955 he enjoyed unprecedented success with his legislature. Yet in the early months of 1956 the Montgomery bus boycott showed no signs of weakening; Citizens' Council membership exploded; Nat King Cole was physically attacked on stage in Birmingham; the state legislature passed a barrage of anti-school desegregation laws; and a mob prevented black student Autherine Lucy entering the University of Alabama under court order. Folsom had so lost his ability to exert a moderating influence over racial policy that he was defeated by a three to one margin for the post of Democratic National Committee chairman. Meanwhile, the two supposedly liberal Alabama senators stood by and watched. By the summer of 1956 both Hill and Sparkman were speaking at Citizens Council rallies.[24]

Senator William Fulbright of Arkansas had achieved a liberal reputation as a fervent internationalist. Along with Spessard Holland of Florida and Price Daniel of Texas, Fulbright considered the Russell draft of the Manifesto to be too bitter and inflammatory. They insisted on changes but the changes they insisted on were stylistic not substantial. A statement of support for interposition had already been eliminated by the Russell drafting sub-committee. Fulbright and his friends did delete the references to "naked power" and "flagrant and unjustified" decisions but they were content with these cosmetic changes. Fulbright's signing of the Manifesto was consistent with his refusal to endorse the Brown decision and his steadfast silence later during the Little Rock crisis of 1957 where he refused repeated pleas from former governor McMath and congressman Brooks Hays to support the Court ordered desegregation of Central High School. Fulbright refused to condemn governor Faubus's use of troops or to denounce the mob of violence which denied blacks admission to the school. In 1956 segregationist forces were not yet in the political saddle in Arkansas; Fulbright's preference for signing the Manifesto was a part of a wider refusal of community and political leaders in the state to mobilise in support of compliance with the law of the land - a refusal which would leave Orval Faubus looking in vain in 1957 for support from those leaders when he came under pressure from newly invigorated segregationist pressure groups in Little Rock. Seeking, but finding no backing from these leaders, Faubus felt he had little option but to defy the federal courts.[25]

Another southern moderate who signed the Manifesto was Kerr Scott of North Carolina. Scott, the candidate of the "branchhead boys" had upset the established political leaders of North Carolina to win the governorship in 1948. Scott was the first governor of the state to appoint a black to the state board of education, just as he was the first governor to appoint a woman to the state appeals court. Scott had caused heart failure among the state conservatives by appointing Frank Porter Graham, the former president of the University of North Carolina, to a vacant senate seat. In 1954 Scott was elected to the Senate, his campaign managed by the young Terry Sanford, despite a last minute, post-Brown, racial smear by his opponent. Yet in 1956 Scott agreed to sign the Manifesto. He changed his mind over a weekend, aware that it was inconsistent with almost everything he stood for in his political life. He rang his legislative aide, Bill Cochrane, on the Monday morning to get Cochrane to take his name off the document. Cochrane explained that Senator George was about to read the Manifesto in the Senate within an hour. The press already had the document. To remove Scott's name at this stage would draw more attention than if he let his name stay on. As Cochrane recalled, "I was already sad that we couldn't get his name off there. Senator Scott never had any problem with black people and he never went in for that kind of strong stuff."[26]

The moderates who signed the Manifesto may have been coerced by their perception of the overwhelming nature of mass white racial prejudice, but they were also expressing their conscious personal preference for maintaining segregation. They professed to condemn extremist on both sides. Yet they equated the NAACP which was upholding constitutional rights through the courts, with the Ku Klux Klan, which denied those rights through vigilante violence. They professed to favour gradual change: they contended that racial change would not come in the South until white opinion accepted it. Yet the Lister Hills and William Fulbrights of the world made no effort to lead or persuade that majority opinion to accept gradual racial change.

III

The experience of those small number of southern politicians who refused to sign the Manifesto suggest the frailty of southern racial moderation, its idiosyncratic nature and the narrowness of its base in southern politics.

The three southern senators who did not sign - Lyndon Johnson from Texas, and Estes Kefauver and Albert Gore from Tennessee - all had some sort of national political aspiration that offset their regional ties to some extent. All three would go on to vote for the 1957 Civil Rights Act.

The drafters of the Manifesto did not ask Lyndon Johnson to sign. They argued that they did not want to compromise his position as majority leader. Johnson himself was following a delicate balancing act: keeping his power base in the Senate and Texas, yet trying to establish a record on civil rights that might win him northern support for a presidential bid. He conveyed the impression that he would not have signed the Manifesto, even if it had been presented to him. He allegedly said that the document was simply designed for home consumption. Richard Russell, however, was adamant, "I DO NOT BELIEVE THAT LYNDON JOHNSON MADE ANY SUCH STATEMENT". After 1956 Johnson's balancing act was even harder to maintain. By 1958 Russell was saying that Johnson was not really a southerner although he was still willing to give Johnson the benefit of the doubt. He did not yet feel betrayed by his protégé, as he would later in 1964.[27]

The Manifesto was issued in the midst of Estes Kefauver's battle in the Democratic primaries for the 1956 presidential nomination. As a southerner chasing national office, he had little choice but to denounce the Manifesto. He reiterated the stand he took in 1954 when he had stressed that the Supreme Court decision must be upheld as the law of the land. Indeed, Kefauver was much more condemnatory of the southerners who signed than Adlai Stevenson, who was anxious not to lose votes in the forthcoming Florida primary.

Albert Gore shared Kefauver's hostility to big business, his support for public power, and his support for progressive taxation, although his power base in Tennessee was different from Kefauver's. Like Kefauver, Gore was committed to support the 1954 Supreme Court decision. In addition, he was hankering after the vice-presidential nomination in 1956. As indeed was the governor of Tennessee, Frank Clement. It was said in Tennessee in 1956, "in America it is possible for any man to run for the president. In Tennessee they all are."

Both Gore and Kefauver were challenged at the polls for their racial views: Kefauver in 1954 and 1960; Gore in 1958 specifically for signing the Manifesto and voting for the 1957 Civil Rights Act. Each time they fought off well-financed opposition. Of course, it was easier for liberals to win elections in Tennessee than in some other southern states: a greater percentage of voting age blacks were registered in Tennessee; organised labour was a force to be counted; the TVA had a liberalising impact; there were newspapers who supported compliance with the Supreme Court. But in these respects Tennessee was not so very different from North Carolina and Arkansas at least. What was different in Tennessee was that both senators and the governor chose to seek public support for compliance with the court. In such circumstances when the three leading politicians, despite their mutual distaste for each other, set the terms of the political debate in a particular way, racial moderation had a chance of success.[28]

The evidence from Tennessee therefore tentatively suggests that there was more room for manoeuvre than southern moderates were prepared to credit. The evidence from North Carolina is more ambiguous. First, it suggests what an idiosyncratic and personal matter taking a moderate stand on racial matters was. Second, the fate of the congressmen who did not sign, does suggest that the political perils were not imaginary.

Apparently there was considerable disquiet in the North Carolina

90

house delegation about signing the Manifesto. In the end, however, only three congressmen did not sign. All faced immediate primaries in which their failure to sign was a salient issue: two of the three were defeated.

It is difficult to imagine three more disperate congressmen than Charles Deane, Harold Cooley and Thurmond Chatham and three more diverse routes to racial moderation.

Deane was easily the most liberal of the entire North Carolina delegation. He was regularly endorsed by the CIO; his loyalty to the national party made him the fair-haired boy of northern Democratic leaders. He was one of the few North Carolina politicians who achieved a positive rating from the Americans for Democratic Action. His support for the Supreme Court came part from his liberalism, part from his Baptist faith, (he was prominent among the state Baptists), and part from his support of moral rearmament. He toured Europe with an integrated moral rearmament group presenting "moral" plays.[29]

Harold Cooley had not entirely lost the vestiges of liberalism which saw him elected to the House as a New Dealer in 1934. As chairman of the House Agriculture Committee, he saw himself as part of the national Democratic leadership; he had to work with northern and western representatives of other farm commodities to ensure favourable treatment for tobacco; and he may have had thoughts of his own of the vice-presidential nomination in 1956. Not lacking in the sense of his own importance, Cooley resented being presented with the Manifesto as a sort of fait accompli, when House members had been kept out of the discussion leading up to its drafting.[30]

The most surprising racial moderate of all was Thurmond Chatham. Chatham was the millionaire chairman of the board of directors of the family Chatham mills. In the 1930s he was a Roosevelt-hating member of the Liberty League. In 1940 he supported Wendell Willkie. Elected to Congress on an anti-union platform in 1948, Chatham remained firmly opposed to unionisation, particularly of his own mill, and opposed to raising the minimum wage.

As a student at Yale however in 1916, he had sat next to a Negro in two of his classes and became friendly with him; in the Navy in World War II he had seen desegregation in operation; on the House Foreign Relations committee he had become friendly with younger liberals, Abraham Ribicoff and Lloyd Bentsen. His support for national Democrats on foreign policy began to spill over into the domestic field. He favoured recognition of Red China. When the Supreme Court decision came in 1954 he said he had been expecting it, he was confident that the South would take it in its stride, and he was pleased that the decision was out of the way. America would be able to turn to "the greater problems which face us in the international sphere."[31]

The effect of the Manifesto in the primaries that followed is not easy to disentangle. The clearest influence is in Charles Deane's primary battle. Deane had not faced serious opposition in 1952 and 1954. No opponent had filed against him in 1956 until he failed to sign the Manifesto. An ambitious, young, and well connected politician immediately announced and made the Manifesto his main issue. Deane himself was convinced he was defeated because of his failure to sign and there is no reason to doubt his analysis.[32]

In the case of Chatham and Cooley the evidence is more mixed. The first letter Chatham received after not signing the Manifesto told the congressman "you express yourself like a Damn Yankee. If you like the Negro you can have him but I think you are dead duck." Two days after not signing the Manifesto, Chatham was told "your not signing along with the rest of the southern congressmen in opposition of desegregation (mongrelizing) will I'm sure place you in favour with senator Hubert Humphrey and his Negro worshippers." The North Carolin Patriots (the North Carolina equivalent of the Citizens Council) targeted Chatham for special opposition with particular success in two of the counties in his district.[33]

As for Cooley, he had no opposition until after he refused to sign. Then he was opposed by local broadcaster W.E. Debnam, who had written the popular racist track *Then My Old Kentucky Home*. Debnam labelled Cooley the NAACP candidate.[34]

As with so many southern political campaigns there were local and personal factors in their races as well. Chatham had faced surprisingly stiff opposition in 1952 and 1954 from political unknowns who had capitalised on his absentee record in congress. In 1956, irrespective of the Manifesto, he was going to face opposition from a substantial local politician, the district solicitor, who represented counties that felt they had been overlooked in congressional representation. His opponents stressed Chatham's absenteeism, his foreign trips and his earlier support of Republican candidates. There was also a whispering campaign about Chatham's alcoholism (and indeed Chatham died of cirrhosis of the liver in 1957).[35]

Cooley had long since ceased to keep his political fences mended and he too enjoyed foreign junkets. He was attacked as the "globe trotting gad fly". Voters were told "the district needs a full time congressmen". There were even deeper personal factors. The first person to denounce Cooley for not signing the Manifesto, and to consider running himself was Pou Bailey, the man who later allegedly persuaded Jesse Helms to run for the Senate. Bailey's cousin was the man Cooley defeated to get into Congress twenty two years earlier;

92

Bailey's uncle had defeated Cooley's father for the same congressional seat in 1916.[36]

Two facts emerge, however, from these cross currents of local and national issues. Chatham remained unapologetic for his refusal to sign the Manifesto and was defeated. Rudimentary analysis suggests he ran best in high income white urban wards and in black wards: an early portent of the cross-class biracial alliance that would play an important part in southern politics in the 1960s. Cooley won - but he racebaited the racebaiter to do so. He had started off by stressing the false hopes that the Manifesto aroused and the fact that as a lawyer he could not attack the Court in the language of the Manifesto. While he still asserted that he was proud of his decision not to sign, by the end of the campaign he was proclaiming that he hated and despised the Brown decision. And he then attacked his opponent for advocating the desegregation of public transport and public playgrounds and for having eaten a meal with the NAACP's Roy Wilkins in Wilkins's home in New York City. His opponent, said Cooley, had said "let the negro eat where he pleases, sit where he pleases and sleep where he pleases. This is exactly what Debnam's friend Roy Wilkins has been advocating for years." Flanked by Senator Sam Ervin, Cooley blasted his district with his segregationist propaganda and overwhelmed his opponents by a two to one margin.[37]

IV

Philip Elman, assistant to the solicitor general under Truman and Eisenhower, reported that he had heard that,

> Hugo (Black) was telling the brethren that you cannot constitutionally defend *Plessy*, but if and when they overruled it, it would mean the end of southern liberalism for the time being. The Bilbos and the Talmadges would come ever more to the fore, overwhelming the John Sparkmans and Lister Hills. The guys who talked nigger would be in charge, there would be riots, the army might have to be called out - he was scaring the shit out of the justices, especially Frankfurter and Jackson.[38]

Black was right in his ultimate description of what happened but wrong in his analysis of how it would happen. Black feared the massive nature of poor white racism which would be exploited by unscrupulous demagogues. The evidence of the Southern Manifesto suggests that defiance of the Court was not simply a response to

93

popular outrage. Southern conservative leaders, concerned at the indifference of southern popular opinion and fearing compromising forces in their own ranks, were prepared to launch a righteous crusade to stir up white opinion in defiance of the Court, to convince white southerners that desegregation could be prevented. Southern white moderate politicians were not simply overwhelmed by mass racism, but contributed to their own downfall. In many cases reluctant personally to envisage the end of segregation, they hoped the issue would go away or that token integration could be slipped in quietly without any fuss. What they were not prepared to do was to lead a campaign to mobilise public opinion in favour of compliance with the Court and racial change. Consequently, they were no match for conservative leaders who were prepared to take the issue to the public.

The task for moderate leaders was not easy and they could probably have made no difference in South Carolina or Mississippi, for example, and there were dangers elsewhere. But there was room for manoeuvre and most of the time southern moderates did not act. Even if they had, in the long run it would have made little difference. After 1960 no southern whites could dictate the timetable of racial change. The civil rights movement, from below, and the federal government and judiciary, from outside, forced the substantial racial changes on the South that neither southern liberals nor the forces of economic modernisation could create from within.

REFERENCES

1.   Frank Freidel, *FDR and the South*, Baton Rouge: Louisiana State University Press, 1965, p. 66. Morton Sosna, *In Search of the Silent South: Southern Liberals and the Race Issue*, New York: Columbia University, 1977, pp. 60-87.

2.   Numan V. Bartley and Hugh Davis Graham, *Southern Politics and the Second Reconstruction*, Baltimore: Johns Hopkins University Press, 1975, pp. 24-50.

3.   Numan V. Bartley, "The Era of the New Deal as a Turning Point in Southern History", in James C. Cobb and Michael V. Namaroto, *The New Deal and the South*, Jackson: University Press of Mississippi, 1964, pp. 135-46.

4. Richard Kluger, *Simple Justice: The History of Brown v. Board of Education and Black America's Struggle for Equality*, New York: Random House, 1975, pp. 714-47.

5. Hodding Carter, Interview, Southern Oral History, Southern Historical Collection, Chapel Hill. Charles Morgan, *A Time to Speak*, New York: Harper and Row, 1964. Frank Smith, *Congressman from Mississippi: An Autobiography*, New York: Pantheon, 1964, p. 321.

6. J. Harvie Wilkinson, *From Brown to Bakke: The Supreme Court and School Integration, 1954-1978*, New York: Oxford University Press, 1979, pp. 78-127.

7. Numan V. Bartley, *The Rise of Massive Resistance in the South: Race and Politics in the South during the 1950s*, Baton Rouge: Louisiana State University Press, 1969, pp. 82-117. Neil R. McMillen, *The Citizens' Council: Organized Resistance to the Second Reconstruction, 1954-64*, Urbana: University of Illinois Press, 1971. Comment, Dan T. Carter, 14 April, 1984. Dorn's private correspondence gives not the slightest hint that he had any qualms about his segregationist rhetoric in the 1950s, *William Jennings Bryan Dorn Papers*, Columbia, S.C.: Caroliniana Library.

8. Killian quoted in Anthony Lake Newberry, "Without Urgency or Ardor: The South's Middle-of-the-road Liberals and Civil Rights, 1945-1960", Ph.D: Ohio University, 1982, p. 4. Carl Rowan, *Go South to Sorrow*, New York: Random House, 1957, p. 206.

9. Charles B. Deane to Hayes Mizell, 10 April, 1962, *Hayes Mizell Papers*, Columbia, S.C.: Caroliniana Library. I am very grateful to Hayes Mizell for making his material on the Southern Manifesto available to me.

10. *New York Times*, 12 March 1956. Senator Thurmond made available to Hayes Mizell copies of the successive drafts of the Manifesto which are now in the Mizell Papers.

11. Comment, James L. Sundquist, 8 April 1987. Robert Sherrill, *Gothic Politics in the Deep South*, New York: Ballantine, 1969, pp. 255-276. Dan T. Carter, "Southern Political Style", in Robert Haws, ed., *The Age of Segregation: Race Relations in the South, 1890-1945*, Jackson: University of Mississippi Press, 1978, p. 47.

Comment, Robert Burts, August, 1984. Howard Quint, *Profile in Black and White: A Frank Portrait of South Carolina*, Washington: Public Affairs Press, 1958.

12. James W. Ely, Jr., *The Crisis of Conservative Virginia: The Byrd Organization and the Politics of Massive Resistance*, Knoxville: University of Tennessee Press, 1976, pp. 30-50. James Howard Hershman, Jr., "A Rumbling in the Museum: Opponents of Virginia's Massive Resistance", Ph.D. University of Virginia, 1978, pp. 1-188. Guy Friddell, *Colgate Darden: Conversations with Guy Friddell*, Charlottesville: University of Virginia Press, 1978, pp. 157-166. William Bryan Crawley, Jr., *Bill Tuck: A Political Life in Harry Byrd's Virginia*, Charlottesville: University of Virginia Press, 1978, pp. 228-232.

13. Albert Gore, *Let the Glory Out: My South and Its Politics*, New York: Viking Press, 1972, pp. 102-5. *The State*, 14 Feb. 1956. C.B. Deane to Hayes Mizell, 10 April 1962, *Mizell Papers*, Sherrill, *Gothic Politics in the Deep South*, pp. 66-70.

14. Ernest B. Furguson, *Hard Right: The Rise of Jesse Helms*, New York: Norton, 1956, p. 59.

15. Richard B. Russell to Hayes Mizell, 30 April 1962, (not sent) *Richard B. Russell Papers*, Richard B. Russell Library, University of Georgia. Daniel David Potenziani, "Look to the Past: Richard B. Russell and the Defence of Southern White Supremacy", Ph.D., University of Georgia, 1981, pp. 121-37, 154, 176.

16. Potenziani, "Look to the Past", pp. 45-97, 176.

17. Sherrill, *Gothic Politics in the Deep South* 49. Potenziani, "Look to the Past", pp. 180-82. Richard B. Russell to R.A. Howard, 14 Jan. 1959, *Russell Papers*.

18. Smith, *Congressman from Mississippi*, pp. 70-99.

19. Sherrill, *Gothic Politics in the Deep South*, pp. 189-234. Chester M. Morgan, *Redneck Liberal: Theodore G. Bilbo and the New Deal*, Baton Rouge: Louisiana State University Press, 1985. Jessica Mitford, *A Fine Old Conflict*, London: Michael Joseph, 1977, p. 145. James W. Silver, *Mississippi: The Closed Society*, New York, Harcourt, Brace and World, 1964. P.D. East, *The Magnolia Jungle: The Life and Times of a Southern Editor*, New

York: Simon and Schuster, 1960. Thomas E. Williams, "Children and Welfare in a Segregated Society: Mississippi, 1900-1970", ms in the author's possession. Will D. Campbell, *Brother to a Dragonfly*, New York: The Seabury Press, 1977, pp. 126-27.

20. Paul R. Clancy, *Just a Country Lawyer: A Biography of Senator Sam Ervin*, Bloomington: Indiana University Press, 1974, pp. 171-4. William C. Powell ed., *Dictionary of North Carolina Biography*, vol. I A-C, Chapel Hill: University of North Carolina Press, 1979, pp. 324-25.

21. William H. Chafe, *Civilities and Civil Rights: Greensboro, North Carolina and the Black Struggle for Freedom*, New York: Oxford University Press, 1980, pp. 48-60.

22. James C. Davis to John W. Williams, 2 July 1956; Davis to Roy Harris, 1 Feb. 1957, *James C. Davis Papers*, Emory University Library. Rowan, *Go South To Sorrow*, p. 213. Potenziani, "Look to the Past", pp. 133, 136. Bartley, *The Rise of Massive Resistance*, pp. 289-91.

23. Drew Pearson, "Washington Merry-Go-Round", Clipping, *Mizell Papers*. Jack Bass, *Unlikely Heroes*, New York: Simon and Schuster, 1981, p. 65.

24. George E. Sims, *The Little Man's Big Friend: James E. Folsom in Alabama Politics, 1946-1958*, University, Ala.: University of Alabama Press, 1985, pp. 161-88. John Bartlow Martin, *The Deep South Says 'Never'*, London: Victor Gollancz, 1958, p. 107.

25. Jim Lester, *A Man For Arkansas: Sid McMath and the Southern Reform Tradition*, Little Rock: Rose Publications, 1976, pp. 231-36. Bartley, *The Rise of Massive Resistance*, pp. 251-69. Brooks Hayes, *A Southern Moderate Speaks*, Chapel Hill: University of North Carolina Press, 1959, pp. 130-194.

26. "North Carolina's Man on the Hill", *Carolina Alumni Review*, Spring 1984, pp. 13-14. H.G. Jones, Interview, 13 August 1984.

27. Stanford P. Dyer, "Lyndon Johnson and the Politics of Civil Rights, 1935-1960: The Art of 'Moderate Leadership'", Ph.D., Texas A&M, 1978, pp. 102-107. Charles J. Block to Richard B. Russell, 21 March 1956; Russell to Arch H. Rowan, 27 March 1956, *Russell Papers*. Potenziani, "Look to the Past", pp. 182, 219.

28. *New York Times*, 12 March, 3 April 1956. Hugh Davis Graham, *Crisis in Print: Desegregation and the Press in Tennessee*, Nashville: Vanderbilt University Press, 1967, pp. 29-90. James B. Gardner, "Political Leadership in a Period of Transition: Frank G. Clement, Albert Gore, Estes Kefauver and Tennessee Politics, 1948-56", Ph.D., Vanderbilt University, 1978, pp. 500-670. Joseph Bruce Gorman, *Kefauver: A Political Biography*, New York: Oxford University Press, 1971, pp. 184-5, 236-39, 314-48. Charles Fontenoy, *Estes Kefauver: A Biography*, Knoxville: University of Tennessee Press, 1980, pp. 239-40, 290-92, 335-340.

29. *Greensboro Daily News*, 2 Sept. 1955. *Winston-Salem Journal*, 12 Sept. 1955.

30. *Hendersonville Times-News*, 14 March 1956 (clipping), Harold D. Cooley to H.Q. Dorsett, 13 March 1956, *Harold Dunbar Cooley Papers*. Chapel Hill: Southern Historical Collection.

31. Ralph J. Christian, "The Folger-Chatham Congressional Primary of 1946", *North Carolina Historical Review*, 53, 1976, pp. 25-53. *Raleigh News and Observer*, 18 May 1954. *Winston-Salem Journal*, 18 May 1954.

32. C.B. Deane to Hayes Mizell, 10 April 1962, *Mizell Papers. Winston-Salem Journal*, 17 March 1956. *Raleigh News and Observer*, 13 May 1956. *Charlotte Observer*, 17 May 1956.

33. Anon letter to Thurmond Chatham n.d., Dallas Gwynn to Chatham, 24 March 1956, I.F. Young to Chatham, 13 May 1956, *Thurmond Chatham Papers*, North Carolina Division of Archives and History.

34. Debnam Adverts, *Cooley Papers. Raleigh News and Observer*, 17 March 1956.

35. L. Van Noppen to Chatham, 8 March 1956, Scott Adverts, *Chatham Papers. Greensboro Daily News*, 10 April 1956, 13 April 1956. *Winston-Salem Journal*, 19 April 1956.

36. Ermine B. Hampton to Barbara Dearing n.d., Debnam Adverts, *Cooley Papers. Raleigh News and Observer*, 14 March 1956. *Raleigh News and Observer*, 6 April 1956. Anthony J. Badger, *North Carolina and the New Deal*, Raleigh: North Carolina Division of Archives and History, 1981, p. 89.

37. Cooley to E.L. Cannon, 3 April 1956, Nashville speech, 7 April 1956, Henderson speech, 17 May 1956, WTVD speech, *Cooley Papers*. Chatham to Hiden Ramsey, 31 May 1956, Chatham to Ralph Howland, 5 June 1956, *Chatham Papers*.

38. Kluger, *Simple Justice*, pp. 593-4. The author wishes to acknowledge the generous award of a Fellowship from the American Council of Learned Societies which enabled him to carry out research for this paper.

8. JUSTICE BLACK, DR. KING AND THE PUBLIC FORUM

Richard King, University of Nottingham

During the "civil rights" decades few white southerners acquitted themselves with moral or civic distinction. Initial reactions to the momentous Court decision of 1954 were mixed, but few whites in positions to make a difference recommended more than grudging compliance. Most professed outraged at what they considered the violation of constitutionally protected states rights and a time-honoured way of life. And though McCarthyism waned nationally after 1954, a variant emerged below the Mason-Dixon line at about the same time. Teachers and ministers were fired; books were banned; schools closed and a few politicians removed from office in this Red Scare, southern-style. White-sheeted Klansmen and white-collared Citizens Council members constituted committees of vigilance to root out those who wanted to change the southern way of life.

Of those few white men and women who do deserve mention, Supreme Court Justice Hugo L. Black would rank near the top of the list. Born in Clay County, Alabama in 1886, Black was elected to the U.S. Senate in 1926 and named to the Court in 1937 despite considerable controversy surrounding his earlier membership in the Klan during the 1920s. But Black was hardly championed by conservatives. An increasingly cranky H.L. Mencken wrote, "I can see little in Black except a Cracker demagogue." As a fervent New Dealer Black had carried the water for the President more than once and earned a certain notoriety for his investigations of big business earlier in the decade. Self-taught in the most important things, Black possessed a tenacious mind; he was a battler and he was stubborn. Though he tended to be a "joiner" and protected his political flanks quite carefully, he was no insider in the Senate. In fact his closest associates were "radical republicans" such as George Norris, Robert Lafollette Jr., William Borah and Bronson Cutting. And despite Black's one-time membership in the Klan, the NAACP's Walter White was later to remember his "superiority of intellect and character" over his southern colleagues in Congress.[1]

Indeed it is a measure of Black's influence on the Court that the "Warren Court" was known to some as the "Black Court". Whatever the case, the Supreme Court over which Warren presided did not become "his" Court fully until he forged a working alliance with Justice Black after the mid-1950s. Black was obviously engaging in a bit of white southern "Tomming" when he claimed to be a "rather backward country fellow"; in reality, as John Hart Ely has recently observed, Black was "only posing as a rustic".[2] During Black's time on the court, his great jurisprudential adversary was the former Harvard law professor, Felix Frankfurter, a man with whom he established something of a "love-hate" relationship. Undoubtedly Black learned from the schoolmasterly Frankfurter. But though one could imagine the Warren Court without Frankfurter, it would be well-nigh impossible to imagine it without Black. "In the end", claims Warren's biographer, "it was Black, not Frankfurter, who best served the court and the nation."[3]

Considering his southern roots, Black's constitutional position on segregation might seem the most interesting topic to pursue. In fact Black's most valuable contribution was to breathe life into the First Amendment not just as a protection of individual free speech and expression, but also as a guarantee of political speech and conduct. This work was to prove as valuable to the civil rights movement as was his interpretation of the Fourteenth Amendment. In what follows I want to trace out Black's position in these areas and to suggest that Black was less a liberal than a republican, insofar as his constitutional jurisprudence can be translated into political terms.[4] Finally I want to place alongside, and then juxtapose against, Black another southerner, Martin Luther King, who, along with the rest of the movement, probed the limits of Black's First Amendment jurisprudence and revealed certain of his (and its) limitations through the theory and practice of non-violent direct action and civil disobedience.

For our purposes, Black's constitutional theory is a tale of two amendments - the Fourteenth and the First. The Fourteenth Amendment is probably the most controversial and hence most studied amendment to the Constitution. During Black's tenure on the Court, its meaning was analysed and the intentions of its framers investigated in reference to school desegregation ("inconclusive" announced Warren in the *Brown* decision), segregation (answers went both ways), and protection of voting rights (again disagreement). But for Black the Fourteenth Amendment was important above all, as his oft-cited dissent in *Adamson v. California (1947)* made clear, as a mandate of incorporation: "My study ... persuades me that one of the chief objects that the provisions of the Amendment's first section, separately and as a whole, were intended to accomplish was to make the Bill of Rights applicable to the States."[5] Though never fully accepted by the Court, this theory of incorporation stood at the centre of Black's understanding of the post-Reconstruction Constitution.

It would be wrong to maintain that Black's incorporation theory led directly to the *Brown* decision in 1954. The Fourteenth Amendment explicitly applied to the states and so incorporation was not at issue. At the same time Black's idea of incorporation was part of a nationalising tendency which pressured the Court to rule on the question of school segregation, a matter traditionally left to the states to decide. Black's role in the whole process was peculiar. As the Court "radicals", Black and William O. Douglas had for several years been ready to rule on the constitutionality of segregated schooling. But when the final rounds of argument came in 1952 and 1953, Black deliberately kept a low profile so as not to alienate his two adversaries, Robert Jackson and Frankfurter, who were seeking a criticism-proof way to outlaw segregation and might have been pushed in the opposite direction by an overly enthusiastic Black.[6] Indeed, the Court transcripts of the arguments in the Segregation Cases read like a private colloquy between Frankfurter and the lawyers arguing the cases. In the end, Chief Justice Warren's skillful leadership and, it should be added, Frankfurter's skillful politicking among his brethren, paid off in a unanimous ruling against school segregation.

Only in 1965 did Black reveal the constitutional reasoning behind his concurrence in *Brown*. While Warren's opinion grounded the decision in the changed historical circumstances which made public education so important in national life *circa* 1954 as opposed to 1868 (not to mention the notorious social scientific data mentioned in a footnote), Black asserted that the Brown decision was "compelled by the purpose of the Framers of the Thirteenth, Fourteenth, and Fifteenth Amendments completely to outlaw discrimination against people because of their race or color."[7] In other words segregated schools were already unconstitutional by 1870.

It should be added that Black, one of the three southerners on the Court which outlawed segregation (Tom Clark and Stanley Reed were the other two), did not venture back to Alabama for over 10 years; and in fact the *Brown* decision ruined his son Hugo's political career there. All this confirmed his prescient warning in the midst of the *Brown* deliberations that a decision striking down segregation would "mean the end of southern liberalism for the time being."[8]

But Black had much more difficulty with the various cases that came to the Court in the 1960s having to do with the sit-ins and various novel forms of direct action. Black's general opinion was that "no one spoke to the issue (of public accommodations) in the congressional debates" in the aftermath of the Civil War and that the Fourteenth Amendment did not "without Congressional legislation, prohibit owners of restaurants ... to refuse service to Negroes."[9] Still he did vote to sustain the 1964 Civil Rights Act based as it was on

102

Congressional power to regulate commerce. In a television interview in 1968 he allowed that the Court's order in 1955 that school desegregation proceed with "all deliberate speed" had been a mistake.[10] Finally it was a significant tribute to Black that when Thurgood Marshall was sworn in as the first black Court justice, he chose one-time Klan member, Black, to administer the oath of office to him.[11]

On first glance it is not obvious why Black's championing of the First Amendment should be relevant to the transformation of southern race relations and politics in the 1950s and 1960s. Since the 1950s the First Amendment has been linked in the popular mind to obscenity cases or to cases involving prayer in the public schools. Before that First Amendment issues had mainly to do with matters of free political speech, membership in allegedly subversive organisations and the status of loyalty oaths. In those areas, particularly in the late 1940s and 1950s, Black and Douglas had remained steadfast in their attempts to shelter individuals and groups against restrictions on their First Amendment rights. Black made his views clear in a lecture in 1960 when he wrote that there were "absolutes" in our Bill of Rights and that they were "put there on purpose by men who knew what words meant, and meant their prohibitions to be 'absolute'." This meant to Black that Congress "should not make any law with respect to these subjects" and that the Court should not seek to "balance" First Amendment rights against what it took to be the interests of the nation. "The Framers themselves", he asserted, "did this balancing when they wrote the Constitution and the Bill of Rights."[12]

Despite the apparent simplicity of Black's reading of the First Amendment, much ink has been spilled as to what "absolute" means and what sort of things the First Amendment actually protects. It is important to note that, though Black spoke of absolutes, he did not claim that all the first nine amendments were absolutes; rather there were absolutes *in* them, e.g. protection of speech and religious observance, separation of church and state, due process and parts of the Sixth Amendment.[13] Moreover, within the First Amendment, the Court might properly balance "speech" against "conduct"; penalties and restrictions could be exacted regarding "conduct" not "beliefs".[14] Put another way, freedom of assembly did not have the same status as free speech. Indeed, the place and time, i.e. the context as opposed to content of speech could also be regulated. These distinctions were to remain crucial in Black's First Amendment jurisprudence and become increasingly sharpened as public demonstrations and marches gave way to riots and group violence as the 1960s unfolded.[15]

Finally, in the late 1960s Black made clear that nothing in the First Amendment referred to "only political speech."[16] Not only did Black refuse to censor pornography; he declined to view the films or read the materials in question when the Court was asked to rule on them. Black objected to censoring pornography primarily because of the knock-on effect such censorship might have: "while it is 'obscenity and indecency' before us today ... this type of elastic phrase can, and most likely will, be synonymous with the political, and maybe with the religious unorthodoxy of tomorrow."[17] The habit of censorship easily became an addiction.

Despite his blanket opposition to abridgement of speech, it is generally clear that Black considered political speech and beliefs most worthy of protection. Early in his tenure on the Court, he contended that "Freedom to speak and write about public questions is as important to the life of our government as is the heart to the human body" whose "continued existence ... depends upon the right of free discussion of public affairs."[18] Near the end of the 1940s, he wrote that more than the "rights to vote and privately to express an opinion on political matters" were involved in "Real popular government".[19] His emphasis fell repeatedly upon the need to cultivate the "sound thinking of a fully informed citizenry".[20] Finally, in his *A Constitutional Faith* (1968) Black again affirmed that "Free speech plays its most important role in the political discussion and arguments which are the lifeblood of any representative democracy" and that with First Amendment rights secure, "people develop a sturdy and self-reliant character which is best for them and best for their governments."[21]

Generally, if there are three ways to justify free speech - as a way of attaining the truth, i.e. intellectual or academic freedom; as a means of self-expression, i.e. artistic creation or personal development; or as the very core of collective self-determination and self-government,[22] Black's emphasis as a constitutional theorist and as a political thinker fell upon the third, political justification. Indeed we might say that, though the First Amendment was a constitutional absolute for Black, his political philosophy made it a means to ensure the existence of an informed citizenry and by extension popular "limited" government. From this perspective, Black was not a liberal but a republican (in the generic sense). Indeed there is surprisingly little talk in Black of rights; much more of freedoms and liberties; little, as one critic objected, about the dignity of the individual and rather more about self-government and an informed citizenry.[23]

All this is to say that Black's importance to the civil rights movement, despite his later difficulties with the constitutional status, the political value or the social desirability of what he considered intrusive public demonstrations and protests, was his life-long effort to keep alive and strengthen what Harry Kalven has called (in a context critical of Black) the "public forum",[24] that virtual space of political debate and consideration created by the Constitution, but not coincident with any one of the branches of government or the "State" generally. This, it seems to me, is an American version of the *res publica*. Thus despite the theoretical dubeity of his absolutist position, Black's near deification of the First Amendment did establish solid constitutional backing for those concerned not just with private or artistic expression but also ensured that political expression would not be "balanced" out of existence.[25] Black's "republican" reading of the First Amendment was thus to prove invaluable to the civil rights and anti-war movements insofar as it helped create a space of speech and action within which public protest could take place, even if Black retreated from his expansive reading in the 1960s.

This leads in turn to Black's theory of constitutional hermeneutics. One is tempted to describe it as a positivist theory, for Black's absolutism seemed at times to imply a deductive procedure whereby on certain crucial matters application could be read off from principle, aside from the individual values or preferences of the Court. In fact, in several cases Black's decisions did stand at variance with his own stated preferences. He was opposed to the Vietnam War yet ruled against school children wearing arm bands against the war; he had no objection to birth control yet dissented from striking down a Connecticut law forbidding dissemination of information relating to birth control; and he found no Constitutional prohibition against the poll tax as such, though he was not personally in favour of it.[26] Yet to call Black a positivist is to assume that he regarded the Constitution as a value-free document, a kind of decision machine. Such was clearly not the case. Rather it represented a set of values and institutions, occasionally at odds with his own preferences. The Constitution, for Black, was not infinitely flexible.[27]

Black's theory of interpretation might more accurately be called "fundamentalist" or "Protestant", for he was suspicious of interpretation or construction altogether. Such a description has a certain validity, but not even Black was so simple-minded as to rule out the need for interpretation on occasion and he recognised that it "may result in contraction or extension of the original purpose of constitutional provision."[28] But just for that reason, he developed a republican hermeneutics to decide those cases where meaning was not self-evident. It is appropriate to call it republican, since it was founded on the principle of a return to the first principles of the republic. That having been done, the "language and history", i.e. meaning of the words and, that failing, the intentions of the framers rather than "reasonableness or desirability"[29] determine constitutional validity. As he wrote in *Adamson*, "where construction becomes necessary, we are to place ourselves as nearly as possible in the condition of the men who framed that instrument ...".[30] To Black this use of history as the source of original meaning had to be distinguished both from the use of history in the form of judicial precedents or from an appeal to contemporary history, i.e. present needs and context. The Court was *not*, as Woodrow Wilson once said, "a Constitutional Convention in continuous session".[31] Indeed Alexander Bickel was absolutely correct to suggest that Black, unlike his colleagues on the Warren Court, was neither a rationalist nor a believer in "progress".[32]

It is also crucial to enumerate those criteria, besides precedents and circumstances, which Black excluded as possible criteria for constitutionality. As we have seen, neither the Court nor the Congress (with approval by the Court) could balance absolutes off against other compelling interests. For Black it was just the difference between the American and the British systems that the former was not founded upon Parliamentary supremacy.[33] More importantly Black was dead set against allowing any notion of natural law or natural right to creep into constitutional interpretation. The historical reason for this grew out of the decisions of the Court in cases such as *Lochner* where legislative action to regulate economic and social affairs had been struck down because it allegedly violated natural law.[34] Black also felt that Frankfurterian criteria such as "reasonableness" or "desirability" or "the decencies of civilized conduct" or "natural justice" were non-technical ways of pirating in natural law. To Black the Court could "roam at will" if it adopted such standards.[35] Thus appeal to metaphysical standards was in truth an appeal to subjective preference.

Again we see that Black had no liberal commitment to *natural* law or rights. Rights and liberties were not discoverable by a "bevy of Platonic guardians"[36] or read off from the nature of things. To Black's way of thinking, rights had been *constructed* by the framers of the Constitution and by the architects of the Reconstruction amendments.[37] They were historical rather than natural facts. In other words Black refused to recognise the validity of principles that fought free of the specific language - and in some cases, the general intentions - of the Constitution. Though it was the "best Constitution in the world ... it is not perfect";[38] a repository of human insight and wisdom not an incarnate expression of metaphysical principles.

Though an extended critique of Black's republican hermeneutics is impossible here, several points should at least be mentioned. First, since he was not a literary critic, Black spent little or no time exploring what an intention is nor did his "law office history" leave him time to decide whose intentions counted in determining an authoritative reading of the Constitution.[39] Nor did he consider that, as one student of the subject has recently shown, Madison apparently intended that his intentions not be binding.[40] Nor did he explicitly distinguish, as recent Constitutional theorists such as Ely and Sotorios Barber have done, between "immediate needs and focus" and "aspirations".[41] More importantly Black failed in practice to clarify which one - the meaning of words *or* the intentions - were privileged. In the case of the First Amendment, Black adverted to words and intentions, but privileged the words. In the case of the incorporation doctrine as sanctioned by the Fourteenth Amendment, he privileged intentions (and that of one man) and clearly went beyond the literal words of the Amendment.[42]

There are other ways in which Black's jurisprudence was a republican one. Though it is easy to read Black's defence of free speech as a marketplace notion in which truth emerges from the competition among ideas, this seems to me a misreading: Black allows that citizens will err, and, as stated, what is fundamental for Black is the idea of an informed citizenry coming to a decision together rather than as isolated individuals.[43] Black's assertion of the right of storekeepers to serve whom they wished, if their criteria were not racial, might be read less as a commitment to petty bourgeois capitalism than as a defence of property as a guarantor of autonomy, a venerable republican dogma.[44]

Most clearly, one can detect throughout Black's writings the traditional republican anxiety that without constant vigilance the republic will be eclipsed. Not progress but returning to and keeping faith with original principles was at issue. Republican historical consciousness is "monumentalist" in nature, a kind of self-denial in the face of original historical greatness.[45] In the 1940s and 1950s Black expressed this anxiety in his libertarian defence of free speech and association against the depredations of State authority, while in the 1960s he increasingly located the threat to the republic in social disorder: "Government by clamorous and demanding groups is far removed from government by the people's choice at the ballot box." Only by maintaining the system of government and freedoms could "people develop a sturdy and self-reliant character which is best for them and best for their governments."[46]

These last words of Justice Black were written in the year that Martin Luther King was assassinated, after the apogee of the civil rights movement and in the midst of anti-war protest. King is relevant to our inquiry here, since if any black southerner saw the need for his people to "develop a sturdy and self-reliant character"

107

i.e., self-respect, it was King. Like Black King voiced a quite American faith in American uniqueness. "The goal", wrote King, "of America is freedom." And both men in particular treasured the foundational documents of the republic which King called "the great well springs of democracy."[47]

But in several respects they differed significantly and these differences illuminate most clearly the important constitutional and political matters at issue. First, and most importantly, King did believe in the existence of a moral or natural law: "some creative force ... works for universal wholeness ... though the arc of the moral universe is long, it bends toward justice." These "constitutional or God-given rights" were the standards against which human legal and constitutional orderings were to be measured.[48] Thus King's theory of incorporation had it that the Constitution and the Declaration articulated the human understanding of natural law. Closely linked with this was King's belief in the dignity and value of each person created in God's image. Thus, though King often evoked the Constitution and the Declaration, one of his crucial achievements was to translate constitutional language having to do with federalism, equal protection and freedom of speech and assembly into more accessible (and inspiring) moral and political language.

Indeed King's constitutional thinking with its emphasis upon rights can be located more comfortably in the tradition of radical liberalism than in the republican tradition as such. He not only emphasised natural rights and individual dignity, but was also committed to progress, despite his appeals to the first principles of the republic. His concern was with deliverance from oppression not a return to some ideal state of origins, with fulfillment of ideals in the future not return to a time in the past when they had been efficacious. (Indeed the substantive content of King's social vision - the achievement of the beloved community - went beyond liberalism's defence of rights and individual dignity.) What Black saw as decline and disorder represented for King and the movement the unfortunate results of a "dream deferred". Finally in King we can see the understandable reluctance of black Americans to locate the ultimate source of rights in any human polity.

This is not to say that King was unaware of the importance of a stable framework of laws. In one of his early speeches in Montgomery, ho voiced a claim that he was to repeat in one of his last speeches in Memphis in 1968: "the great glory of American democracy is the right to protest for right." This claim bore a close resemblance to Hannah Arendt's discussion of the "right to have rights" in *Origins of Totalitarianism*. For Arendt this was not an appeal to natural rights but a description of the situation in which one has the right "to live in a framework where one is judged by one's actions and opinions" and "to belong to some kind of organized community."[49] If we read King's assertion in light of Arendt's explanation, we can say that King was asserting the right of black Americans to be included in the polity rather than being in the situation of an alien asking for naturalisation. Indeed to protest publicly was itself to assume that the protestors already belonged, that a space of public appearance waited to be occupied by them. To assert and act on this was a kind of performative assertion, creating, as it were, what it asserted in the act of asserting it.

The question then became, how was one to speak and act within this space and under what conditions? Here we have yet another difference between Black and King. In the context of the 1960s, it was impossible for King and the movement to separate the articulation of their political beliefs from action upon those beliefs. In constitutional terms, this was an implicit assertion that the right "peaceably to assemble" should enjoy the same protected status as speech; in political terms, it contradicted the neat division Bayard Rustin drew between "protest" and "politics". But ultimately this emphasis upon public action in the form of sit-ins, marches, and picketing raised the problem of civil disobedience. Direct action was (and is) not synonymous with civil disobedience but the experience of the 1960s suggests a close connection.

The problem here is that, according to Fred Berger, "there is still no clear cut jurisprudence of civil disobedience to which the American legal system is committed."[50] Indeed, during the 1960s the Supreme Court twisted and turned without ever quite confronting the phenomenon of civil disobedience. Though the Court was inclined to find ways to vacate convictions for criminal trespassing and violations of injunctions in the various cases involving sit-ins and demonstrations, the Court did not - and perhaps could not - formulate any constitutional justification of civil disobedience.[51]

No one more than Black was disturbed by the notion of civil disobedience. Indeed in *A Constitutional Faith* he asserted that the right to assembly did not "guarantee that people will be supplied by government or by private parties with a place to assemble even though their assembly is peaceful."[52] The problem with this view was that, interpreted loosely, it merely pointed to regulation of context and was nothing new. But read with Black's clear animus in mind, an animus that had grown considerably over the years, such pronouncements seemed to make public protestors unduly, even unreasonably, dependent upon public authorities/private individuals for permission to exercise First Amendment rights to assemble peaceably. As Eric Severeid responded to Black in the 1968 CBS interview, groups "can't assemble in the air".[53]

Central to Martin King's understanding of civil disobedience and its relations to the natural law idea is his analysis of just and unjust laws in his "Letter from Birmingham Jail". King began by citing Aquinas to the effect that "An unjust law is a code that is out of harmony with the moral law" and one "not rooted in eternal law and natural law". Yet King realised that few people thought in natural law terms and thus shifted to a psychological-moral standard in his claim that an unjust law "degrades human personality". Still, this begged the question of what it was about an unjust law that was degrading. King's answer was that segregation implied a "false sense of inferiority to those who were discriminated against and reduced them to the status of things." He then moved back to theological language by quoting theologian Paul Tillich to the effect that "sin is separation". Thus if segregation is separation, then segregation is sin.

Even then King was not satisfied. He moved finally to legal and political criteria by asserting that a just law had to apply to a majority as well as to a minority; in Constitutional terms it had to provide equal protection and due process. He went on to add an explicitly political provision when he contended that no law, even if it met the previous criterion, was just if it was inflicted on a minority who "had no part in enacting or devising the law." Thus if we take this participatory criterion as overriding, or at least as a necessary condition for calling a law just, then King seemed to imply a basic citizen right to have an active voice in the making of laws, something that has generally not been the case among higher law and natural rights advocates.

Finally, opposition to unjust laws implied for King a form of civil disobedience, the ultimate meaning of the right to protest for right(s). Within the framework of liberal freedom, freedom as equal status before the law, civil disobedience is the attempt to rectify aberrations in a fundamentally just structure of laws and institutions. It is liberal rather than revolutionary, since the civil disobedient is willing to suffer the consequences of breaking the law by going to jail. Thereby he or she demonstrates the highest devotion to the "spirit" as opposed to the "letter" of the law. "One who breaks an unjust law", wrote King, "must do so openly, lovingly, and with a willingness to accept the penalty."[54] Indeed, appeal to higher law/natural law doctrines can be understood as a way of reassuring the audience of citizens that one is not aiming at anarchy or revolution.

Finally, then, King's concern with freedom as equal standing which was undergirded by natural rights/law provided the foundations for his doctrine of civil disobedience. But in the American context this implied a commitment as well to the public forum, i.e. the *res publica* constituted by the Constitution in the form of the First Amendment. Nor was the meaning of the public forum exhausted by voting, as ironically Black had agreed several decades before, or holding office. Its full meaning was manifested in its provision of a place to speak and act together in public.

In a broad sense, at issue between Black and King were two different understandings of what is properly said and done in the public forum and whether there is a useful constitutional distinction to be made between speech and action.

In certain obvious cases there is an intuitively convincing difference to be drawn between speech and action. Speaking in support of a group that advocates armed revolution or even advocating revolution must be distinguished from committing a violent or illegal action. But once one excludes the obvious cases and focusses on situations such as arose in the 1960s in connection with the civil rights movement and the anti-War movement, at least where violence was neither advocated nor undertaken, the situation is quite different. It is not just that speaking may imply a form of action, e.g. the words "I now pronounce you husband and wife" is a performative utterance, but that acts of civil disobedience are also intended to communicate ideas about the unfairness of a law. They are, as Berger notes, "statute-violating acts that demonstrate, in their commission, the protested injustice or policy." Indeed, Berger has argued that the First Amendment should protect such action or conduct if conventional channels are blocked, if the purpose is "to foster open, unfettered, informed debate" by, for example, revealing conditions which the public may not be informed about or want to confront, and if we take "persons as a value". Surely, he argues, we can distinguish types of conduct that "infringe no basic political and moral rights from those that do." Clearly, though "there must be some limits, ... they are not marked by what is a 'normal' matter of expression."[55]

In constitutional terms Berger is saying that the right to peaceably assemble should assume equal status with free speech. In both cases a distinction should be made between abridgement and regulation. But the larger point is that the same sort of criteria must be applied to action as to speech. Indeed Berger suggests that ultimately there is no important distinction to be drawn between political speech and non-violent political action.

But in addressing these problems raised by the protest movements of the 1960s, ones that worried Black so much, Hannah Arendt took a more radical tack in her essay "Civil Disobedience". No defender of disorder and anarchy, Arendt pinpointed the fallacy in the kind of legal argument Black had advanced in linking social and civil disobedience: "Since disobedience and defiance of authority are such a general mark of our time, it is tempting to view civil disobedience as a mere special case." On this view, breaking the law is breaking the law, whether it is done for criminal or political reasons. But this, Arendt claimed, was a mistake. The criminal commits his crime in secret while the civil disobedient acts publicly and usually in concert with others. One is a social, the other a political phenomenon. Moreover, though "law can indeed stabilize and legalize change once it has occurred, ... the change itself is always the result of extra-legal action."[56]

What was needed, continued Arendt, was some explicit recognition of "Consent and the right to dissent", the two characteristics of the "spirit" of American law, which would by-pass the issue of whether assembly and speech enjoyed the same First Amendment protection. She identified this spirit of the laws with what Tocqueville called "voluntary associations" and then claimed that civil disobedience was a prime example of it. Arendt urged further that "civil-disobedient minorities" be recognised in the same way that other special interest groups are and asserted that neither in "language or in spirit" does the First Amendment cover "the right to association as it is actually practiced in this country." "If there is anything", she concluded, "that urgently requires a new constitutional amendment and is worth all the trouble that goes with it, it is certainly this."[57]

Finally, however utopian and unrealistic Arendt's proposal seems, the spirit informing it seems worth considering. Indeed in present-day America the spirit which sustains the public realm seems to be in eclipse. Citizens seem consumed by private concerns, while those who violate the letter and the spirit of the laws occupy some of the highest offices of the land. It would seem an appropriate time again to remember those first principles so cherished by Justice Black and to recall the efforts of those like Dr. King who extended and enriched the public realm established by the spirit of the Constitution. The arguments of the judge and of the activist will always be in tension; they cannot, and probably should not, be resolved. But both remind us in their different ways that the public forum is not coincident with the State and that *raison d'état* is not the same as the *res publica*. What happened in the South between 1955 and 1965 should have taught us that.

112

REFERENCES

1. Gerald T. Dunne, *Hugo Black and the Judicial Revolution*, New York: Touchstone Books, 1977, pp. 179, 167.

2. Hugo Black, "Justice Black and the First Amendment 'Absolutes': A Public Interview", in Irving Dillard, ed., *One Man's Stand for Freedom*, New York: Alfred Knopf, 1963, p. 472; John Hart Ely, *Democracy and Distrust*, Cambridge, Mass, 1980. p. 3.

3. Dunne, *Hugo Black*, p. 197; Bernard Schwartz, *Super Chief: Earl Warren and His Supreme Court*, New York: New York University Press, 1983, p. 48.

4. Ely describes Black as "liberal", a mistake as I will try to make clear in the main text. There are clearly problems in trying to figure out the political philosophy of Justice Black (or any Justice) from his/her written decisions. Justices are not required to articulate a complete political philosophy and their decisions on constitutional issues may be at odds with their own particular or general preferences. Nor finally do Supreme Court justices seem very well educated in anything but law.

5. Black, "Adamson v. California" (1947), *One Man's Stand*, p. 165.

6. Richard Kluger, *Simple Justice*, New York: Alfred Knopf, 1976, chapter 23; Dunne, *Hugo Black*, chapter 4.

7. Black (dissenting), "Harper v. Virginia State Board of Education", 383 *US* 663, 1966, p. 179; see also Dunne, *Hugo Black*, p. 315.

8. Kluger, *Simple Justice*, p. 593.

9. Monrad Paulsen, "The Sit-In Cases of 1964: 'But Answer Came There None'", *Supreme Court Review*, ed. by Philip Kurland, Chicago: University of Chicago Press, 1964, p. 156; Dunne, *Hugo Black*, p. 392.

10. Hugo Black with Eric Severeid and Martin Agronsky, "Justice Black and the Bill of Rights", CBS News Special, December 3, 1968.

11. Dunne, *Hugo Black*, p. 405.

12. Hugo Black, "The Bill of Rights", *One Man's Stand*, p. 33; "Public Interview", *One Man's Stand*, p. 472; "Bill of Rights", p. 46.

13. CBS Interview.

14. Black, "American Communications Association v. Doud" (1950), *One Man's Stand*, p. 212.

15. See particularly Black's dissent in "Cox v. Louisiana" 379 *US* 559 (1965) and "Tinker v. Des Moines Independent Community School District 393 *US* 503, 1969. Harry Kalven, Jr., "The Concept of the Public Forum: Cox v. Louisiana", *Supreme Court Review*, 1965: 1-32; and Ira Michael Heyman, "Civil Rights 1964 Term: Responses to Direct Action", *Ibid.*: pp. 159-86 are also valuable here.

16. Hugo Black, *A Constitutional Faith*, New York: Alfred Knopf, 1968, p. 46. This is a thinly-veiled rejection of Alexander Meiklejohn's interpretation of the First Amendment as protecting political speech alone. See *Political Freedom: The Constitutional Power of the People*, New York: Oxford Galaxy, 1965.

17. Black, "Smith v. California", 1959, *One Man's Stand*, p. 362.

18. Black, "United Public Workers v. Mitchell", 1947, *Ibid.*, p. 160.

19. Black. "Milk Wagon Drivers Union v. Meadowmoor Diaries", 1941, *Ibid.*, pp. 76, 82.

20. Black, "Kovacs v. Cooper", 1949, *Ibid.*, p. 198.

21. Black, *Constitutional Faith*, pp. 59, 63.

22. These three rationales for free speech are put forward in David Cole's interesting essay applying Harold Bloom's theory of the "anxiety of influence" to dissenting court opinions "Agon at Agora: Creative Misreadings in the First Amendment Tradition", *Yale Law Journal*, 95, 5, April 1986, pp. 857-907. Cole focusses on Holmes, Brandeis and Brennan.

23. These differences in emphasis help account for Sylvia Snowiss's unease with Black's jurisprudence as expressed in "The Legacy of Justice Black", *Supreme Court Review*, 1974, pp. 187-252, an

article which helps clarify the ways in which Black was not a liberal.

24. The definition I give to the term "public forum" is suggested by but not identical with Kalven's use of the term.

25. See Charles Black, "Mr. Justice Black, The Supreme Court and the Bill of Rights", *Harpers*, February 1961, pp. 63-68 for a defence of the strategic and rhetorical (as opposed to the philosophical or historical) validity of the concept of constitutional absolutes.

26. Robert Cover, *Justice Accused*, New Haven: Yale University Press, 1975, analyses the positivist jurisprudence in the ante-bellum slavery debate. For Black's specific dissents which express constitutional positions at odds with his own political preferences, see "Tinker v. Des Moines School District", 1969, "Griswold v. Connecticut", 1965, and "Harper v. Virginia State Board of Education", 1966.

27. Sotorios Barber, *On What the Constitution Means*, Baltimore, Md.: Johns Hopkins University Press, 1984, makes the simple but crucial point that for the Constitution to mean anything, that is, for it to be a Constitution, it cannot mean anything we want it to mean, however morally correct or important our unconstitutional view may be. The Constitution is a yardstick of a specific length not a tape measure of infinite extension.

28. Black, "Griswold v. Connecticut", 381 *US* 479, 1965, p. 539; See H. Jefferson Powell, "The Original Understanding of Original Intent", *Harvard Law Review*, 98, 5, March 1985, for a brief discussion of the deep suspicion of construction lodged in the Protestant ethos.

29. Black, *Constitutional Faith*, p. 8.

30. Black, "Adamson v. California", 1947, *One Man's Stand*, p. 165.

31. Quoted in Merrill Peterson, "Thomas Jefferson and the Constitution", *This Constitution: A Bicentennial Chronicle*, 13, Winter 1986, p. 15.

32. Alexander Bickel, *The Supreme Court and the Idea of Progress*, New York: Harper Torchbooks, 1970, pp. 13-4.

33. Black, "The Bill of Rights", *One Man's Stand*, pp. 36-7.

34. In both "Adamson v. California" and "Griswold v. Connecticut", Black adverted to the Lochner case as the prime example of the constitutional mischief worked by natural law doctrines.

35. See, for example, Black "Rochin v. California" , 1952, *One Man's Stand*, pp. 232-3 for a typical enumeration of what he considered illegitimate standards of constitutionality; Black, *A Constitutional Faith*, p. 36.

36. Quoting Learned Hand in "Griswold v. Connecticut", 1965, p. 540.

37. I use "constructed" here as the opposite of "discovered" or "natural". Most contemporary rights theorists such as Ronald Dworking or John Rawls adopt the view that rights are not natural but constructed within a political and legal community. See Joseph F. Fletcher and Patrick Neal, "Hercules and the Legislator: The Problem of Justice in Contemporary Political Philosophy", *Canadian Journal of Political Science*, XVIII, 1, March 1985, pp. 57-70.

38. CBS Interview.

39. See Alfred H. Kelley, "Clio and the Court: An Illicit Love Affair", *Supreme Court Review*, 1965, pp. 119-58 for the phrase "law office history", though Black receives better marks than some from Kelley. Kelley's distaste for the Court's uses of history goes over the top when he compares the recent Court's use/abuse of history to the notorious ideological distortions of biology mandated by Lysenko in the Soviet Union. It might be added here that Kelley worked on the NAACP's research team which explored the conditions under which the Fourteenth Amendment had been framed and adopted. His experience was that what he found as an historian conflicted with the needs of the NAACP in the case. He apparently served as "devil's advocate" in briefings. Kluger also mentions a paper by Kelley in which he "put Thurgood Marshall and his team of attorneys in the most unfavorable light possible." Kluger, *Simple Justice*, p. 820. See also pp. 635-41. The strongest point in Kelley's argument is his implicit claim that when justices and their clerks do history, they don't do it the way professional historians do it; his weakest point is the implication that professional historians can arrive at a non-controversial

conclusions and "get it right". His comparison with Lysenkoism makes a fundamental error of confusing standards of evidence and proof in biology with those in history.

40. Powell, "Original Understanding", pp. 885-948.

41. Barber, p. 33.

42. In fact if one defines natural law/rights as that which functions to trump all positive laws, then Black's absolutes do function in the same manner as natural laws/rights, except for the fact that they can be repealed. Nor is it the case that natural law/right always had reactionary implications. Anti-slavery lawyers used natural law/right to attack slavery prior to the Civil War. What changes in the post-Civil War period is the concept of nature. Once having taken on a Darwinian cast, nature becomes the locus of competition rather than the embodiment of spiritual force.

43. Snowiss charges Black with having a marketplace model of free speech; but David Cole points to the close historical connection between the marketplace model and that of the informed citizenry. See Black, "Barenblatt v. U.S.", 1959, *One Man's Stand* for Black's view that "It is this right, the right to err politically, which keeps us strong politically as a nation." p. 358. The idea of making errors is hard to square with the marketplace model in which making errors is not at issue.

44. See Paulsen, "Sit-In Cases", pp. 137-70 and also Steven Hahn, *The Roots of Southern Populism: Yeoman Farmers and the Transformation of the Georgia Upcountry, 1850-1890*, New York: Oxford University Press, 1983. Hahn links southern Populism and republicanism through the importance of property in the producer ideology. Since the connection between Black and Populism (or better populism) has often been suggested, the republican tinge to Black's jurisprudence may have something to do with his populist heritage.

45. See J.G.A. Pocock, "Civic Humanism and Its Role in Anglo-American Thought", *Politics, Language and History*, New York: Athenaeum, 1971, pp. 80-103 and *The Machiavellian Moment*, Princeton, N.J.: Princeton University Press, 1975 for the definitive explication of the anxious historical consciousness of republicanism. The point about "monumentalism" derives from

Nietzsche's *The Use and Abuse of History* and can imply a Bloomian self-denial vis-à-vis one's precursors.

46. Black, *A Constitutional Faith*, p. 63.

47. Martin Luther King, *Why We Can't Wait*, New York: Signet, 1964, pp. 93, 94.

48. King, *Stride Toward Freedom*, New York: Harper and Row, 1958, p. 107; the second part of the quotation is found in K. Zepp and F. Smith, *Search for the Beloved Community*, Valley Forge, Pa.: Judson Press, 1974, p. 113.

49. King, *Stride*, p. 62; Hannah Arendt, *The Origins of Totalitarianism*, 2nd ed., Cleveland, Ohio: Meridian, 1958, p. 296.

50. Fred Berger, "Symbolic Conduct and Freedom of Speech", *Freedom of Expression*, Belmont, Cal.: Wadsworth Publishing Company, 1980, pp. 134-47.

51. See Thomas P. Lewis, "The Sit-in Cases: Great Expectations", *The Supreme Court Review*, 1963, pp. 101-51; Paulsen, "The Sit-In Cases of 1964", pp. 137-70.

52. Black, *A Constitutional Faith*, p. 45.

53. CBS Interview. Authorities are bound to grant permits for marches and assemblies under reasonable circumstances, but this in itself raises the problem of prior restraint.

54. This discussion is found in *Why We Can't Wait*, pp. 82-4.

55. Fred Berger, "Symbolic Conduct ...", pp. 150-2.

56. Hannah Arendt, "Civil Disobedience", *Crisis of the Republic*, New York: Harcourt Brace Jovanovich, 1972, pp. 73, 80.

57. *Ibid.*, pp. 94, 101.

9. THE BEGINNING TEXT: IMMIGRANT AUTOBIOGRAPHIES AND CONSTITUTIONAL ALLEGORESIS (OR, ALL'S WELL THAT BEGINS WELL)

William Boelhower, University of Venice

If they are to be connected at all, the three nouns in the title of my essay will have to be submitted to a process of syntactic triangulation between a topic (the beginning text), a genre (immigrant autobiography), and a method (constitutional allegoresis). Since the signifying form of the above genre is itself generated by the narrator's *quest* for a beginning code (or text), and since the very space of autobiographical questing reproduces the semiotic activity of constitutional allegoresis laid out along a horizontal axis, a merely thematic approach would inevitably prove insufficient.[1] Based solely on the semantic control of the presence and absence of allusions to the United States Constitution in various immigrant autobiographies, a thematic analysis must necessarily remain *within* the problematic I wish to explore here. I confess, it would be flippant to give an immigrant preparing for his citizenship examination a Michelin guide to the United States instead of a copy of the country's Constitution; so, in similar spirit, I will avoid treating you as tourists by placing my favourite constitutional chestnuts from immigrant autobiographies - just how many I've gathered counts little indeed - within a larger horizon of representation.

As a text-type immigrant autobiography is architectonically a narrative of constitutional allegoresis. This means that its very attempt at coherence - its desire to *be* a text and achieve closure - actually depends on its success in verifying its own beginnings, having as it does the Constitution as its ultimate object. Subject to the imperative of verification as it is, the autobiographical quest of the immigrant narrator becomes inquest, while the constitutional object proves to be inseparable from this object's reconstruction. Consequently, what we are presented with is an "analytic".[2] In order to *make* sense, the process or order of autobiographical progression and spatial journeying within American cultural boundaries - an order of events, objects, scenes of contact and conflict, and so forth - must be submitted to the order of interpretation, to the act of storytelling itself. In a semiotically rich way, therefore, the problem of beginnings will tie the immigrant autobiographer to the endlessly turning wheel of interpretation.

As Anzia Yezierska in her autobiographical piece "America and I" says, "Between my soul and the American soul were worlds of difference that no words could bridge over. What was that difference?"[3] In her slightly earlier autobiography, *The Promised Land*, Mary Antin offers us what could be taken as a gloss on this query by underlining the word "worlds". As she and all other immigrants quickly learn, "America is not Polotzk".[4] Concerning the form of content of our genre, Yezierska's difference is largely due to the juxtaposition of two spatially conceived cultural models. For the immigrant narrator who has crossed worlds, such a radical geographical and cultural shift poses a fundamental difficulty inherent to the genre's analytic. "I wanted order, order in my head", Yezierska cries out in her essay "Mostly About Myself";[5] but her desire to design a self as being-in-the-world, to establish a principle of narrative congruence, suggests that our analytic is also a *system of translation*. Again, in Yezierska's words, this system is expressed as "What shall I keep, and what shall I throw away?"[6]

Significantly, this very dilemma becomes the motive for Louis Adamic's coming to America in the first place; that is, "to adventure in understanding".[7] But, frankly speaking, this is a minimal formulation of immigrant autobiography's *raison d'être*. A stronger designation of the genre's beginning intention is, simply, "How does one become American?" As we see, our analytic has as its typological goal the *process* of becoming a citizen, and this goal must in turn be based on the "Great Code" of the Constitution.[8] Even Adamic, who is so full of the political vinegar of the 1930s, suggests as much:

> In America everything was possible. There even the common people were "citizens", not "subjects", as they were in Austria and in most other European countries.[9]

The fact that he puts the distinction citizen/subject in quotation marks is most important as I shall show.

There is, therefore, a necessary relation between the idea of immigrant autobiography's originating germ and the need to locate a founding text.[10] Americanisation (with citizenship as the desired goal) requires that on internalise a regime of constitutional statements (*éconcés*). Not surprisingly, this schooling process is manifest as a narrative program in the titles of the best known and perhaps most important immigrant autobiographical texts. Thus, there are Jacob Riis's *The Making of an American* (1910), Edward Bok's *The Americanization of Edward Bok* (1920), Edward Steiner's *From Alien to Citizen* (1914), and Marcus Ravage's *An American in the Making* (1917). Others, like Mary Antin's *The Promised Land* (1911) and

120

Constantine Panunzio's *The Soul of an Immigrant* (1921) literally choose the topos of the school to structure their protagonist's conversion *Bildung*.[11]

Before bestowing a sharper configuration on immigrant autobiographical beginnings - which will then plunge us in a more dramatic study of the genre's yearning for closure or a conclusive logos - I will need to provide at least a brief identikit of the genre under examination. The building up of a model will also allow me to treat immigrant autobiographies as an epistemological index by describing quite inclusively a normative set of narrative constants. In the case of my text-type, the generative principle - its incipit - expresses an opening desire which commits the narrative to a definite system of inferencing. In *Immigrant Crossroads*, Constantine Panunzio defines the object of his desire as follows: "One of the forces which make for Americanization and one which is seldom recognized is found in the very idea of America which the newcomer brings with him."[12]

To reach the desired object or goal, however, the immigrant narrator must send the protagonist on a spatial journey across the sea and across the topology of American culture. That is, the pretext is a conduit metaphor the extension of which raises a problem both of narrative *texere* and of finding the ordering text of American identity and nationality.[13] As the discourse of a journey, our genre's completed spatial form (*textus*) is correlative to the spatial semiotics of the United States elaborated as cultural geography; while the latter is founded by the Constitution's own authoritative act of representation, externality, and dissemination. Thus, the immigrant autobiographical analytic will seek conventionally to recapitulate the theory of representation of that ultimate Text which is responsible for converting presemiotic land into the political form of *patria*. As Daniel Webster once declared, the Constitution "is all that gives us a NATIONAL character."[14] The only way for the immigrant analytic to do this is to have the protagonist travel around the country and along an axis of local heterogeneous spaces (the larger the sample, the more prepared the protagonist) so that the narrator can set about testing, reinterpreting, or simply confirming his/her original desire. Since narrative closure must be guaranteed through a centrifugal process of description, its own totalising act will thereby suffer undermining. That is, the very process of analytico-referential expansion the immigrant protagonist must defer to in decoding his new habitat not only elaborates but simultaneously threatens the autobiographer's search for narrative coherence. As such, the formal achievement of this text-type hopelessly reveals itself to be "*un espacement de la lecture*" of the nationally extended authority of the Constitution.[15]

For the United States is already framed, being already inscribed by a master-plot. The immigrant autobiographical narrator must simply position himself/herself in it as citizen. To sum up, if the formation of the protagonist goes hand in hand with the gathering of information, then the Constitution is necessarily the in-forming text, charged with establishing the nation's juridico-cultural liminality. Caught up in having to verify its own beginnings, immigrant autobiography ends up investigating the constitutionality of the founding text's current historical visibility.

There is now one final point to clarify concerning our genre's identikit, and it directly addresses the interpretative gap existing between the non-discursive materialisation of the Constitution and this same text as the originating discursive source of *patria*. The problem of representation in immigrant autobiography is largely due to this gap. Earlier, I alluded to the juxtaposition of two cultural topologies which accounts for the inherent tension in the genre's narrative form. We have also seen that this juxtaposition is due to the act of immigration itself. Such a momentous journey implies a fundamental break in narrative continuity, almost always presented dramatically as a long and violent ocean-crossing. The journey itself is a departure, and part of leavetaking includes abandoning home, family, property, patrimony, and genealogical attachment. The pathos of this scene is evident at the immigrant's arrival in America, when he walks down the gang plank with what remains: a suitcase, perhaps a trunk, and most likely nobody willing to help carry it. So much material and cultural subtraction often overwhelms. These words from Marcus Ravage's autobiography ring through many immigrant narratives, "In fact, a person gone to America was exactly like a person dead."[16] Here death usually means cultural translation, although at any one moment - it is impossible to say when or why or how - the immigrant subject may suddenly come back to life by shifting cultural, if not physical, topologies; especially if the founding dream or pretext is undermined during the immigrant's constitutional across the American continent.

In the words of Mary Antin, and in spite of premature death notices, the immigrant is inevitably "a heroine of two worlds".[17] (This she announces in the vary last pages of her autobiography in a chapter tellingly entitled "The Heritage".) There are, then, two ways of seeing at stake, one founded on what was left behind and the other on an exquisitely modern text. Again and again, immigrant narrators will return in the final pages of their works to the type of query Marcus Ravage proposes here:

Deep down in my soul, so deep I was scarcely aware of it, these questions were constantly tormenting me: Was it worth while? Could you not have got all that America has given you - of education, of self-development, of opportunity and of happiness - without quitting your home, your loved ones and your country?[18]

We are witness here to two fundamentally different modes of representation and dwelling, resulting in a semiotic clash which invests the very relation between incipit and closure in immigrant autobiographies.

By singling out the two principal definitions of representation in the *Oxford English Dictionary*, I can perhaps better display the issue here, which is that of the third term of the critical triangulation set forth in the introduction, namely constitutional allegoresis. One meaning of the Latin etymon *repraesentatio* comes from the past participle *repraesentatus* and suggests that representation pertains to the mimetic order and that this type of appropriation of the world is best presented as a model or picture. One has here a completed simulacrum to work with. On the contrary, a second and radically different meaning of representation derives from the infinitive *repraesentare*, which yields the idea of performance. In this instance representation signifies an act in which meaning is not so much the result of mimetic copying as of producing. Since the two meanings are opposed to each other, a choice of one implies a radical shift in representational theory. Now, willy nilly, the problem of this shift is precisely what immigrant autobiographies are faced with in having to reconcile two cultural models in order to achieve narrative closure.

I can perhaps best illustrate this issue of representational modes by now selecting a number of incipits among the works already cited, all of them stereotypical. Autobiographical coherence depends on a "system of boundaries and inner constraints",[19] and these are textually incarnated by the concepts of incipit and closure. In employing these terms, I will also have to coinvolve the Constitution as a correlative text in this discussion, it being the *forma mentis* of the nation's cultural topology which the immigrant narrator must scan in order to achieve spatial form for his narration.

The incipit is immigrant autobiography's narrative locomotive. Moreover, the motor of desire it runs by is the same which stimulates the act of immigration in the first place. It is almost always expressed as an original insight or seductive opening metaphor. This is Marcus Ravage's in *An American in the Making*: "For we have glimpsed a vision of American, and we started out resolved that, whatever the cost, we shall make her our own."[20] There is yet a more figuratively striking version of immigrant autobiographical beginnings with a Passover script as frame in Mary Antin's *The Promised Land*. In place of the Exodus refrain "May we be next year in Jerusalem", the Antin family substitutes the words "Next year - in America!"[21] From that point on in the narrative, "America" (again put in quotation marks) will become the object of the girl's obsessive dream.

In both autobiographical instances there is also an announced intention which is so forcefully stated as to imply as well a method of representation. While, referentially speaking, the vision of the object generates desire, which in turn requires the journey to new shores for its fulfillment, syntactically the opening metaphor initiates what Joel Fineman has called a "structure of continual yearning".[22] Here the formal destiny of the word "America" becomes that of extending its metaphorical power over the entire space of immigrant autobiographical representation. Obviously, this effort to overcome diachronic sequence is literally impossible, although the so-called visionary method can still have a totalising effect by means of a strongly encoded figurative strategy. The latter, which becomes specifically a strategy of speaking-the-other, is traditionally subsumed under the practice of allegory or allegoresis. In immigrant autobiographies the Other is the beginning trope of the dream to which all the mute empiria strung along the spatial route is to be accommodated. The problem, though, is how. What the immigrant protagonist tries to do at the referential level - make his dream of America come true, perhaps at all costs - the narrator as autobiographical writer tries to do at the storytelling level. In other words, to use Quintilian's definition of allegory, he will simply seek to continue the originating metaphor until it not only spans but also permeates the entire autobiographical narrative as logos.

Ravage's "at all costs" - an interesting economic coinage and koiné - may imply a certain violence at various levels of the autobiographical text and I think we would agree that the "do or die" attitude is as much a part of the Americanisation process as it is of immigrant autobiography, as I shall show. Jacob Riis, for example, unabashedly says at one point in his account *The Making of an American*, "I resolved that I would reach the top, or die climbing."[23] But this forceful approach is not the single mode of representing the economy of Americanisation. Indeed, Riis himself notes that he came to America equipped with "a strong belief that in a free country, free from the dominion of custom, of caste, as well as of men, things would somehow come right in the end ... if he took a hand in the game."[24] Later on, he will even suggest that the "game" is based on luck and that "The thing is to get *in the way* of it and keep there till it comes along, then hitch on, and away you go."[25] There is here a basic opposition between the modes "making" and "reaching" and "things coming right" and "coming along". The former mode is productive, performative, and may involve some violence of interpretation, while the second implies a mimetic strategy of copying, of reading out the already completed model. Both modes, of course, contribute to make up an immigrant autobiographical analytic.

Riis's stance, I think, is a bit precocious and not the best example I could have chosen to reinforce Mary Antin's more central remark, "It is painful to be consciously of two worlds" or (for my purposes) caught between two different theories of representation.[26] Edward Steiner affords us a more appropriate "primal structural scene" in his autobiography *From Alien to Citizen*. One day, when but a little boy, Steiner happens upon a famous fortune-teller who was visiting his village in Hungary. After paying a goodly sum given to him by his mother, the boy receives an envelope in which his fortune is contained. Running home with the news, he bursts in the door with these words on his lips, "Mother, I am going to America, and I am going to marry a rich wife."[27]

This figural scene (an allegorical trope) is somewhat semantically closed as an incipit, especially if one recalls Hayye Drosher the wigmaker's words to Mary Antin's mother as they are about to set out for the new world: "And may God grant you an easy journey, and may you arrive in a propitious hour, and may you find your husband well, and strong, and rich, and may you both live to lead your children to the wedding canopy, and may America shower gold on you. Amen."[28] The difference between the two representations, Steiner's and Antin's, is the one Hawthorne's young Robin Molineux learns at the moment of his passage from a rural, physiocratic economy based on the family, to an urban, democratic economy of the individual. Steiner's opening trope pertains to the first stage of Molineaux's rite of passage, or to an anti-modern economy of representation.

Concerned with a new life and new foundations, all the incipits I have quoted so far address the problem of dwelling in terms of the etymon *OIKONOMIKOS* (economics), which has both syntactic and semantic implications for the issue at hand. The word can be broken down further into the components *OIKOS* (house), *NOMOS* (manager) and the verbal root of the latter *NEMEIN* (to distribute). While *OIKONOMIKOS* means to be skilled in household management, but also alludes to a system of government in general, the English word "economics" - always according to the *Oxford English Dictionary* - refers to this system as a science or art of the production, distribution, and consumption of commodities. By putting the all-inclusive issue of dwelling under the etymological roof of *OIKONOMIKOS*, we will also have good foundations for including both constitutional and immigrant autobiographical texts within a common definitional space. Furthermore, both the Constitution and immigrant autobiography share the same representational concerns.

To return now to Steiner's rather felicitous incipit of marrying a rich wife, I think we can now easily see why the metaphorical fusion of "rich" and "wife" is a systematically closed proposition. His gay metalogism (ultimately, success in America) reveals a very specific type of household management, in that the metaphor eliminates any possibility of randomness between the two terms. As this script would have it, the immigrant dream will come true within the four walls of the home. Steiner will become rich by marrying, not become rich and then marry. We can even guess who will be chief steward. We have here, in other words, a re-enactment of an old genealogical dream, with its components of inheritance, patrimony, family, and so forth - a rather reposing paradigm.

There is, however, a stick between the spokes of our representational wheel, as there always is in immigrant autobiographical storytelling. Steiner's incipit, his fathering pre-text and family dream, must still undergo its textual journey in order for his hero to slip between the sheets and begin spinning sweet dynastic memories. Needless to say, the distance between dream and bedroom door is the continental carpet of the incorporated Constitution. The wigmaker's blessing in Mary Antin's autobiography seems, in comparison, to be a representationally open trope. Its repeated isolating of clauses by means of the ritualistic "and" nicely juxtaposes getting rich and building family through marriage within a loose combinatory syntax. Such a metonymic patterning is already geared to absorb the shock of spatial distribution the immigrant journey will necessarily plot out.

Yet, by wishing the Antins an "easy journey", Hayye Droshe surely intends to be as homiletically assertive as Steiner. The wish remains, "May your dreams come true in America". Thus, regardless of the above differences between the two incipits, both presume or hope that their beginning trope will be natural and that the immigrant protagonist will *find* the desired object to be as originally imagined. Positioned in the old world as the primal structural scene is, its mode of representation is mimetically oriented around the quest for a completed, a closed, cultural model. Such an anticipated closure is definitionally allegorical, since the implied method is to stay within one continuous frame, the opening one. And the frame will remain one if all that unfolds from it can be accounted for as a single extension of it. If the incipit can compose the variety of narrative microstructures within its own representational economy, then it will have completed an allegorical *coup* of generalisation and unification.

The result will be the completed model of America as a homogeneous cultural space, an *adaequatio rerum et idearum.*

As Joel Fineman has noted, this type of allegoresis works "to extent that it can suggest the authenticity with which the two coordinating poles bespeak each other ..."[29] What invariably challenges the authenticity of the incipit's claim of coordination in the immigrant autobiographical genre is once more the horizontal axis of the immigrant narrator's journey. This axis is extended as a descriptive system which, in the intentions of the incipit, should serve to confirm its own figural statute and practice, thus leading quite naturally to closure. As the principal semiotic vector of American constitutional topology, the road-axis in immigrant autobiography formally elaborates an open series of discrete contact frames yielding a topo-analysis of American national dwelling.[30]

But before going down this road with our dreamy-eyed immigrants to see if it leads to closure, we should first consult the text that not only precedes but also occasions the immigrant autobiographical incipit. The Constitution shares the same central issue of juridical/political extension as immigrant autobiography. The goal too is the same: to define an incorporating model of citizenship. Faced with such a vast and various land, how can one create a common ground of national dwelling? The problem was one of method, of how to transform local topography into the topology of the nation-state. In his book *Explaining America*, Garry Wills calls this issue "a variation on the problem of the one and the many".[31] Finding a solution required spatial thinking capable of applying the scientific laws of checks and balances, separated powers, and representational distribution. It was also a matter of the type of three-dimensional writing needed to build a system of *OIKONOMIKOS.* Like the incipit of immigrant autobiography, the constitutional text too had a horizontal allegory in mind. By intending a single order of circulation and communication, a blueprint for Union, it gave way to an altogether modern household: which immigrant after immigrant has named "a tremendous adventure", as if the house were a ship and the land really a *nomos* of the sea.[32]

In this case, too, the problem of closure was anchored to the Preamble, the Constitution's primal structural scene: "We, the people of the United States, in order to form a more perfect Union, establish justice, insure domestic tranquility, provide for the common defence, promote the general welfare, and secure the blessings of liberty to ourselves and our posterity, do ordain and establish this Constitution for the United States of America". A single sentence, a pre-stroll preface before setting out on a textual journey that led to the possession of a continent. And like our immigrant incipits, it states a preliminary desire (the ritualistic "ordains and establishes") out of which will spring the representational syntax (the Constitution) which we also know as the Republican form of nation-ness.

The intention and method are familiar in the sense that the Constitution's own autobiographical quest for a national identity will involve a spatial economy of cohesiveness. But the achieved type of "domestic tranquility" - at least from the point of view of the immigrant autobiographer - is scandalously new! While the motive of forming "a more perfect Union" promises to be a good allegorical programme, perhaps a confirmation of Edward Steiner's script of marrying a rich wife, the opening designation of a "We" protagonist can only explode any pretensions of representational compactness. By announcing a plural subject as representational paradigm, our household now lacks a fathering steward, a synthetic center, a single perspective. On the basis of this new conception of dwelling, the Constitution actually imposes the people on themselves as a form of representation. As if one could have allegory from below! In this regard David McKay has recently observed in *Politics and Power in the USA*, "The individual, not the state, is what matters. In fact, Americans have some difficulty conceptualizing what 'the state' is."[33] To put it in terms more germane to the discussion at hand, the traditional representational form of our *OIKOS* - as home, city, state, and nation - has become a dwelling without walls.

As one may now guess, such an extreme form of distribution poses a severe obstacle to the quest for allegorical closure in both our text-types. In opening rather than closing the land, however, the constitutional framers did not have reason to suspect the new type of cultural semiotics they were authorising. No threat to national cohesiveness was foreseen in making representation and spatial extension complementary terms. It was, after all, to be nature's nation. There was perfect transparency between the natural and the state orders. The Constitution, in other words, could be considered a mimetic text, a completed model of Republicanism as signifying form.[34] There is here perhaps no more astounding evidence of allegorical authenticity than the Land Ordinance of 1785, which is certainly part of the same episteme that gave birth to the Constitution. What is more, there is no more vivid picture of a political economy in which land is measured, divided into democratically equal lots, and made into a form of currency.

It is by way of describing a regime of constitutional *énoncés* (statements) that I would now like to take up the problem of closure in immigrant autobiography. And this brings us full circle, back to the analytic of constitutional allegoresis, the only term of the title of my essay which has not yet been discussed. By the mere act of

128

descending the gang plank, the immigrant protagonist is already on the threshold of the house the Constitution built. He/She must now trek along the roads of the Republic to learn, in Steiner's words, how "to stand in this conglomerate of races and nationalities which flow into our nation and be able to say without cant: We the People."[35] It is precisely this plural subject that produces an order of constitutional *logoi* in the form of common, free-floating *énoncés*. There is, in fact, a passage from Mary Antin's autobiography that helps to explain the relation between this order of an ongoing originating constitutional source and the stricter text of the Constitution itself as originated source: "And the route we took from the tenements of the stifling alleys to a darling cottage of our own ... was surveyed by the Pilgrim Fathers, who transcribed their field notes on a very fine parchment and called it the Constitution of the United States."[36] This order of discourse has a much broader and deeper extension than the restrictive thematics of Michael Kammen's "popular constitutionalism".[37] Moreover, the way this order is generated and distributed responds as much to the rarefying constitutionals of our immigrants - their physical and cognitive journeying - as to the actual concern for constitutionality.

Indeed, I might more aptly call these maxims a form of democratic "we-speak" or constitutional populism, for it is this type of political-cultural koine the people use to dwell nationally as citizens. Such undialectical "constitutional" communication is, to use a concept of Michel Foucault's, extremely rarefied in that its peculiar order is coextensive with American cultural and political liminality. In Edward Steiner's words once again, "there is a vast, unlimited field over which broods the spirit of a noble idealism, the spirit of America."[38] But there is also a certain banality about this constitutional allegoresis that invests its semiotic authority with the truth-content of clichés. In fact, the banality of these utterances is specific to the modes of thought and action of the American "I am" as part of a national "we". To sum up, such utterances serve as rules of passage allowing the immigrant protagonist to move from one local space to another along the specifically national level of nomothetic circulation: the nation as a single extended household.

It is primarily at this discourse level of a projected continuum that the nation as a field of representation can be read as a homographic text and offer the immigrant an extended "horizontal comradeship", to borrow from Benedict Anderson.[39] And this same level of transit becomes the very axis - the road of the immigrant's autobiographical schooling and Americanisation. Earlier, however, I said that the journey itself makes the extension of the autobiographical incipit problematical. That is, it inevitably breaks down into the distribution of an open series of local spaces, into the serialisation of local contact frames. By means of this geopolitics of the local, the immigrant protagonist encounters all that is empirical, discontinuous, unrepeatable, and anomalous.

Time and again in his autobiography, Jacob Riis deals with this *leçon des choses* by fleeing, but also by scripting events biblically: "Inwardly raging, I shook the dust of the city from my feet, and took the most direct route out of it ..."[40] While the homiletic angle may suggest that he has not abandoned his faith in the standard immigrant autobiographical incipit, yet he does go elsewhere to attempt to legitimate it. This way of handling the culturally heteromorphic level of local space does leave topological gaps of signification within the space of allegorical distribution. For Italian immigrant Emanuel Carnevali, getting on and off the road means an endless string of jobs which he narrates in the form of a mere list: my first job ... my second ... my third ... and so on, until he is led to conclude, "The days I was not employed by work I was employed by hunger."[41] Here again, in this rhetoric of contiguity one senses that no possible synthesis will be able to gloss over this pathology of the global structure of the nation: a significant spread of "internal extraterritorial places", to use an expression of Paul Virilio's.[42] Indeed, the descriptive journey into modern American space so multiplies the local that no synthetic form is forthcoming. An even stronger sense of randomness and of a missing totality is evident in this passage from Pascal D'Angelo's autobiography *Son of Italy*: "Everywhere was toil - endless, continuous toil ... - toil. In Hillsdale, Poughkeepsie, Spring Valley, New York, Falling Water, Virginia, Westwood, Remsey, New Jersey, Williamsport, Maryland ... Utica, New York, White Lake Corner, Otterlake, Tappan, Statsburg, Oneanta, Glen Falls, and many other places ..."[43] In the light of this economy of representation, ultimately commensurate with the vast fields of the Republic, it is hard to speak of a successful substitutional practice based on the strategy of repeating or continuing with the beginning rhetorical trope of immigrant autobiography's conventional incipit.

Since immigrant autobiographies do not find their incipit mimetically confirmed or citizenship self-evident (if this were the case, allegorical verification would be intrinsic to the referential order of American cultural description), they simply produce this confirmation through constitutional allegoresis. As Edward Bok notes in his work *The Americanization of Edward Bok*, "where there is no vision the people perish".[44] But vision, the only means of connecting semantically an open series of local cultural topoi, is achieved through a structure of citationism which I have already defined above as an analytic of constitutional utterance. Jacob Riis helps to explain such an economy of representation when he says towards the end of his autobiography, "I did my work and tried to put into it what I thought citizenship ought to be, when I made it out."[45] To sum up, constitutional allegoresis *is* what it means to be an American citizen. Or, inversely, to become an American, one must learn to practice constitutional allegoresis.

No longer read mimetically, constitutional discourse becomes a principle of floating interpretation; for as Louis Adamic notes on behalf of all immigrants in *Laughing in the Jungle*, "As a foreigner, always on the alert, trying to know and understand America, I had become ... aware of too many things that were not in tune with what appeared to be the Wilsonian idea of justice and other such principles."[46] At the same time, however, immigrant autobiographies show that constitutional utterances are a necessary fiction for producing American dwelling. As we have already seen, it is precisely by means of constitutional utterances that Jacob Riis climbs in and out of local places as though he were really going from same to same. Relying on a compulsive strategy of repetition, immigrant narrators remain on the road, in transit, but as nationals.

Transit, then, also means transport, with constitutional citationism being the code for translating the immigrant protagonist into the authoritative language of citizenship. In this way is closure provided and our autobiographical genre itself defined. We have here, in conclusion, a real structural sleight of hand: immigrant autobiography achieves closure by repeating the incipit, but now as constitutional allegoresis. In other words, nothing is being cancelled here, neither opening trope nor any of the subsequent space of the textual journey. In effect this means that the incipit's elaboration as closure does not in the least trace a continuum but, on the contrary, functions as an act of redundancy, one more rhetorical figure in a metonymic series of figures.

This type of combinatory closure, based on constitutional allegoresis, is more a local gesture than it is an expanded teleology; more a discrete practice than an ongoing ideological progression. To gain access to the national circuit of the nation-state, to the universal level of the subject as citizen, the immigrant narrator simply quotes the originating constitutional source. Thus, from the Jewish pits of turn-of-the-century Boston, Mary Antin delivers such lapidary maxims as "In America everything is possible", "All occupations were respectable, all men were equal in America";[47] while Edward Steiner, himself no newcomer to bottom-dog status, shows such constitutional good sense as: "Young man, in this country you must remember that God helps those who help themselves"; and "freedom to all who obey the law".[48] As for Jacob Riis, I might cite his "Right in the end does prevail over might"; or "The light comes as we work toward it".[49] Still, as empirical subject, Riis is known to friends as "the man of coincidences",[50] thus making him both existential *homme* of the locally aleatory moment and global citizen of the necessary nation-state.

If, then, we have many highly discontinuous narrative frames, we also have a single interpretative practice. In a moment of healthy soul-saving didacticism, Constantine Panunzio declares in his autobiography *The Soul of an Immigrant*, "If my experience has any significance at all, it lies in the fact that it shows what a transformation in the thought-life of the foreign groups could actually take place ..."[51] Immigrant autobiography is not only the discourse of a journey, therefore, but also the journey of a type of discourse - due to the shift that takes place in economies of representation. By learning to re-use the constitutional text according to the modified field of American extension, our immigrant narrator converts his autobiographical incipit's attempt at interpreting America as an Old World allegory into a New World allegory of interpretation. Indeed, in the words of Marcus Ravage, the very self as citizen is "an invention", "just a character in my book".[52] Such a subject has a fictive identity, no different than that constructed by the narrative *texere* of immigrant autobiography. The two share the same linguistic status. Just as the state itself is not an essence but a practice, so too does the immigrant narrator, through speech-act situations, designate the autobiographical self as citizen. For our immigrant autobiographical genre, therefore, constitutional allegoresis becomes a necessary fiction: in the end there is only the beginning. And all is well that begins well.

REFERENCES

1. For a full treatment of the signifying form of immigrant autobiography as a distinct genre, see my essay, "The Brave New World of Immigrant Autobiography", *MELUS*, Vol. 9, No. 2, Summer 1982, pp. 5-23.

2. By the term "analytic" I simply mean the following: meaning is the result of a relational economy between the order of the mind (or - in our case - signifying text) and the order of reality and is based on the interaction of these two poles. Semiosis, in other words, is produced by means of inevitable transformations of this interaction, depending on a shift of emphasis between mind and reality or text and the referential order.

3. Anzia Yezierska, *Children of Loneliness*, New York: Funk & Wagnalls, Co., 1923, p. 49.

4. Mary Antin, *The Promised Land*, New York: Houghton Mifflin, Co., 1912, p. 193.

5. Anzia Yezierska, *Children of Loneliness*, p. 17.

6. *Ibid.*, p. 11.

7. Louis Adamic, *Laughing in the Jungle*, New York: Harper & Brothers, 1932, p. 326.

8. See Michael Kammen, *A Machine That Would Go of Itself*, New York: Alfred A. Knopf, 1987, p. xx.

9. Louis Adamic, *Laughing in the Jungle*, p. 6.

10. See, for the notion of "originating germ" and "founding text" Edward Said's suggestive discussion in his book *Beginnings*, New York: Basic Books, Inc., Publishers, 1975, pp. 3-12.

11. Marcus Ravage, *An American in the Making*, New York: Dover Publications, 1971; orig. 1917; Jacob Riis, *The Making of an American*, New York: The MacMillan Co., 1924; Edward Bok, *The Americanization of Edward Bok*, New York: Charles Scribner's Sons, 1923; Edward Steiner, *From Alien to Citizen*, New York: Fleming H. Revell Company, 1914; Constantine Panunzio's *The Soul of an Immigrant*, New York: Arno Press, 1969; originally published in 1928.

12. Constantine Panunzio, *Immigrant Crossroads*, New York: Mac-Millan Co., 1927, p. 256.

13. For examples of the Constitution as the ordering text of American identity, see Michael Kammen, *A Machine That Would Go of Itself*: Jefferson Davis in 1858 notes, "we became a nation by the Constitution; whatever is national springs from the Constitution; and national and constitutional are convertible terms" (p. 62); Andrew Johnson, in his third annual message to Congress, said, "The Union and the Constitution are inseparable ... Without the Constitution we are nothing; by, through, and under the Constitution we are what it makes us" (p. 118). The "ordering text" I am referring to, of course, is the sort of constitutional

universalism that made the actual Constitution possible: this text as spirit rather than letter, concept rather than reality.

14. *Ibid.*, p. 94.

15. See Edward Said, *Beginnings*, p. 10.

16. Marcus Ravage, *An American in the Making*, p. 10.

17. Mary Antin, *The Promised Land*, p. 361.

18. Marcus Ravage, *An American in the Making*, p. 324.

19. See Edward Said, *Beginnings*, p. 9.

20. Marcus Ravage, *An American in the Making*, p. xiv.

21. Mary Antin, *The Promised Land*, p. 141.

22. Joel Fineman, "The Structure of Allegorical Desire", in Stephen J. Greenblatt, ed., *Allegory and Representation*, Baltimore: Johns Hopkins paperback, 1986, p. 45.

23. Jacob Riis, *The Making of an American*, p. 85.

24. *Ibid.*, p. 21.

25. *Ibid.*, p. 197.

26. Mary Antin, *The Promised Land*, p. xiv.

27. Edward Steiner, *From Alien to Citizen*, p. 20.

28. Mary Antin, *The Promised Land*, pp. 165-6.

29. Joel Fineman, in *Allegory and Representation*, p. 31.

30. A "frame" is a structure of data that serves to represent a stereotypical situation; as such it is a prefabricated script amounting to a virtual text or condensed story that is hyper-codified. See Umberto Eco, *Lector in fabula*, Milan: Bopiani, 1979, p. 79ff. For the notion of "topo-analysis", see Gaston Bachelard, *La poetica dello spazio*, Italian tr. Ettore Catalano, Bari: Dedalo Editore, 1975, pp. 36-42. It refers to the spatial

localisation of our memories and of our being; locates the various functions of our dwelling in topological terms.

31. Garry Wills, *Explaining America, The Federalist*, Harmondsworth, Middlesex: Penguin Books Ltd., 1981, p. 98.

32. For the words "tremendous adventure", see Mary Antin, *The Promised Land*, p. 166; For the notion of house as ship and the nomos of the sea, see the brilliant essay by Carl Schmitt, *Terra e mare*, Italian tr. Angelo Bolaffi, Milan: Giuffrè Editore, 1986).

33. David McKay, *Politics and Power in the USA*, Harmondsworth, Middlesex: Penguin Books Ltd, 1987, p. 30.

34. As James Fenimore Cooper wrote in 1830 "(W)e are unique as a government, and we must look for our maxims in the natural corollaries of the Constitution." Quoted in Michael Kammen, *A Machine That Would Go of Itself*, p. 94.

35. Edward Steiner, *From Alien to Citizen*, p. 321.

36. Mary Antin, *The Promised Land*, p. 357.

37. See Michael Kammen, *A Machine That Would Go of Itself*, p. xi. For the notion of an order of discourse that is territorially coextensive with the political and cultural identity of the nation-state, I am deeply indebted to Gilles Deleuze, *Foucault*, Paris: Editions de Minuit, 1986.

38. Edward Steiner, *From Alien to Citizen*, p. 250.

39. For the words "horizontal comradeship", see Benedict Anderson, *Imagined Communities*, London: Verso Editions, 1983, p. 16.

40. For the notion of "leçon des choses" as a *savoir*, see Gilles Deleuze, *Foucault*, p. 58ff; the quotation is from Jacob Riis, *The Making of an American*, p. 32.

41. *The Autobiography of Emanuel Carnevali*, compiled by Kay Boyle, New York: Horizon Press, 1967, p. 84; for a discussion of this text, see William Boelhower, *Immigrant Autobiography in the United States*, Verona: Essedue, 1982, pp. 137-77.

42. Paul Virilio, *Velocità e politica*, Italian tr., Milan: Multhipla Edizioni, 1981, p. 68.

43. Pascal D'Angelo, *A Son of Italy*, New York: MacMillan Co., 1924, p. 74.

44. Edward Bok, *The Americanization of Edward Bok*, p. 430.

45. Jacob Riis, *The Making of an American*, p. 273.

46. Louis Adamic, *Laughing in the Jungle*, p. 172.

47. For the quotes from Antin, see her *The Promised Land*, pp. 352, 193.

48. For the quotes from Steiner, see his *From Alien to Citizen*, pp. 50, 44.

49. Jacob Riis, *The Making of an American*, pp. 60, 210.

50. *Ibid.*, p. 29.

51. Constantine Panunzio, *The Soul of an Immigrant*, p. 276.

52. Marcus Ravage, *An American in the Making*, p. 290.

10. THE INFLUENCE OF THE AMERICAN CONSTITUTION ON DUTCH LAWYERS, JUDGED BY THE DUTCH DEBATE ON JUDICIAL REVIEW

Bart van Poelgeest, University of Leyden

As an "example in the distance", in the words of J.W. Schulte Nordholt, the American Revolution drew the admiring attention of the 18th century Dutch patriot party.[1] The prominent lawyer Pieter Paulus noticed a striking resemblance between the Union of Utrecht from 1579, the constitutional basis of the Republic of the seven united Dutch provinces, and the recently adopted Articles of Confederation. Paulus took it for granted that the Americans had used the Dutch document as an example.[2] That opinion was shared by another Dutch lawyer with regard to the U.S. Constitution of 1787, Gerhard Dumbar. Dumbar was the learned secretary of the city of Deventer and like Paulus a supporter of the progressive Dutch patriot party that opposed the stadtholder and the ruling oligarchy around him. The first translation of the U.S. Constitution and some of the Federalist Papers in a non-English language was made by Dumbar. He published it in three volumes between 1793 and 1796 and added his comments on both the Constitution and the Federalist Papers.[3] Although the interest in the American constitutional experiments was certainly more widespread in the Dutch Republic than in most other continental countries, the assumptions of Paulus and Dumbar on the importance of the Dutch Republic for the Founding Fathers had little to do with reality. Schulte Nordholt has clearly demonstrated the naive overestimation of the two Dutch lawyers in this respect. Some of the Founding Fathers, and J. Madison in particular, had made a study of the Dutch Republic, but that had at best had only an indirect and negative influence. Not surprisingly so, for the contemporary Dutch Republic did not exactly offer an attractive alternative. It was dominated by a virtual aristocracy of regent families under the supervision of an hereditary stadtholder with quasi-monarchical powers. The patriot party had successfully challenged the stadtholder since the beginning of the fourth Anglo-Dutch war in 1780, during which they humbled William V by officially recognising the United States as an independent state in 1782. In 1787 however, during the Constitutional Convention in Philadelphia, the weaknesses of the Dutch Republic became evident. The internal quarrels threatened to reach the stage of an open civil war but that was

137

prevented by an Anglo-Prussian counterrevolutionary *coup d'état* that restored the stadtholder and forced the pro-American patriots to escape to France. In those circumstances the Dutch example lost all its potential charm for the Founding Fathers.[4]

The American interest in Dutch constitutional practice then disappeared definitively with the signing of the Constitution in 1787. But did the American example also loose all its attraction for Dutch lawyers? The question is more easily put then conclusively answered. Undoubtedly some Dutchmen were influenced by parts of American constitutional law but it is difficult to trace and assess that inspiration. Only rarely does an author directly suggest an American solution for a Dutch problem. More often the American example is quoted alongside that of other countries or no explicit reference is made at all, even when it seems obvious that the author had the U.S. Constitution in mind. This problem will be approached from two angles. The most active kind of interest, Dutch publications on the U.S. Constitution, is relatively easy to measure. To get some impression of the more indirect influence of the American example, the Dutch debate on judicial review will be examined as far as it shows the use of American sources. As federalism and the American version of the separation of powers differed too much from the Dutch constitutional monarchy to offer useful comparisons, judicial review as the third prominent feature of American constitutional practice for a long time seemed the most relevant idea to the Dutch.

Judicial review of legislation did not exist in the days of the Dutch Republic (1579-1795). The constitutional arrangements under the Union of Utrecht indeed resembled those under the Articles of Confederation. Although the Union of Utrecht came close to a federal constitution, no federal court existed to enforce its provisions. The high courts of the seven provinces were explicitly forbidden by the provincial estates to adjudicate any political case. This led the Zeeland regent Lieven de Beaufort in 1737 to make a cynical comment on the value of constitutions: "The people can trust such documents as safely as a paper armour that at any time can be thorn into pieces and thrown into the fire."[5]

The Old Regime in the Low Countries collapsed with the arrival of the French revolutionary troops. The stadtholder fled to England in 1795, never to return. The new Dutch government made a peace treaty with France and soon became a French satellite state. France left the Dutch, especially the patriots returned from their exile in France, room enough to debate a new constitution for the republic. The favourite examples were of course the French and the American constitutions. The radical party strove for a strongly centralised state according to the French model. Their political opponents, known as

138

"the federalists" (in exact opposition to what that label meant in the U.S.A.), claimed the support of the American constitution for their more conservative views. They wanted to preserve more of the old, extremely federalist structure of the old republic.[6]

The National Assembly delegated the task of preparing a draft of the constitution to a committee of 21. One of its members was a revolutionary tailor from Utrecht, Jacob van Manen, a self-educated man of much humbler social origins than most of his colleagues in the Assembly.[7] He proposed the introduction of judicial review for the new national Supreme Court in 1796. This Supreme Court should also have the power to decide conflicts between the legislature and the executive but if both branches of government disagreed with the decision of the Court, the electorate had to decide. Although Van Manen nowhere refers to any foreign example, it is likely that he drew his inspiration from the texts of the U.S. Constitution and the Federalist Papers just published by Dumbar. The concept of judicial review was foreign to the Dutch tradition and did not appear in the French constitution. Van Manen may claim to have been the first on the continent to introduce judicial review, basing his conclusions on the texts only. That was seven years before Chief Justice John Marshall activated this slumbering power of the Supreme Court in Marbury v. Madison. Van Manen could not persuade the committee to accept his idea. His most important opponent in this matter was the radical textile-merchant from Leyden, Pieter Vreede, who preferred to leave the power of review in the hands of the legislature because that branch of government was closest to the people.[8]

In the following years many constitutions were drafted and rejected or abolished after a short period of time. One of them, the constitution of 1801, established a new institution, the National Syndicate, that was given the task to supervise the constitutionality of all actions of the state, including legislation. When the Syndicate discovered a possible violation of the constitution by the state, it could bring the case before the Supreme Court that had to decide the matter. This type of judicial review was, most likely, copied from the French constitution of 1799 that knew a similar institution, the "Sénat Conservateur". The Dutch version wasn't much of a success because of personal problems and lack of cooperation by the executive. The National Syndicate disappeared with the new constitution of 1805.[9] After a short period of incorporation into the French Empire (1810-1813), the Dutch regained their independence after Napoleon's defeat in 1813.

The son of the last stadtholder returned from England to accept the sovereignty of the new monarchy of the Netherlands "under the guarantee of a wise constitution". William I appointed a committee to draft such a constitution. The chairman of the committee was Gijsbert Karel van Hogendorp, a brilliant conservative who had visited the United States in 1783.[10] He was an expert in American affairs but in his draft for the national constitution he chose to remain as close as possible to the traditions of the old Dutch Republic. Van Hogendorp proposed to leave the power of review of legislation in the hands of the legislature but he showed himself willing to accept judicial review by the Supreme Court at the suggestion of his colleague Count Van Lynden. A majority of the committee, however, shared the opinion of Lord Elout who rejected judicial review because it would make the Court a political institute while it was not adequately equipped for such a responsibility.[11] The constitution of 1814 then opted for legislative review of legislation. That provision disappeared for unknown reasons during the revision of the constitution in 1815, made necessary by the enlargement of the Kingdom with the southern Netherlands (the present Belgium) at the congress of Vienna.

Although the constitution of 1815 left the matter of review of legislation undecided, the practice was clear. An executive order of the King, the so-called "Conflictenbesluit", had severely curtailed the powers of the judiciary by reserving all conflicts between the administration and the judiciary to the King. That left little room to the judges in political cases, let alone room for judicial review.[12] The "Conflictenbesluit" provoked the criticism of two lawyers who also referred to the question of review of legislation. According to the Amsterdam lawyer C. Backer the interference of the King in judicial affairs was wrong but Backer also showed himself an opponent of judicial review of legislation because he considered the legislation as the most important body in the state.[13] The catholic lawyer H. van Sonsbeeck reached the opposite conclusion in his disapproval of the "Conflictenbesluit". He favoured judicial review with the argument that the judge took an oath to preserve the constitution. Van Sonsbeeck did not only quote French and German literature as Backer had done but also a French article on judicial review in the United States. That reference was made only casually and did not support one of his arguments in any way.[14]

This shows that the American constitution and its practice were virtually unknown in Holland during the first half of the 19th century, reflecting a more general lack of knowledge and interest in the United States, in contrast to the situation in the last quarter of the 18th century. The only Dutch publication on the subject was a thesis of 1835 by O.A. Baron Lewe van Aduard about the legal arguments used by the colonies in the conflict with Great Britain. It was just a translation into Latin of some English and American literature on that issue.[15] Apparently Lewe's professor, the famous liberal professor in constitutional law and history J.R. Thorbecke, hadn't shown any interest. More striking perhaps was the total silence in Holland after the publication in Paris of Alexis de Tocqueville's *De la démocratie en Amérique*. While the book caused a sensation in France, Germany and other European countries, it seems to have been widely ignored in Holland for more than thirty years.[16]

Tocqueville described the importance of the American judiciary and the practice of judicial review. Unfortunately it is unknown whether the young lawyer D. Donker Curtius had read the book before 1841 when he argued in court that the courts should exercise the power of review with regard to the ordinances of the provinces, explicitly leaving aside the question with regard to acts of parliament.[17] In 1847 Van Sonsbeeck jr. defended his father's opinion in favour of judicial review in his thesis without any reference to the United States.[18] That same year, 3 years after the withdrawal of the "Conflictenbesluit", the Hoge Raad der Nederlanden, the Dutch Supreme Court, decided a case in a way that came close to assuming the power of judicial review.[19]

Judicial review became the subject of an important debate the next year. In 1848 the French monarchy had collapsed and the revolution spread to other countries, including the Netherlands. King William II was afraid to lose his throne and overnight appointed the leader of the liberal opposition, the Leyden law professor Thorbecke, as chairman of a committee to revise the constitution. Donker Curtius was also a member of that commission. It presented the King with a revised constitution within a month. William II then appointed a new cabinet with Donker Curtius as minister of Justice to introduce the amendments in parliament. For political reasons the spiritual father of the changes, Thorbecke, was kept out of the cabinet.

The cabinet then made some changes in the committee's drafts. The original version of Thorbecke had not mentioned the attribution of review of legislation to any branch of government as in the old constitution but now a new article was added that simply stated "the laws are inviolable". In its explanation to the parliament the cabinet held that this provision meant to exclude judicial review of acts of parliament. The idea had come from Donker Curtius who had remarked in the cabinet that "judicial tyranny is the worst of all". The Council of State supported the cabinet in this matter over the dissent of counsellor Van Sonsbeeck sr. who opposed the cabinet's proposal by saying: "Now the minister places the legislature above everything."[20] During the parliamentary debates some members expressed grave doubts about the new article but they were a minority. Only two members referred to the exclusion of judicial review in their speeches; other issues such as curtailing the power of the monarch were clearly more important. Albarda opposed the article because it would subordinate the constitution to the normal legislative process while his colleague Sloet supported the cabinet's proposal because he feared judicial review would create a judicial omnipotence that was more dangerous than any arrogance of the legislature or the executive.[21] Finally the article was accepted by the majority and it remained part of the constitution until 1983.

The explicit constitutional exclusion of judicial review was rather exceptional. First among the critics was of course professor Thorbecke who called it "the strangest jump in the air a legislature ever made". He argued that the constitution could only be supreme as long as the judiciary prevented the legislature from encroachments on the constitution.[22] Probably Thorbecke also was afraid that the article was an open invitation to the conservative majority in parliament to undermine his liberal constitution by adopting unconstitutional laws. He got the support of C.W. Opzoomer, an Utrecht law professor, who defended judicial review on statutory grounds. Opzoomer quoted the American example. In a footnote he referred to the works of Justice Story, the Federalist papers and the opinions of the Supreme Court in general. The first edition of Opzoomer's book in 1848 contained no quotations at all. It is likely that he had made up his mind on the subject before he learned about judicial review in the U.S.A. and only later added it as an extra argument.[23]

The first 19th century Dutch lawyer who showed some knowledge of American constitutional law was W.A.C. de Jonge who worked at the Ministry of Justice. In 1849 he wrote an article on judicial review in which he also shortly described the American practice, using Tocqueville as his only source of information.[24] Later that reference was taken over by the Amsterdam law professor J. de Bosch Kemper. In his textbook on Dutch constitutional law he explained the American choice for judicial review as a logical consequence of the historical distrust of a dominating legislature. The Dutch legislative process was good enough, according to De Bosch Kemper, to make any fear of a dictatorial majority in parliament, expressed by Tocqueville, seem unreal.[25]

The second half of the 19th century showed an increase in the interest of Dutch lawyers for American constitutional law. That was probably due to the publicity around the Civil War and the growing importance of the United States. In 1878 P.J. Löben Sels wrote a very biased thesis on the right of the states to secede from the Union. He had married the daughter of the Dutch consul in San Francisco and knew the United States from his own experience. Sels adopted the southern point of view, as laid down by A. Stephens, without any reservation. Even more uncompromising was his judgement on the Americans. The high ideals of 1787 had been perverted by an unchecked lust for money. So it is all the more surprising that Sels, who advised the Americans to adopt the excellent moral standards of the Dutch, emigrated to the United States to establish himself as a lawyer in San Francisco and founded a ranch in California (still in the possession of his descendants).[26] Further, there were three other Dutch theses that dealt with the United States. W. Suermond described an American trade union (1890),[27] C. Bake made a comparison between federalist states, including the United States (1881),[28] and J. Paulus advocated a change in the Dutch First Chamber that would make its composition similar to that of the United States Senate (1886).[29]

The debate on judicial review got a new impetus after a decision of the Dutch Supreme Court in 1865 that had declared a provincial ordinance unconstitutional.[30] A member of the provincial assembly angrily wrote that the court should not interfere with any legislative process. He called judicial review not only "questionable and reprehensible" but also "a profound constitutional heresy and highly revolutionary". Two young lawyers responded in less emotional terms in the same magazine in 1866.[31] That appeared to be no more than the prelude to what still had to come. In 1867 the prominent magazine *De Gids* published an extensive review article by a judge in the court of Arnhem, D.J.Mom Visch, of Tocqueville's *De la démo-cratie en Amérique*, more than thirty years after the first edition. In a footnote under the passage dealing with judicial review, Mom Visch expressed his view that the Dutch prohibition was absurd.[32] Until the First World War the Dutch debate on judicial review was influenced by the Tocquevillean fear of a dictatorial parliamentary majority and the political struggle for the extension of the franchise. The American example of judicial review became more and more important in this discussion.

That the issue had attracted the attention of Dutch lawyers was shown by two theses that appeared in 1867 and 1868. The first thesis was written by J.Ph.T. du Quesné van Bruchem and publicly defended in Utrecht on June 29th. Just a few weeks earlier Lord F.J.Th. Beelaerts van Blokland got the idea to devote his thesis to the same subject, judicial review of legislation. When Beelaerts learned about Quesné's book, he first considered choosing another subject but after reading the book he decided to stick to his original intention because he rejected Quesné's conclusion. Beelaerts defended his thesis in Leyden on May 29th, 1868.[33] The differences were not limited to the conclusions. Whereas Beelaerts's work was widely praised as a masterpiece, Quesné's thesis passed into oblivion. Their careers also

143

reflect that. Quesné became a lawyer who produced honey-sweet poems and would have been completely forgotten had he not married a sister of Vincent van Gogh's.[34] Beelaerts made a brilliant career. He worked on several important legislative projects at the Ministry of Justice and became a distinguished member of parliament. Three times he turned down an offer to become the minister of Justice or a law professor.[35]

There were also similarities. Neither of them had ever visited the United States. They both used the same sources (the commentaries on constitutional law by Story and Kent) and shared Tocqueville's pessimistic view on the development of democracy. Quesné and Beelaerts saw his fears become reality in the heavy political turmoil of the Reconstruction. Both were convinced that the constitutional monarchy embodied the highest grade of perfection in the organisation of a state. Quesné thought that the United States could not do without judicial review to maintain democracy. The Dutch system was threatened by the same disintegrating forces as the United States but as the Dutch constitution provided more guarantees for the quality of the legislative process a milder version of judicial review would suffice. Quesné proposed to give the courts the power not to apply a law in a specific case (as applied) instead of the American practice to invalidate the law. Beelaerts pointed out that the informal practice of "stare decisis" in the Dutch courts made that an unworkable solution. He also put the debate on a proper footing by attacking the rhetoric of Quesné and Opzoomer that the judge could not be forced to apply unconstitutional laws. Beelaerts argued that the real question was which branch of government was most suited to exercise the power of review. To him it was clear that parliament was more qualified than the judiciary because of the political nature of review and the safeguards in the legislative process. Lord Beelaerts did not mention the democratic mandate of the parliament as an argument. At that time only slightly more than ten percent of the male population could vote. Beelaerts opposed all liberal proposals to enlarge the electorate, perfectly in tune with his Tocquevillean fear of mass democracy. The aristocrat felt deeply humiliated when, at the end of his life, he was forced to win votes for himself by giving one campaign speech before the elections for his seat in parliament. In his thesis Beelaerts did not refer to any foreign example of judicial review because Quesné had already done that but it was clear that he mainly had the American system in mind. One year later, in 1869, Beelaerts published a long article on judicial review in the United States, the first major Dutch publication on American constitutional law since Dumbar's translation of the constitution. Beelaerts accused his opponents of quoting the American

144

example in support of their views without ever taking the trouble to demonstrate how it actually worked. Then he went on to consider all the arguments put forward in favour of judicial review such as history, the text of the constitution and federalism, rejecting all of them by comparing them to the situation in other countries. The sole explanation could only be the historical distrust of the legislature and the traditional respect for the judiciary. Beelaerts regarded the American judiciary as the necessary and even useful check on the evils of mass democracy, especially since "the colored element" also got the right to vote. To him the conclusion was self-evident: although judicial review was good for the United States, it would be wrong for the Kingdom of the Netherlands.[36] The Groningen lawyer W.A. Reiger reached the same conclusion as Beelaerts in a review of his thesis but he put more faith in the freedom of speech and the wisdom of the electorate as arguments against judicial review.[37] An eccentric response came from J. Levy, a lawyer and member of parliament, who argued that the judiciary had the power of review because it was part of the executive, the supreme branch of government. Levy considered Beelaerts's American excursions interesting but irrelevant.[38]

At the end of the 19th century the gradually growing electorate seemed to make the warnings of Tocqueville more acute. The influential Leyden law professor J.Th. Buys still supported the constitutional exclusion of judicial review to prevent the law from becoming uncertain[39] but his former student Beelaerts began to express some doubts. Wouldn't it be better to trust the judiciary more than the parliament that became more and more democratic? In 1887 the parliament debated a major revision of the constitution that made a larger electorate possible. Another proposal was the appointment of the justices of the Supreme Court by the parliament. Beelaerts reacted furiously because the enlarged electorate made the independence of the judiciary more necessary than ever. He asked parliament "to look to America. There one can see that the dangers, inherent to democracy, in the opinion of the best and ablest statesmen can be avoided most effectively by taking care of the complete independence of the judiciary while, on the contrary, demagogues do everything to make the judges dependent of the legislature and the electorate ... Tocqueville warned against the increasing tendency of legislative assemblies to enlarge their power and to influence the judiciary ... A judiciary free from all influence of the people and the legislature, that is the most urgent demand of our time."[40] He persuaded the parliament on that point. The appointment of the justices remained in effect with the Supreme Court itself. Beelaerts's opinion was echoed by a more important party leader, the Amsterdam law professor Lord

A. de Savornin Lohman. In his handbook on constitutional law Lohman agreed with the article about judicial review but added: "One may ask whether, in case of an increase of the direct influence of the people upon parliament, the guarantee of a free, independent and thus fair decision on the constitutionality (of acts of parliament) will be weakened".[41]

The Voting Rights' Law of 1896 enfranchised half of the adult male population. In his Leyden thesis of 1905 about judicial review, J.Ph.Chr. van der Burgh showed no sign of alarm or fear. He was the first to ignore Tocqueville's gloomy predictions. Van der Burgh made a thorough analysis of the American legislative process with the aid of the books by J. Bryce and W. Wilson. He concluded that judicial review was a good answer to some deficiencies in the committee system and the composition and size of the constituencies in the American system but that it was undesirable for the Dutch constitutional monarchy. The Anglosaxon tradition of an active judiciary was alien to the Netherlands. Van der Burgh trusted the electorate more, even under universal suffrage, than the judiciary.[42] His Leyden law professor H. Krabbe took a different view in 1906. Krabbe favoured judicial review, not for antidemocratic reasons but as a means of increasing the possibilities for the judiciary to react to new social developments in general.[43] This approach was shared by Lord C.H.J. van Haeften, a lawyer in the Hague, but he mixed it with the old Tocquevillean concept. In his book on judicial review Van Haeften quoted, for the first time in a Dutch publication, some jurisprudence of the Supreme Court, including *Lochner v. New York*. Van Haeften had no confidence in the electorate and argued that judicial review was a democratic institution because it took into account the sense of justice of the people: "Exercised by a highstanding judiciary, it prevents a majority of the people from having its own way and it lets justice prevail as an expression of aristocratic democracy".[44]

That was the last echo of Tocqueville in the Dutch discussion about judicial review. In 1917 universal suffrage for adult males was introduced, followed by universal suffrage for adult women in 1919. From now on the direct perception of events in the United States became the dominating factor in the use of the American example of judicial review. The wider news coverage of the United States in the Dutch press after the important contribution of the country during the final stages of the First World War made direct reactions possible. The leading expert on constitutional law in that period was the Amsterdam professor A. Struycken. He criticised the United States for not respecting Dutch neutrality during the First World War and stimulated Dutch participation in the new League of Nations.[45] In the chapter on judicial review in his handbook, Struycken took the

146

position that each constitution should be judged in its national, historical context. That meant that the American practice of an activist judiciary was not suitable for the Netherlands. But he also noted that the Americans had problems with their own heritage. On *Lochner v. New York* Struycken commented: "That decision made clear that the judiciary had assumed the role of interpreter for the more conservative elements of the people ... This anti-social jurisprudence has conjured up a powerful movement aimed at ending judicial supremacy ... This movement in America that does harm to the confidence in the judiciary, may be a warning for countries such as ours not to cause such constitutional conflicts by lifting the prohibition on judicial review."[46]

More ambivalent towards the American experience was the lawyer who succeeded Struycken as Amsterdam law professor in 1914 and who later took over the Leyden chair from Krabbe in 1927, R. Kranenburg. More than Struycken, who died at an early age, it was Kranenburg who influenced generations of law students by his lectures and widely used book on Dutch constitutional law. He had already shown his warm interest in American constitutional history in an article on the creativity of the Founding Fathers. He praised, in contrast to the famous Leyden professor of history J. Huizinga, the genius of Alexander Hamilton and compared him to such heroes of Dutch history as Oldenbarneveldt and De Wit. Kranenburg also pointed out the similarities between the Dutch revolt and the American revolution.[47] In his inaugural speech at Leyden he started with a quotation from John Marshall in *Marbury v. Madison* to demonstrate the advantages of comparative law.[48] Kranenburg devoted much attention to American constitutional law and was the first Dutch professor who offered his students examinations on the subject. He was more positive on judicial review than Struycken and thought that its disadvantages were to a large extent compensated by the restraint of the judiciary, as was the case in the United States. Still, Kranenburg did not advocate judicial review for the Netherlands as "for the moment" the Dutch situation gave no cause for alarm.[49] The "for the moment" signifies both the charm the American example had for him and his rather pragmatic political views.

That same phrase "for the moment" got a new dimension during the constitutional crisis of 1937 when president Roosevelt put pressure on the Supreme Court to accept his New Deal legislation. The conflict also attracted the attention of Dutch lawyers. It inspired a student of Kranenburg, F. van Reigersberg Versluys, to devote his thesis to the subject. Although Van Reigersberg visited the United States and proclaimed himself to be an "objective, foreign observer for whom neither judicial review is a dogma nor the Supreme Court sacred", he was very biased in his support of Roosevelt and unrestricted criticism of the Supreme Court and judicial review in general.[50] Other Dutch commentaries were more sophisticated although none supported the Supreme Court. Kranenburg added a paragraph to his handbook in which he called Roosevelt's threats "constitutionally doubtful" and took the crisis as an example of "what undesired tensions judicial review may cause in the life of a state".[51] Another comment by A. Hartogh in the leading Dutch law journal showed sympathy for Roosevelt. Still, Hartogh condemned the president's infringements on the independence of the judiciary and wondered why he had not used his immense popularity to get his way by the more cumbersome but constitutionally correct procedure of an amendment.[52] The definite legacy of this crisis was laid down in the handbook by the Groningen law professor C.W. van der Pot. His book later replaced Kranenburg's book and Van der Pot used the New Deal conflict as an extra argument against judicial review.[53]

The most important Dutch author on American constitutional law since Beelaerts was M.V. Polak, who was the first to signal the approaching conflict between the White House and the Supreme Court in an article of 1935 with the title "Judicial government".[54] Polak also wrote a well-documented survey of the historical origins of judicial review in the United States in 1937.[55] That same year he published an article in which he addressed the Dutch parliament to take notice of the recent Supreme Court jurisprudence on the freedom of speech at a time that the Minister of Justice had proposed a law abridging that freedom.[56] Polak was a teacher of Dutch constitutional law at a Leyden school. He also prepared law students for their university examinations in Dutch and American constitutional law by professor Kranenburg.[57]

The German occupation led to the closing of Leyden university. It also made further publications of Polak impossible. After the war the general admiration for the American victor found its academic expression in no less than six dissertations with an American subject.[58] One of the more interesting from a comparative perspective, was the thesis by J. van den Houten. His study of American federalism strongly suggested the adoption of that model for Europe although his introduction rejects the notion that any particular state should be the example. Van den Houten forgot to suppress his enthusiasm in the English summary when he wrote: "By the formation of a federal state immense perspectives of prosperity and peace can be opened; of the latter the United States are the best proof".[59] In another thorough study of the procedure of amending the U.S. Constitution, W. Nolen was much more reserved in his praise for America than the others.[60] The fact that the United States had

148

forced the Netherlands to its most dramatic constitutional revision of the century, the transfer of sovereignty to its former colony Indonesia, gave a bitter actuality to Nolen's thesis. The unanimous admiration for the United States was soon replaced by the traditional, more ambivalent attitude of the Dutch towards America. Among lawyers the best proof of that was given by the prominent jurist H. Drion, a Leyden law professor and later justice of the Dutch Supreme Court. The philosophically-oriented Drion wrote a review article in 1948 on the works of B. Cardozo whom he compared to the Dutch law professor P. Scholten. Drion concluded that he preferred the more realistic European Scholten to the typically American philosophy of naive humanism and optimism represented by Cardozo.[61]

Less philosophical was the important contribution M.V. Polak made to the knowledge of Dutch lawyers of American constitutional law. His influence cannot be underestimated. Almost yearly he wrote one or more articles in the prominent law journal *Nederlands Juristenblad* about recent decisions of the Supreme Court. Between 1945 and 1970 Polak held a monopoly as the Dutch watcher of the U.S. Supreme Court. He also wrote the only Dutch handbook on American constitutional law.[62] The book was very popular among Leyden law students, many of whom used it as their basis for the oral examinations in American constitutional law by professors Kranenburg and J.V. Rypperda Wierdsma. Polak showed a gradual development in his judgement on the desirability of judicial review, not dissimilar from the change M. Shapiro noticed in generations of American court critics.[63] Polak firmly remained on the progressive side of the political spectrum all his life. That brought him to his disapproval of the Supreme Court's decisions against the New Deal but on the other hand he was fascinated by the active role of the American judiciary in the field of civil rights. The German occupation must have made him, as a Jew, acutely aware of the serious shortcomings of his beloved America in matters of race discrimination and civil liberties. He did not hesitate to compare the segregation in the South and later Mcarthy's persecution of communists with measures of the Nazis.[64] His tone became even more critical during the Cold War but the decision in *Brown v. Board of Education of Topeka* marked a definite change in his attitude. He praised the justices of the Warren Court "for their mighty help to enlighten the spirits of a people that has assumed the leadership of the democratic world" (1954).[65] From then on the Warren Court fulfilled all his wishes case by case and he presented all the landmark decisions to his Dutch audience in the most laudatory terms. It persuaded Polak to set aside his frustrations of the 'thirties and embrace judicial review wholeheartedly as a means to encourage the constitutional consciousness of the people.[66] In his last article of 1970, shortly before his death, he expressed the hope that the Warren-court decisions would survive the imminent attack by president Nixon.[67]

The postwar debate on judicial review was revived by the Amsterdam law professor G. van den Bergh who was a fervent opponent. In 1951 an academic polemic on the subject in the *Nederlands Juristenblad* remained undecided. Polak showed that Van den Bergh's argument about the inherently undemocratic character of judicial review should be moderated in the light of American court decisions that protected communists.[68] The socialist Van den Bergh was probably still under the spell of the events of 1937. Two years later parliament forced the cabinet to accept an important constitutional change that allowed judicial review of legislation under self-executive provisions of international treaties. That was due to the traditional Dutch championing of international law and a strong European sentiment. The second, direct challenge of the constitutional ban on judicial review of legislation was made by the Tilburg law professor H. Jeukens in his inaugural speech of 1963. He mainly used arguments drawn from the Dutch legal system to support his plea for judicial review but his quotations and footnotes clearly showed his wide knowledge of the American practice.[69] Jeuken's main academic opponent was the Amsterdam law professor L. Prakke. He had studied at Columbia University in New York where he had gathered the material for his thesis on judicial review. Prakke came to the conclusion that judicial review as such was wrong because of its antidemocratic character. For historical reasons it might suit the United States but it certainly did not fit the much more timid Dutch judiciary.[70]

The contributions of Jeukens and Prakke showed a knowledge of the importance of judicial review in the United States that had become more or less familiar to many Dutch lawyers. The issue resonated outside the walls of Academia for the first time since 1848 during the nineteen sixties and seventies. The political climate seemed ready for constitutional changes and a government committee published a draft, *De Proeve*, for a new constitution, made by some experts, including Jeukens. He proposed the provision that would introduce judicial review. The Supreme Court supported Jeuken's idea, the Council of State opposed it. Neither of the institutions quoted American sources in their advice. A second committee, which was instructed to use the draft as the basis for a definite proposal to revise the constitution, divided on the issue of judicial review. A majority, however, was willing to accept judicial review if it was limited to the classic human rights in the constitution. The cabinet rejected the majority opinion of the committee and opposed judicial review. This proposal then was introduced in the parliamentary committee in 1969. The members of that committee also divided on judicial review without expressing a clear majority opinion. During the following procedure of the successive readings of the amendments between 1969 and 1982, all cabinets, regardless of their political colour, refused to introduce judicial review. In the crucial parliamentary debate there seemed to be a silent majority in favour of judicial review as only the Liberal Party opposed it on principle. The Socialists showed no interest and the Christian-Democrats who supported judicial review did not push the issue when it might have had a chance of success.[71] References to the American example were made only casually. Everyone agreed with the remark of the commissioner of the government that judicial review was appropriate for traditionally undemocratic countries like Germany and Italy but unnecessary for the Netherlands. He also stated that the American example was irrelevant because judicial review in the United States was closely connected with the federal system and the presence of ethnic minorities.[72] Some complicated compromises that were introduced by the democratic party also failed.[73] The old formula "the laws are inviolable" was replaced by a new provision in the revised constitution of 1983 that explicitly forbids the judiciary to test an act of parliament upon its constitutionality. That seems to leave room for judicial review under general principles of law but no court has yet drawn that conclusion.[74]

Although the American example of judicial review was not adopted, the impact of other parts of American constitutional law on Dutch law has grown considerably from the late sixties onwards. The activist approach in the area of civil liberties by the Warren Court opened the eyes of several young Dutch lawyers to new, still dormant dimensions in Dutch constitutional law. There were enough opportunities to learn more about American constitutional law. The law faculty libraries together possessed a wide range of magazines, books and journals according to a list of the early seventies.[75] A small number of Dutch students also visited American law schools. But there were educational facilities in the Netherlands as well. In 1963 the first Columbia Summer Program in American Law started in Leyden. The initiative was taken by the Dutch-born Columbia law professor H. Smit. The courses in the Program are taught by members of the Columbia law faculty to a mainly European audience with a fairly large proportion of Dutcsh students. Constitutional law was part of the program from the beginning.[76] The Program later got a Dutch "counterpart" when prof. T. Koopmans encouraged one of his assistants, A. Zuydwijk, to teach a course in American constitutional law in the Leyden law faculty. The course became obligatory for students of political science but remained voluntary for law students. Most of the teachers of this course, such as C. Flinterman, J. Peters, T. Zwart and M. Kroes, also published on American constitutional law.[77] Flinterman and Peters wrote dissertations in which they compared Dutch and American constitutional law. Flinterman studied the act of state doctrine, while Peters introduced some American doctrines on the freedom of speech to Dutch lawyers.[78] The latest important comparative work was a thesis by B. Sloot who proposed some American solutions to the problems concerning affirmative action.[79] It remains difficult however to assess the direct influence of American ideas on Dutch law. Some decisions of the Dutch Supreme Court, however, seem to owe something to American jurisprudence but it is impossible to trace a direct impact as the court does not reveal its sources of inspiration in the opinions.[80]

The increasing awareness among Dutch lawyers of civil liberties, institutionalised in the Dutch lawyers' committee on human rights, in the late sixties and early seventies certainly was strongly influenced by the American example. However, once the debate on judicial review had been decided in parliament, the attention gradually shifted towards the remaining possibilities under the existing system. That meant a growing interest in the use of international treaties, especially the European Convention on Human Rights, as a tool to strengthen the civil liberties aspect of cases before the courts. As the Burger Court seemed less inspiring than the Warren court in this area and the European Courts appeared to be quite activist in their protection of basic human rights, more Dutch lawyers tried to persuade their judges to apply the international guarantees. In the eighties the Dutch judiciary slowly but definitely moved in that direction. That was the background of the inaugural speech of the Leyden law professor E. Alkema who noted that judicial review was no longer a matter for debate. The only question was how long the growing legal unity in the EC will permit the Dutch exception to the general European rule of judicial review of legislation.[81] Although the study of American constitutional law partly caused a shift of interest towards international and European law, there seems no reason to assume that Dutch lawyers will abandon the study of American legal practice. The traditional Dutch interest in the "example in the distance" may claim a pedigree of more than two centuries old and has become an established part of Dutch legal studies.

REFERENCES

1. J.W. Schulte Nordholt, *Voorbeeld in de verte. De invloed van de Amerikaanse Revolutie in Nederland*, Baarn, 1979.

2. *Ibidem*, p. 19; J.W. Schulte Nordholt, "The example of the Dutch Republic for American federalism", *Bijdragen en Mededelingen betreffende de Geschiedenis der Nederlanden*, 94, 1979, pp. 440-441.

3. *Ibidem*, p. 441; G.J. Mecking, "Mr. Gerhard Dumbar, een verlicht historicus?", *Overijsselse Historische Bijdragen. Verslagen en mededelingen van de vereeniging tot beoefening van Overijsselsch regt en geschiedenis*, 100, 1985, pp. 167-193; G. Dumbar, *De oude en nieuwe constitutie der Vereenigde Staten van Amerika uit de beste schriften in haare gronden ontvouwd*, Amsterdam, 1793-1796, 3 vol.).

4. Schulte Nordholt, *The Example of the Dutch Republic*.

5. G.J.B. Besier, *Specimen iuris publici de legum fundamentalium indole et ambitu*, Utrecht, 1849, pp. 90-91.

6. S. Schama, *Patriots and liberators. Revolution in the Netherlands 1780-1813*, New York, 1977.

7. *Nieuw Nederlandsch Biografisch Woordenboek* VIII, pp. 1098-1102.

8. G.J.Th. Beelaerts van Blokland, *De onschendbaarheid der wet*, Leyden, 1868, pp. 146-153; L. de Gou, ed., *Het plan van constitutie. Chronologische bewerking van het archief van de eerste constitutiecommissie ingesteld bij decreet van de Nationale Vergadering van 15 maart 1796*, 's Rijks Geschiedkundige Publicatiën, kleine serie 40, The Hague, 1975, pp. 142-144.

9. Beelaerts, *De onschendbaarheid*, pp. 154-168; A.M. Elias, *Het Nationaal Syndicaat 1802-1805*, Bussum, 1975.

10. J.W. Schulte Nordholt, "Gijsbert Karel van Hogendorp in Amerika, 1783-1784", *Tijdschrift voor Geschiedenis*, 88, 1975, pp. 39-62.

11. H.T. Colenbrander, ed., *Ontstaan der Grondwet*, 's Rijks Geschiedkundige Publicatiën, kleine serie nr. 1, The Hague, 1908, pp. 407-409, 418-419; Beelaerts, *De onschendbaarheid*, pp. 169-176.

12. J. Drion, *Administratie contra rechter tot de intrekking van het Conflictenbesluit*, The Hague, 1950.

13. C. Backer, "Verhandeling over het voorwerp van regterlijke beslissing in burgerlijke zaken, vooral in afscheiding beschouwd van den werkkring der administratie", *Bijdragen tot regtsgeleerdheid en wetgeving*, 3, 1828, pp. 56-62.

14. H. van Sonsbeeck, *Proeve over de zelfstandigheid der regterlijke magt*, Zwolle, 1829, vol. 2, pp. 84-88, 233.

15. O.A. Lewe van Aduard, *De iuris controversia Magnam Brittaniam inter et dissidentes ab ea, seculo superiore, colonias Americanas*, Leyden, 1835.

16. A. Lammers, *Verheffend en opbeurend voor de geest*, Leyden, 1986, p. 6.

17. *Weekblad van het Regt*, 23, 1841, nr. 224.

18. B. van Sonsbeeck, *De munere judicis*, Leyden, 1845.

19. Beelaerts, *De onschendbaarheid*, p. 186.

20. *Ibidem*, pp. 209-210.

21. *Handelingen van de regering en de Staten-Generaal over de herziening der Grondwet 1847-1848*, The Hague, 1848, dl. 3, pp. 135, 280.

22. C.W. de Vries, ed., *Bijdrage tot de herziening van de grondwet van mr. J.R. Thorbecke*, The Hague, 1948, pp. 60-63.

23. C.W. Opzoomer, *Aanteekening op de wet, houdende algemeene bepalingen der wetgeving van het Koningkrijk*, Leyden, Amsterdam, 1848, 4th ed. 1884, p. 198.

24. W.A.C. de Jonge, "De wetten zijn onschendbaar", *Themis*, 10, 1849, pp. 353-364.

25. J. de Bosch Kemper, *Handleiding tot de kennis van het Nederlandsche staatsregt en staatsbestuur*, Amsterdam, 1865, pp. 216-220.

26. P.J. van Löben Sels, *Beschouwingen over den Noord-Amerikaanschen statenoorlog van 1861-1864*, Utrecht, 1878; Lammers, *Verheffend*, pp. 12-13; *Nederlands Patriciaat*, 52, 1966, p. 343.

27. W. Suermondt, *Een Amerikaansche arbeidersvereeniging en hare eischen*, Rotterdam, 1890; Lammers, *Verheffend*, pp. 13-14.

28. C. Bake, *Beschouwingen over den statenbond en den bondsstaat*, Amsterdam, 1881.

29. J. Paulus, *De Hoogerhuizen van Europa en Amerika. Proeve van een kritisch-historisch onderzoek omtrent hun samenstelling en grondslag*, The Hague, 1886.

30. *Weekblad van het Regt*, 1864, nr. 2646, 1865, nr. 2664.

31. *Weekblad van het Regt*, 1866, nrs. 2777, 2783, 2784.

32. D.J. Mom Visch, "Alexis de Tocqueville", *De Gids*, 31, 1867, pp. 405-452; *Nederlands Patriciaat*, 52, 1914, p. 419.

33. J.Ph.T. du Quesné van Bruchem, *De bevoegdheid der rechterlijke macht, met opzigt tot wetten die de grondwet schenden. Eene staatsregtelijke proeve naar aanleiding van art. 115 al. 2*, Grdwt, Utrecht, 1867; Beelaerts, *De onschendbaarheid*.

34. *Nederlands Patriciaat*, 10, 1919, p. 361.

35. J.H. Hora Siccama, "Levensbericht van jhr.mr. G.J.Th. Beelaerts van Blokland", *Levensberichten der afgestorven medeleden van de Maatschappij der Nederlandsche Letterkunde te Leiden 1899-1900*, Leyden, 1900, pp. 197-281.

36. G.J.Th. Beelaerts van Blokland, "De bevoegdheid van den Amerikaanschen rechter tot ongrondwettigverklaring der wet", *Nieuwe Bijdragen voor Rechtsgeleerdheid en Wetgeving*, 19, 1869, pp. 5-61.

37. W.A. Reiger, "Is de rechter bevoegd de grondwettigheid der wet te beoordelen?", *Bijdragen tot de kennis van het staats-, provinciaal en gemeentebestuur in Nederland*, 15, 1869, pp. 291-324.

38. J.A. Levy, "De rechter, zelfstandig drager der koninklijke rechtsmacht (rechterlijke aanbevelingen)", *Nieuwe Bijdragen voor Rechtsgeleerdheid en Wetgeving*, 1877, pp. 107-108.

39. J.Th. Buys, *De grondwet. Toelichting en kritiek*, vol. 1, Arnhem, 1883, pp. 630-638.

40. *Handelingen over de herziening der Grondwet*, The Hague, 1886-1888, p. 1.

41. A. de Savornin Lohman, *Onze constitutie*, Utrecht, 1901.

42. J.Ph.Chr. van der Burgh, *Opmerkingen over des rechters toetsingsbevoegdheid*, Leyden, 1905.

43. H. Krabbe, "De heerschappij der grondwet", *De Gids*, 1906, pp. 393-400.

44. C.H.J. van Haeften, *Rechter en grondwet in verband met de vrije rechtspraak*, Amersfoort, 1911, pp. 60-61.

45. *Biografisch Woordenboek*, I, pp. 565-566.

46. A.A.H. Struycken, *Het staatsrecht van het Koninkrijk der Nederlanden*, Arnhem, 1928, pp. 115-116.

47. *Biografisch Woordenboek*, I, pp. 324-325; R. Kranenburg, "Noord-Amerikaansche staatsvorming", *Studiën over recht en staat*, Haarlem, 1953, pp. 202-221.

48. R. Kranenburg, *Staatswetenschap, sociologie en rechtsphilosophie*, Leyden, 1927.

49. R. Kranenburg, *Het Nederlandse staatsrecht*, Leyden, 1958, pp. 288-293.

50. F. van Reigersberg Versluys, *Rechter en grondwet in de Vereenigde Staten van Noord-Amerika*, Nijmegen, 1938.

51. R. Kranenburg, *Staatsrecht*, p. 292.

52. A.F.K. Hartogh, "Supreme Court en New Deal in de Verenigde Staten", *Nederlands Juristenblad*, 1937, pp. 889-896, 913-921.

53. C.W. van der Pot, *Handboek voor het Nederlandse staatsrecht*, Zwolle, 1940.

54. M.V. Polak, "Judicial government", *Weekblad van het Recht*, 1935.

55. M.V. Polak, "De oorsprong van het toetsingsrecht ten aanzien van wetten van het congres door het Supreme Court der Vereenigde Staten van Noord-Amerika", *Tijdschrift voor Rechtsgeschiedenis*, 15, 1937, pp. 269-286.

56. M.V. Polak, "De vrijheid van drukpers", *Nederlands Juristenblad*, 1937, pp. 869-876.

57. I thank Mr. J.M. Polak for the biographical information about his father.

58. J. van der Meulen, *The seat of authority. A comparative analysis of the relations between the legislative power and the executive power in the British constitutional system and in the American federal constitution*, Leyden, 1945; G. van Reenen, *De staatskundige en staatsrechtelijke betekenis van president F.D. Roosevelt*, Leyden, 1948; H. van Buuren, *De consolidatie van de onafhankelijkheid der Verenigde Staten van Amerika (1763-1795)*, Utrecht, 1949; M. Heinsius, *De president der Verenigde Staten*, The Hague, 1948.

59. J.N. van den Houten, *Bondsstaat en souvereiniteit*, Leyden, 1945, pp. 6, 144.

60. W.H.D. Nolen, *Beschouwingen over de wijziging van de federale constitutie in de Verenigde Staten van Amerika*, Leyden, 1949.

61. H. Drion, "Bij de 'Selected Writings' van Benjamin Nathan Cardozo (1870-1938)", *Themis*, 1948, pp. 549-559.

62. M.V. Polak, *Schets van het Amerikaanse Uniestaatsrecht*, Leiden, 1951.

63. M. Shapiro, "Fathers and sons: the court, the commentators, and the search for values", V. Blasi, Ed., *The Burger court. The Counterrevolution that wasn't*, New Haven, 1983, pp. 218-239.

64. M.V. Polak, *Schets*, p. 74.

65. M.V. Polak, "Het Amerikaanse arrest tegen afscheiding bij het openbaar onderwijs", *Nederlands Juristenblad*, 1954, pp. 511-514.

66. Polak, *Schets*, 3rd ed. 1956, p. 100.

67. M.V. Polak, "Het Amerikaanse Hooggerechtshof en de rassendiscriminatie", *Nederlands Juristenblad*, 1970, pp. 1241-1250.

68. M.V. Polak, "Rechter, wet en grondwet", *Nederlands Juristenblad*, 1951, pp. 660-663.

69. H.J.M. Jeukens, *De wetten zijn onschendbaar*, Alphen a/d Rijn, 1963.

70. L. Prakke, *Toetsing in het publiekrecht*, Assen, 1972.

71. M.C. Burkens, "The complete revision of the Dutch constitution", *Netherlands International Law Review*, 29, 1982, pp. 323-336; C.A.J.M. Kortmann, *De grondwetsherziening 1983*, Deventer, 1983, pp. 30-34, 306-308.

72. H. van Maarseveen, ed., *De parlementaire geschiedenis rond de algehele grondwetsherziening*, 1b, pp. 144-147.

73. A.K. Koekkoek, W. Konijnebelt, "Het raam van hoofdstuk 1 van de herziene grondwet", A.K. Koekkoek, ed., *Grondrechten. Commentaar op hoofdstuk 1 van de herziene grondwet*, Nijmegen, 1982, pp. 11-16.

74. H. van Maarseveen, "Rechter en onrechtmatige wetgeving", *Nederlands Juristenblad*, 1987, pp. 717-720.

75. E.H. Hondius, W.M. Peletier, *Amerikaanse en Canadese rechtsliteratuur in Nederlandse bibliotheken*, Deventer, 1973.

76. M.V. Polak. "Leyden-Amsterdam-Columbia Summer Program in American Law", *Ars Aequi*, 1982, pp. 644-646.

77. C. Flinterman and J.A. Peters, "Watergate, de President en de Constitutie", *Nederlands Juristenblad*, 1974, pp. 629-639, 937-943; A.J. Heringa and T. Zwart, "Dienstplicht alleen voor mannen ontoelaatbaar? De zaak Rostker v. Goldberg", *Nederlands Juristenblad*, 1982, pp. 1029-1038; M. Kroes, "Ratificatie van multilaterale mensenrecht-verdragen in de Verenigde Staten", *Americana*, 1987, pp. 43-51.

78. C. Flinterman, *De Act of State doctrine. Een rechtsvergelijkende studie naar de plaats van de Act of State doctrine in het Amerikaanse en Nederlandse recht*, Leyden, 1981; J.A. Peters, *Het primaat van de vrijheid van meningsuiting. Vergelijkende aspecten Nederland-Amerika*, Leyden, 1981; A comparison of the VS and Canadian systems: S. IJbema, *Constitutionalism and Civil Liberties*, Leyden, 1973.

79. B.P. Sloot, *Positieve discriminatie, maatschappelijke ongelijkheid en rechtsontwikkeling in de Verenigde Staten en in Nederland*, Zwolle, 1986.

80. *Nederlands Jurisprudentie*, 1978, pp. 365, 1299; 1979, pp. 436, 495, 1587; 1980, pp. 356, 1183-1184; 1981, pp. 382, 1278, 1282; 1983, pp. 687, 2166-2169; 1984, pp. 803, 2880-2882; 1985, pp. 530, 1721; *Elseviers Magazine*, 42, 1986, nr. 43. 8: Supreme Court Justice Verborgh: "We have become more Anglo-American"; for a current review of judicial review in the Netherlands: J.M. Polak and M.V. Polak, "Faux pas ou pas de deux? Recent developments in the relationship between the legislature and the judiciary in the Netherlands", *Netherlands International Law Review*, 33, 1986, pp. 371-411.

81. E.A. Alkema, *Een meerkeuzetoets*, Leyden, 1986.

11. A EUROPEAN UNION OF AMERICAN DESIGN?

Albert E. Kersten, University of Leyden

Would it not be satisfying to draw the long historical line from the institutional framework of the Republic of the Seven United Dutch Provinces via the Constitution of the United States of North America to a basic law of the Federation of a united Western Europe in the post World War II era? Historical continuity could be illustrated with these three glorious examples, while the inter-relationship between the democratic traditions of the Old and New World could come to the fore. Unfortunately it is impossible for me to deliver such an account, because the third stage was never achieved. Although there has been a considerable amount of thought and discussion on European unification in the twentieth century, the political tide never gave birth to a European federation, let alone a European federation on the design of the American federation. So, my appearance among the contributors to this volume could be very short and end with the apologising statement that a year ago I was overoptimistic in proposing the subject.

Indeed, one cannot discuss the issue of the impact of the American Constitution on a Western European federation, which is the realisation of the United States of Europe. Although, during a very short period in 1952-1953 the prospects for a political unification of Western Europe on a federal basis seemed favourable, it soon proved to be a dramatic intermezzo which stigmatised the protagonists of a European federation and made them believe that a golden opportunity for achieving the federation had been lost by the deliberate opposition of the governments involved. I do not intend to focus on a comparison between the projects for a European Political Community of March 1953 and the American Constitution, because in my opinion it reflects too narrow an approach. It is insufficient to observe that both documents reflect the same Constitutional structure and allocation of powers and that during the discussions on the European Political Community project references were made to the American system. Such an approach would ignore the broader framework of studying the impact of the American Constitutional system on the movement for European unification.

From the foregoing it will be apparent that the well-defined premises of the American Constitution will be left for entering the field of the every-day practice of the American Constitutional system

160

as an example for Europe in solving its economic and political problems ever since the First World War. This pointing to the American system as one out of more alternatives for evading the disastrous armed conflicts and damaging economic protectionism sprang from different sources. The slaughtering of a whole European generation on the First World War battlefields activated the search for alternative political structures which could facilitate the settlement of disputes without the use of force. The establishment of a federation through the transfer of parts of the national sovereignty was propagated by intellectuals as a sovereign remedy. In the twenties, the vast American market was regarded as the perfect basis for a rationalised economic development by an increasing number of European economists. In their view, these conditions should be achieved in Europe too in order to make it competitive with the American economy.[1] Incentives for the unification of Europe sprang from these two sources. The American example counted most in the economic sector, because the European and American economies shared a common set of principles. Less prominent was the American example for the solution of the political problems, because in this field a variety of alternatives was available.

The theme of this exposé can most effectively be explained by summarising the address which the Belgian-American electrical engineer and banker Dannie N. Heineman gave to a distinguished audience in Cologne in November 1930.[2] Heineman, a personal friend of Konrad Adenauer, in those days the governing burgomaster of Cologne, analysed the idea of a European federation from an engineer's viewpoint. He described the industrial era, as a combination of "technical science" and "capital", which had transformed the world during the last fifty years. The world was a living being whose arterial systems were the lines of communication: railways, steamers, telegraphs and airplanes. This giant organism of the European world had two ventricles: one situated in Western and Central Europe, the other in the United States. Contrary to the United States, Europe had gone through a dual development during the last century. Its division into many and unequal states had continued and after the World War the number of states had increased, while "economically the world [tended] towards unification". This strange contradiction between the political and economic institutions had to be changed, because economics and politics were "two functions of the same organism". Heineman, however, did not simply refer to the harmony of economics and politics in the United States as the panacea for the European problems nor did he produce the draft for an ideal Constitution or the blueprint of the future European Federation. In fact, he warned for the illusion of a European Federation as the apt means

161

for ending the political division of Europe. The American Civil War [of 1861-1865] demonstrated "that the most perfect federal Constitution will not suffice to secure the peace of a continent." Lack of inner economic balance had caused the Civil War. After the Civil War the transcontinental railroads, the Interstate Commerce Commission and the Federal Reserve system had created the three-sided basis of the American federation and removed the incentives from which the secession had originated. Therefore, so was Heineman's message, specific infrastructural, administrative and financial preconditions had to be fulfilled before the United States of Europe with a customs union, federal administration, supreme court of justice, congress and senate could become feasible. Such a European federation had to be built on sound economic pillars. At this point of his address Heineman thought that the American experience could act to Europe as an example. First of all the creation of a financial organisation similar to the Federal Reserve System was necessary. The Bank of International Settlements, founded for the smooth transfer of German reparations to other European countries, was in his opinion the basis for such a European Federal Reserve. The most tricky issue, however, was the road toward the abolishment of customs barriers between the European states. Egalisation and reduction of tariffs and general application of the so-called "most favoured nation clause" in intra-European trade were not enough. The escape from this system of equal opportunities by way of specification, hygienic or any other type of indirect protectionist measures should be prohibited. The construction of this second pillar for the European federation could be achieved in several stages, during which increasing collaboration between the great administrations of the various European states should be organised in separate fields. The creation of a European Interstate Commerce Commission would in due time crown this collaboration and pave the way to a European Customs Union. To this goal the Briand Memorandum of 1929 was a sound declaration of intent. In Heineman's view the third precondition for a European federation was the economic harmony and interdependence between the industrial Western and the agrarian Eastern and Central Europe. This could best be promoted by expanding the welfare and purchasing power of the peasants in agrarian Europe through a combination of electricity, road transport and credits.

Heineman was of the opinion that Europe could "easily and quickly erect" this "almost completely unknown" "economic Constitution" of the American federation. He was far too optimistic, but nevertheless his analysis shows a number of points of interest. Most of all, he emphasised the economic interdependence as the necessary foundation for every federation. He also noticed the first useful beginning for the construction of the foundations and believed in its realisation. He further stressed that an economically strong Europe acting as a unity would definitely not constitute a threat to the United States.

Heineman's analysis of the prospects for a European federation is useful for more than one reason. He pointed to the interrelationship of economics and politics and the need for cooperation between politicians, industrialists and bankers in Europe in creating the essential federation. He did not dwell on the differences between the American post Civil War situation and the European scene of the interwar period. To him the age-long history of rivalries between European emperors, kings, princes and states did not impede the growth of the economic interdependence as a precondition for the European federation. He propagated the straightforward application of the American recipes as beneficial. One could label Heineman's message as naive because he neglected the influence of the important historical differences on the process which in his opinion already was developing and as a misrepresentation because developments went different. Of utmost importance was his pointing to the combination of economic and political aspects and to the need for governmental involvement to bring about such a federation. Up to 1930 the movements favouring economic unification on the one hand and political federation on the other had mainly been carried by pressure groups of intellectuals and idealists. Politicians had paid lip-service to these ideals, like for instance the German Minister for Foreign Affairs, Gustav Stresemann.[3] The so-called Briand memorandum on European cooperation and unification also fitted in this pattern.[4] So long as the essential political problems in Europe had not been solved and Germany stuck to its latent aim of regaining territory taken away after the First World War, it was unthinkable that on the governmental level a European federation was considered as a means for the solving of current national and international difficulties. With the deepening of the economic crisis in the thirties, the attention for unification and federalisation diminished. The federalist Paneuropa movement of Coudenhove-Kalergi, which had made such an impressive start in 1922,[5] lost momentum as did the drive among economists for a European customs union.[6] The multitude of expressions and actions favouring European federation quieted down under the gathering storm of the economic and political crisis of the thirties but could be heard again soon after the roaring of cannons had announced the Second World War. To what extent, however, did the American federal experience influence and inspire the supporters of European economic unification and federalisation? In the vast amount of books, articles and pamphlets the references are legion and show two different approaches, the economic and the political.[7] First of all the American federation was seen as the enviable realisation of a vast market, which stimulated and enabled the growth of production as well as the introduction of mass production. This economic achievement seemed unattainable for Europe, because its political fragmentation impeded the creation of such a market. From this point of view the creation of a customs union was the way out to an industrially sound and competitive Europe. This concern about the lack of industrial expansion in Europe did not imply that the United States were automatically the first economic rival of the Old World. The restoration of Europe's strength to face the competition of the United States in the international market was the basic incentive for the movement for the abolishment of the tariff barriers in Europe. The American example generated great enthusiasm among economists, officials and intellectuals, but a thorough strategy for achieving this goal was not produced. The development of such a strategy was also hampered by the inclusion of the European states in the League of Nations network. In that environment a global approach of these issues was emphasised.

The movement for economic unification of Europe was only partly inspired by the American federation. To the promotors of a European political federation, however, the United States offered direct inspiration. Opinions differed on the practicability and desirability of adopting the American Constitutional framework to this end. Count Richard Coudenhove Kalergi deliberately called his movement *Paneuropa* and renounced the current label of "United States of Europe". This detachment from a European federation on the same Constitutional basis as the United States sprang from the awareness of the incongruity of the European and the American situation. In his view the mutual differences in Europe were far greater. Although Coudenhove Kalergi aimed at a confederation he regarded the American federation as proof that a heterogeneous conglomerate of states such as the European, of which every part possessed its own culture, political tradition and level of economic development, could successfully be united within one organisation.

From the foregoing one can conclude that in the interwar years proposals for the solution for the European problems were also developed on the basis on the American experience. Although in this era this approach did not influence the official thinking and policies, it was important that a considerable number of officials got acquainted with this integrationist attitude. The United States government upheld its policy of isolationism towards the European scene, but this could not wipe out that the financial and economic relations were strengthened in those years, and that on both sides of the

Atlantic the leadership of the United States was recognised. It was not unlikely that this awareness of American financial and economic supremacy made the Europeans more receptive to American patterns, if they benefitted from its acceptance. A striking example is the cooperation of the central banks of European countries within the Banks of International Settlements, established on the advice of the American banker, C. Dawes.

The Second World War had an enormous impact on the phenomena which have been discussed so far. American non-involvement in European affairs was transformed into a co-leadership in the total warfare against the Axis. The mobilisation of its vast resources for the war effort impressed the European governments, officials and the resistance movements. Furthermore, the origins of the war were also ascribed to the lack of cooperation in the interwar years, especially during the thirties. This psychological shock of the world war changed deeply the attitude of the neutral European countries. Their stand-offish policies of the interwar period were replaced by an awareness of their political and military vulnerability. Postwar planning of the European governments and of a wide variety of groupings was dominated by the obsession of preventing a repetition of these failures. A secure world without unemployment seemed unattainable without American participation. Of course, differences became manifest concerning the intensity of the future cooperation and concerning the fields in which cooperation had to be achieved. A main point of divergence was the regional or global shape of cooperation. For the short term, i.e. the victory over Germany and the recovery of a war-ridden Europe, the assistance of the United States was regarded as indispensable.[8]

Unanimity did not exist on the long term developments and on the implementation of the lessons of the interwar period for Europe proper. The absence of projects to this end was caused in part by the American preference for global designs for the postwar world: the conference of Bretton Woods produced the basis for a stable international monetary system;[9] the Atlantic Charter and the Lend-Lease treaties contained the principles for an unhampered international trade and economic relations;[10] the United Nations Organisation of San Francisco was constructed on the same global fundament.[11] If the European governments favoured specific European solutions they would have done so within the context of newly established international global organisations. However, they were not ambitious to develop overall European subsystems. The formation of regional groups for economic and political cooperation or merging were deliberated, such as the Czechoslovakian-Polish federation plan.[12] In the end, however, all such schemes ended in failure, with the Benelux the only exception.[13] Nevertheless, the second World War period was decisive to the postwar attitude of the European governments. Many of its Cabinet members and officials had direct contact with the American political and administrative system for the first time in their lives. To their Eurocentric world view an important American dimension was added.

The incapacity of the governments giving shape to their elementary ideas on postwar cooperation contrasted with the abundance of plans, proposals and drafts of the resistance movements, which gave the impression that Europe was ready for federalisation. This tendency was mainly the expression of the renunciation of absolute state sovereignty and exaggerated nationalism, of which the European continent was tasting the bitter fruits. The internal devolution of state authority should check the totalitarian claims of the sovereign state in combination with the transfer of power to a supranational authority. The latter's duty was the safeguarding of peace, democracy and human rights. A wide range of solutions was presented. In general a loose association of states like the League of Nations was rejected; a universal federal superstate to ensure world peace was seen as the probate solution, but to others this aim was beyond reality as long as Europe had not set things right through the creation of a democratic European federation. Foreign policy, economic affairs and defence had to be within the federation's province. Such a federation would offer the remedy for the German question as well.[14]

The manifesto of Geneva, drafted by members of the resistance movements of Denmark, France, Italy, Norway, Holland, Poland, Czechoslovakia, Yugoslavia and Germany in May 1944, reflected this deliberate option for a European federation as the outstanding vehicle for fulfilling the principles of the Atlantic Charter. Only a "Federal Union" would enable the German people to join the European community without menacing other peoples; it would provide the solution to the national minorities problems; it would protect the democratic institutions; it would make possible the economic reconstruction of the Continent as well as the liquidation of monopolies and national self-sufficiency and finally only a Federal Union would allow a logical and natural system for the continental transport. The states had irrevocably to surrender to the federation their sovereign rights in the sphere of defence, external relations, international exchange and communications. A government responsible to the European peoples would form its administration. It would dispose of a federal army while no national armies were permitted. A Supreme Court for the interpretation of the Constitution and deciding cases of conflict between the member States or between the latter and the Union would complete the federal political building.[15]

This blueprint for the political reconstruction of Europe did not gather sufficient support for playing any role in the decision-making of the Allies. It was completely in line with many earlier proposals for a European federation in its lack of attention for the transition from the prewar situation to the federation. Its authors assumed that the collective experience of the German New Order would bring out this solution as natural. Due to the lack of general support within the resistance movement itself and to the non-influential postwar position of the resistance this plan disappeared unnoticed by the policymakers in the Allied capitals.

It is difficult to determine to what extent the American Constitutional framework had inspired this and other projects on the European continent. The emphasis on a democratically controlled federal government is striking as well as the focus on human rights in general and the rights of cultural and ethnic minorities. These characteristics could also be seen as a reaction to the conditions prevailing in Europe at those days. The embryonic description of the federal Constitution in the Geneva Manifesto points in the same direction.

In Britain and the United States groups of Europeans drafted a great variety of proposals for the organisation of postwar Europe. Some amongst them focussed on Europe only, while others encompassed the European problem in a global plan for peace, security and welfare. The creation of a European Federation was presented as a medicine for the security, political and economic diseases of this continent which would enable it to regain its global status and generating economic strength for participation in the international competition. At the same time, a reasonable and safe existence could be offered to the Europeans themselves. Although some linkage between the creation of a federation and the annihilation of all kinds of barriers to economic intercourse was made, a sequence of the political-Constitutional and economic reforms was not discussed or recognised. The American situation was brought up on many occasions as an example for Europe's future economic development and for a balanced democratic system.[16]

The British organisation *Federal Union* made an impressive and mature contribution to the debate on the desirability of a European federation, the preconditions for such a federation and finally its Constitution. It should be emphasised that the activities of this movement, it counted 12.000 members in June 1940 were at their zenith in the beginning of the war when Britain and France were facing Germany. Outstanding and promising political scientists, economists and pro-federalist intellectual as Sir William Beveridge,

167

Patrick Ransom, Lionel Curtis, Ivor Jennings, F. von Hayek, Barbara Wootton and Harold Wilson discussed systematically the European federal union issue during a series of conferences on the constitutional, economic and colonial issues. For a number of reasons this group was more oriented towards the United States, so that the American federal system was considered wit a view to its feasibility for Europe. They propagated a constitutional structure with an executive responsible to a legislature comprising a representative people's house and a states' house, and a division of powers with foreign affairs, defence and certain aspects of economic policy as federal functions. The Constitution itself should be interpreted by a federal court and amended only by a process involving the member states and the federal parliaments. In the economic field the principle of a common currency was accepted. Consensus was missing on the economic powers of the federal government itself and on its relations with the states. This debate reflected the liberal and socialist approaches to the role of the state in the economy as a whole. It was left to the future federal institutions to decide what exceptions there should be to full trade liberalisation, free migration within the federation and the fixed exchange rates.[17]

The Federal Union movement did not stop at the drafting of a full-size and elucidated Constitution; it also studied the preconditions for such a federation and the importance of the American federal experience. Arthur Goodhart, who prepared the first draft Constitution pointed out that the American Constitution had been worked out under "particularly fortunate" conditions in comparison with those prevailing in Europe in 1940/41. One single language versus many, continual internal migration versus migration barriers; a minimum of inter-state jealousy versus a long tradition of intra-European warfare; substantial uniformity in political ideas versus a wide range of political traditions and state practices; and absence of religious division along territorial lines versus religious division along state borders.[18] This enumeration could be supplemented, for instance, with a pre-industrial versus an industrial society. These observations brought forward the question of whether under such unfavourable conditions a federal union had a chance of creation or success. In the opinion of the editor of *The Spectator*, Wilson Harris, the "lamentable state of Europe" offered ample argument for following the American example, because the choice was between taking a first step towards some kind of closer association (with the American situation as final goal) or perishing. Doom-mongering, however, was not the only incentive. Herbert Fisher pointed to the existence of the indispensable real basis of common ideas between the members of the envisaged European federation. Despite the sharp opposition between

168

national ideas in France, Great Britain, Italy and Germany he discerned "many things which the leading peoples in Europe have in common": their common foundation of European culture.[19]

The discussion had mounted to a wide range of evaluations of the feasibility of a federation in Europe and more specifically an American-style federation. Undoubtedly the new European war was the spark for this discussion. The European process of self-destruction had to be stopped, according to the prevailing opinion. However, this last resort birth of the British Federal Union's draft had not resulted in what H.G. Wells called a "pseudo-practical short-sightedness". The problems had been carefully mapped, and the chances for success weighed. The Federal Union supporters had avoided handling the American experience in federation as an exact model for Europe. The psychological confidence that Europe had to unite for its survival was flanked by doubts on the vital conditions for its realisation. Whereas many expected that the war would provide the common basis for the necessary political and economic reconstruction of Europe, some were less confident as to the future development. In their view the realisation of a European federation depended on the active support of the Big Three, though none of them should actually be members. The leading powers, however, had chosen for a global solution to these problems.

Post-World War II: American sponsorship?

The realities facing Europe on V-day were not particularly stimulating for far-reaching concepts like a European federation. The economic and social upheaval absorbed all energy. In order to master these enormous problems a number of temporary international European organisations had been established, but sooner or later their tasks were transferred to the national governments. The attitude favouring intergovernmental cooperation and creation of supranational institutions did not disappear, but was flooded by the daily routine which dominated governmental quarters. Outside these premises a non-structured network of groupings and organisations for European integration was mushrooming. They fostered the wartime conviction that far reaching cooperation was Europe's sole salvation and in their opinion it could be achieved on the short term.

The first postwar decade was undoubtedly the prime time for European unification. In this period several options were presented and uncoordinated initiatives were taken for their realisation. By 1960 the harvest looked rather poor: political unification seemed faraway and six Western European states only were participating in the

169

European Economic Community. In hindsight one can state that in this epoch the stage was cleared for a long term development which may produce the economic preconditions on which a European federation might be created. Three forces have operated in the European arena with diverging goals, namely the private unification organisations, the European governments and the American administration. What were their goals and how did they interact?

The private groups strengthened their position by organising themselves on a European scale. They counted amongst their members influential politicians and intellectuals, so that a direct connection was established with national political parties, trade unions and other pressure groups. Their public appeal increased considerably with the concern about the communist threat, especially after the coup of Prague in February 1948. The organisations tried to cover up important differences of opinion concerning the road to a united Europe. One group stood for a strategy of gradual development and regarded the economy as the best starting point. The European governments should create international bodies in charge of a particular domain of the economy. They should also prepare a customs union and monetary convertibility. In a subsequent phase political unification could be entered upon. The federalists, however, rejected this strategy as unrealistic. The national governments would never reach agreement and infinitely protract the negotiations. A European constituent assembly had to be convened to draft the European federal Constitution. Once the democratically controlled federation had been created it could direct the process of gradual unification. The latter approach appeared to be promising. After the European Movement's Congress at The Hague in May 1948 a proposal to this end seemed to be taken up by the governments of the Brussels Pact, the resulting Council of Europe with its intergovernmental basis and powerless Consultative Assembly was all but a constituent.[20]

The disappointment on the Council of Europe was mainly caused by British policies. The British government occupied in the immediate postwar years a central position in the intergovernmental discussions on unification: it supported only projects for cooperation on intergovernmental basis and opposed any transfer of power from Whitehall to an international body. Because British participation was regarded as essential to the process of unification, France and Italy had to give in. Rome and Paris not only demonstrated sympathy for the institutional approach, but initiated also projects for a customs union. Konrad Adenauer's Western Germany embraced a supranational integration policy too, whereas it offered the best opportunity for restoration of Germany's international position in Europe.[21] The governments, however, were more concentrated on economic unification and despite American pressure this proved to be a very slow and tiring process.

Washington's involvement in the European integration process deserves special attention. As financial sponsor of the European reconstruction it demonstrated a considerable degree of aloofness. It refrained from dictating the European states their unification manifesto, although it regarded unification as the most expedient vehicle for creating a economically strong and politically independent Western Europe. It abandoned its scheme for embodying some power of decision in the OEEC and so gave way to a purely intergovernmental framework as required by Britain and the Scandinavian countries. The same line of policy was followed with regard to the European Payments Union, the liberalisation of intra-European trade and the study of a European customs union.[22] This actual conduct contrasted with the publicly testified support for European unification. This support for the unification concept encouraged greatly the private organisations in their permanent endeavour to keep the European governments on the move.[23]

From this short exposé of the main forces in the process of European integration it is evident that between 1948 and 1954 unification was hastily pursued and that due to the different points of departure and the intensification of the Cold War after the Korean crisis a patchwork-like pattern of unification projects was worked out. In this turmoil everyone tried to realise its most favoured concept. Italy wove the principle of the political unification on a federal or confederal basis into the treaty on the European Defence Community. The study of such a political superstructure was started before the EDC treaty itself had been ratified. The draft for a European federal Constitution was completed by the Ad Hoc Assembly in March 1953, but its acceptance by the governments became most uncertain because on the one hand the ratification of EDC by France became more and more dubious and the Benelux demand for previous agreement on the gradual realisation of an economic union on the other seemed too great a commitment to the other participants. The French rejection of EDC brought about a re-arrangement of Germany's participation in Western defence and the deceit of the institutional approach of European unification. This track had proven to be impassable. Governments and non-federalist organisations turned after considerable unrest to a strategy of building common interests by way of economic integration. To this end the European Economic Community was established.

And what about the American Constitution in this postwar episode? Regarding the Constitution as such I can be short. Supporters of federal unification regarded the American Constitution as a good example of a democratic federal system, which with minor changes could be applied to Europe. To other supporters the direct incorporation of the American political and economic system in Western Europe was less obvious, although they recognised that many lessons from the American practice could be learned. In general, the American system influenced European unification only indirectly. The mixture of global and regional approach to the solution of European economic problems make it very difficult to indicate if and how the American example worked out in the European scene. Furthermore, the economic and military dependence of Western Europe from the United States had changed the focus.

REFERENCES

1. C.H. Pegg, *Evolution of the European Idea, 1914-1932*, Chapel Hill-London, 1983, p. 17.

2. D.N. Heineman, *Outline of a New Europe*, Brussels, 1931.

3. W. Weidenfeld, "Gustav Stresemann. Der Mythos vom engagierten Europäer" in: *Geschichte in Wissenschaft und Unterricht*, vol. 24, 1973, pp. 740-750.

4. J. Hermans, *l'Evolution de la pensée européenne d'Aristide Briand*, Nancy 1965. Pegg, op. cit., pp. 140-148.

5. On Coudenhove-Kalergi's promotion of the *Paneuropa* movement cf. Pegg, op. cit., p. 29-39.

6. Pegg, op. cit., pp. 58-67 and 80-95.

7. Pegg, op. cit., pp. 193-215 provides an extensive survey.

8. W. Lipgens, *Die Anfänge der europäischen Einigungspolitik. 1945-1950. Erster Teil: 1945-1947*, Stuttgart, 1977, pp. 43-80.

9. A. Van Dormael, Bretton Woods. Birth of a Monetary System, London, 1978.

10. A.S. Milward, *The Reconstruction of Western Europe, 1945-1951*, London, 1984, chapter 1.

11. S.C. Tiwari, *Genesis of the United Nations. A study of the*

Development of the Policy of the USA in respect of the establishment of a general international organization, Varanasi, 1968.

12. W. Lipgens, *Europa-Föderationspläne der Widerstandsbewegungen 1940-1945. Eine Dokumentation,* München, 1968, pp. 451-543.

13. A.E. Kersten, "Nederlands-Belgische betrekkingen in ballingschap" in: *Colloquium over de geschiedenis van de Belgisch-Nederlandse betrekkingen tussen 1815 en 1945. Acta,* Gent, 1982, pp. 503-516.

14. Lipgens, *Europa-Föderationspläne,* pp. 1-26.

15. Lipgens, *Europa-Föderationspläne,* pp. 393-398.

16. W. Lipgens, ed., *Documents on the History of European Integration. Vol. 2: Plans for European Union in Great Britain and in Exile 1939-1945* (Berlin-New York, 1986), pp. 23-26.

17. Lipgens, *Documents,* pp. 26-34.

18. Lipgens, *Documents,* pp. 113-118.

19. Lipgens, *Documents,* pp. 174-181.

20. On the origins of the Council of Europe M.T. Bitsch, "Le rôle de la France dans la naissance du Conseil de l'Europe" in: R. Poidevin, réd, *Histoire des débuts de la construction européenne 1948-1950,* Bruxelles Milano Paris Baden Baden, 1986, pp. 165-198.

21. H.P. Schwartz, *Konrad Adenauer. Ein Leben,* München, 1987.

22. Milward, op. cit.

23. P. Melandri, *Les Etats-Unies face à l'unification de l'Europe 1945-1954,* Paris, 1980, gives a detailed record of the public American support.

12. THE HUMAN RIGHTS TRADITION IN THE UNITED STATES

Rob Kroes, University of Amsterdam

I. Introduction: Individualism and Civil Rights

There have been recent trends in the historiography of the early American Republic which make a case for intellectual traditions other than Lockean thought and Puritanism as influences upon the generation of the Founding Fathers. The English Whig tradition, the Scottish enlightenment, the Macchiavellian view as transmitted through Montesquieu, have all been suggested as providing an intellectual context to the extreme individualism of the Lockean and Puritan world views. The latter views indeed stressed man as a self-contained entity, fully cognisant of his individual interests, and centrally motivated by them in his social action. Locke saw him as conceptually separate from society, if not actually predating it. The Puritans too saw him in isolation, directly confronting divine scrutiny.

Despite the recent attempts at redrawing the intellectual world of the Founding Fathers, we can safely say that it is still the accepted view that indeed their political thinking as well as the classical texts to which it gave rise - the Declaration of Independence and the Constitution, including the Bill of Rights - are imbued with the spirit of individualism.[1] It was the spirit of the time.

Or was it? Strictly speaking, if we use the word individualism, we are projecting a view which did not receive its critical coinage until later. Individualism is essentially a Romantic concept, in either the heroic version that Burckhardt gave it, or its more pessimistic Tocquevillean version. Much as the intellectual generation of the Founding Fathers centred their attention on individual man and his pursuit of his rational interests, they always saw him acting in a social context. The thought of men like James Madison, Alexander Hamilton, John Adams and Thomas Jefferson, always critically hinged on the relation between individual liberty and the preservation of the republic. If we look at it this way, we can see more clearly the role played by classical political philosophy and its emphasis on collective political life in a republic. Thus, if we look beyond the Lockean opening statement of inalienable rights in the Declaration of Independence, and go over its list of specific grievances, we enter an intellectual world that is reminiscent of late mediaeval and early modern political thought on the right to resist tyrants. Much as that other remarkable declaration of independence, the Dutch Act of Abjuration two centuries earlier, the American document appeals to local freedoms that were all corporate in character rather than individual. And indeed, some of the vaunted rights guaranteed in the first ten amendments to the Constitution, are not individual in any Lockean sense at all. They are more exactly social freedoms, like the freedom of religion or the freedom of assembly. They are organisational guarantees, more on the level of ordered public life than on any individual level conceived as outside politics or society. Also, whatever their specific thrust, the first ten as much as the later amendments are relational in nature. They all define rights and freedoms within an institutional context. They do not so much define the rights and freedoms in any abstract sense, as worthy causes put to paper, but rather they define them within a Republican context providing the instruments for their protection. They cannot be fully understood unless we bring to bear the weight of political reflection on issues such as the separation of powers, or the institution of a Supreme Court as the pinnacle of an independent judiciary. Such concerns for the pluralisation of political power, or, as in Madison's case, for the pluralisation of organised interests in society, were all the expression of one more central concern: how to prevent their newly established republican order from sliding back into despotism. If there is a continued focus on the individual, it is in his role as citizen within the institutional context of a Republic.

Yet what makes the United States a separate case in the history and development of human rights, on both the levels of thought and implementation, is the longevity of the individualist frame of mind in American society. Until the present day, the American Supreme Court, as the supreme guardian of the civil rights of the American people, in its decisions testifies to this individualist outlook. It may in fact have become more radically individualist over the years. Where individuals, in the parlance of the Founding Fathers, were conceived in their role as citizens, participating in the body politic on an equal footing, they were at the same time seen in their corporate nature, as heads of households, representing the corporate bodies of individual families, and as owners of property, representing, as Marcus Cunliffe has put it, a propertarian view of socio-political stability.[2] With the famous re-apportionment cases of the 1960s, affirming the radical egalitarianism of the one man, one vote principle, the Court has moved toward a more drastically atomistic view of individualism.

If that is one line of legal and political thought in the US, there are others which have rather tended to move human rights conceptions away from their initial individualist, civil rights cast. Woodrow Wilson, in his universalist ideas of the right of national self-determination, transposed traditional individualist ideas of civic equality onto the world stage of individual nations, thus providing nationalist and anti-colonialist stirrings in the world with a powerful vocabulary. Later, Franklin Roosevelt, with his proposed Bill of Social and Economic Rights, outlined ideas which later were integrated into such internationally approved texts as the Universal Declaration of Human Rights.

Domestically, though, such ideas never acquired a legal status on a par with the entrenched civil rights texts. Despite the inherent individualism of these texts, however, they have proved remarkably flexible, capable of development not only toward more radically individualist extremes. Also, they have been made to apply to the radically transformed matrix of social inequality of modern industrial society, sustaining legal opinion as it pertains to the rights of collectivities. As we shall argue more at length, the area of race relations and discrimination has offered strategic ground for the development of civil rights thought in more collectivist directions, applying to group relations rather than relations among separate individuals.

II. Civil Rights - The American Way

The American Declaration of Independence of 1776 invoked a number of truths, held to be self-evident: "That all men are created equal; that they are endowed by their Creator with certain inalienable rights; that among these are life, liberty and the pursuit of happiness; that, to secure these rights, governments are instituted among men, deriving their just powers from the consent of the governed ...". Moving beyond earlier appeals to the British mother country which had all been cast in terms of the rights of Englishmen, it chose to conceive of the American separation from England in the light of universal rights. Some fifteen years later, when Americans had reached agreement on the constitutional arrangements for their republic, they decided to add to their new Constitution of 1787 a list of amendments which is commonly known as the Bill of Rights. Although in one sense the latest outcome of a line of development dating back all the way to the Magna Charta, it was at the same time a highly contemporary document, equally expressive of the spirit of the time as the French revolutionary Declaration of the Rights of Man. As such it is one of the classic versions of early views of human rights, centering on the individual in his political role as citizen.

176

In that sense they are truly *civil* rights. On the one hand they guarantee freedoms: they outline spheres of freedom of the individual citizen outside the reach of government, but within society, such as the freedom of speech and of religion. But on the other hand they also set standards of procedure in those cases where government does affect the life of the individual citizen in order to avoid arbitrariness. In the latter case equality rather than freedom is the guiding principle. Individual equality before the law, the equal protection of the law vis-à-vis every individual citizen, serve as the basic guidelines for government action. Both kinds of rights, the classic freedoms as much as the rights safeguarding equality, aim at protecting the citizen from potential misuse of government power. Yet at the same time the protection of equality vests a high purpose precisely in government, assigning to it the duty to make sure that in fact the protection of the law extend equally to all individual citizens.

For about two centuries now these classic civil rights have served as a guideline to political life in the United States. Their precise sense and meaning have changed through the years, later texts have been added, but all in all there has been a remarkable continuity in the sense of an unbroken line of growth and development. Yet, paradoxically, it has been growth in two, rather contradictory, directions, one increasingly individualist, the other ever more collectivist.

The question as to what the Constitution actually means in any given case can be answered only by giving an opinion as to what it means. And in the United States the operative opinion is that of the Supreme Court, or a majority of it. The opinions are given at such remote distances of time and circumstance from the original text that they depend on inference, coloured as a rule by the reigning world views of a later age. On occasion, however, the Court feels bound to expound on first principles, as happened when the problem of legislative apportionment arose, beginning with *Baker v. Carr* in 1962. Two years later, in *Reynolds v. Sims*, Chief Justice Earl Warren found occasion for a definitive pronouncement of constitutional principle: "Legislators represent people, not trees or acres. Legislators are elected by voters, not farms or cities or economic interests." It had been argued that certain interests deserved to be given special consideration in the electoral system; to this the Chief Justice replied that it was "inconceivable that a State law to the effect that, in counting votes for legislators, the votes for citizens in one part of the State would be multiplied by two, or five, or ten, while votes for other persons in another area would be counted only at face value, could be constitutionally sustainable."

These decisions were fundamental, in the literal sense. They aimed at restoring the American system of government to its foundations. They put into effect a doctrine well understood by the generation of the Founders, that a Republic must return periodically to its founding principles in order to survive - a wisdom as old as Aristotelian thought and transmitted through Machiavelli's wellknown injunction to the Italian Republics to "redurre ai principii". Yet, ironically, Chief Justice Warren, in going back to first principles, at the same time put his own construction on them, casting their implied individualism in a far more radically atomising light. Where political thought in the early years of the Republic had conceived of individual voters as representative of larger corporate entities, such as families, and landed estates comprising those living on them, which together constituted the body politic, the Supreme Court in the 1960s chose to see individual voters as purely representing their own individual interests. Individual voters therefore should be conceived as politically equivalent, entitled to the Court's protection of their equal right to the vote, that is to say of their right to an equal representation of their individual interests.

This recent interpretation is only one outcome of a line of development which tended to take the legal view of relations in society to ever greater lengths of individualism, shedding what corporatist notions may have been implied in earlier views. Thus, during an earlier stage of individualist reconstruction, in the latter part of the 19th century, the novel phenomenon of the industrial corporation, rather than being conceived along more traditional lines as entrusted "by the Publick" with productive functions on behalf of the common weal, came to be defined as purely private property, or more radically still as a private actor, entitled to the full protection of their rights as individual entities. Of course, the ideological implications here vary widely from those inspiring Warren Burger's view of the individual voter. Yet both are equally illustrative of the atomising logic which in the earlier views of civil liberties and equality of the Founding Fathers had still been submerged.

But, as we said, a second line of development is discernable, leading in the opposite direction of a greater awareness of corporate bodies, or at least aggregate categories, as relevant to legal thought and political reflection. Here again it can be said that later developments have a conceptual link to earlier political thought. We have already pointed to the implied corporate view of the individual voter. A telling case in point is the original version of Article I, Section II, of the Constitution apportioning representatives among the various states according to their respective numbers, "which shall be determined by adding to the whole number of free persons ... three fifths of all other persons". It is the famous compromise formula, aimed at

178

giving the slave-holding states added political weight at the federal level by granting their free "electors" a weighted vote. From its inception the Republic of the Free and the Equal has been aware of inequality in its midst, allowing in its legal language for the existence of different categories among its inhabitants. It has always been a source of creative tension, giving rise to a line of legal and political thought quite separate from the heritage of individualism.

Perhaps it is putting it a little too strongly if we use the metaphor of a line of thought, suggesting unbroken continuity. After all, it took the cataclysm of a Civil War before the American public came to see the existence of distinct and unequal categories of inhabitants on American soil in the light of the inspiring creed of liberties and equality. What happened in the adoption of the famous Civil War Amendments to the Constitution was precisely this: the extension of the protection of the initial Civil Rights Amendments, as a high Federal calling, to the entire category of newly freed American blacks. Also, in addition to extending this protection to a whole category of citizens, they widened the Federal reach, explicitly denying to the individual states the right to make laws abridging the constitutional rights of citizens of the United States. Thus the onslaught on entrenched social inequality was doubly corporatist: not only did it apply to the entire body of black citizens, it also directly affected the corporate balance of the federation and the states. The problem of the equal protection of citizens of a different race has ever since remained the responsibility of the federal government. In due course other patterns of group inequalities in society have been deemed equally deserving of government action: inequalities based on national origin, religion, sex. Changes in the climate of opinion in society-at-large have always played their part in this gradual extension of the federal role in the area of group inequalities. We shall have the occasion later on to look at some of the more recent developments in this area. But first I propose to have a closer look at these American trends in the application of civil rights from a comparative perspective.

III. Civil Rights and the international Human Rights debate

In our century, with its clashing ideological systems, it has not been uncommon to be somewhat disparaging of human rights in their classic version of civil rights. People have tended to slight them as merely old hat, representative of an age of individualism which could no longer speak to the modern world with its complex patterns of social differentiation. Others have tended to see them as merely formal rights, unable ever to affect the substance of social inequality. In the eyes of radical anti-liberals they were the mere class privileges of an entrenched bourgeoisie. Both reproaches - of the individualism and of the formalism of classic civil rights - ignore, or are at best unaware of the American civil rights history. Given the context of strife for ideological primacy, it is small wonder that many of these slights tended to come from the Communist world or their sympathisers. Against the classic Civil Rights, boasted by the so-called "Free World", the Soviet Union tended to field its brand of Social and Economic Rights which it allegedly had secured for its citizens.

Such arrogation of a guardianship in the area of what became known as second-generation human rights is not quite sustained by historical fact. As it is, the United States have been among the leading contributors to international thought on the evolution of human rights. President Woodrow Wilson's concepts of a universal world order had not only intended to incorporate the classic civil rights into a body of international law, also, in his ideas concerning the right to self-determination of nations, he had expanded the sphere of individual rights to apply to separate national actors on the international stage. And in 1941 President Franklin D. Roosevelt, proclaiming his "Four Freedoms", would link together such classical liberties as freedom of speech and freedom of worship with more recent conceptions of social rights, such as freedom from want. What he had in mind, were "economic understandings which will secure to every nation a healthy peacetime life for its inhabitants". Ideas like these, later on supplemented by Roosevelt's "Economic Bill of Rights" of 1944, soon developed into a more coherent view of social and economic rights which as a second generation of human rights would add to the classic first generation, not to replace them, but in a happy symbiosis.

When, later on in 1948, the General Assembly of the United Nations voted to adopt the "Universal Declaration of the Rights of Man", both generations were incorporated in the text. This was partly a political compromise, the outcome of pressure on the part of such members as tended to withhold the protection of classic civil rights from their citizenry, but not only so. The Universal Declaration was fully as expressive of changing views in the United States as well.

More recently, in United Nations circles, a debate has been gathering momentum, inspired this time by a number of Third World countries, as to the need for yet a third generation of human rights, to do with the rights of nations. Proposals are proffered concerning the rights of nations to economic development, to peace, to a healthy natural environment, to the sole authority over their natural re-

180

sources, and finally their rights to the common cultural heritage of mankind.

Of course these are all worthy causes and concerns. But one cannot suppress a feeling of witnessing a forward flight, where so much remains to be done in the area of first-generation human rights in so many regions and countries of the world. There are those reproachfully reminding us that emphasising those classic rights is in fact a case of cultural imperialism, of imposing Western values on countries whose national ways and traditions are not receptive to them. Rather surprisingly, out of a misguided sense of cultural relativism, this very point is sometimes made their own by leading thinkers in the West.[3] But in fact such a humble renunciation of Western arrogance is merely Western arrogance in a different guise, resting on the tacit assumption that the protection of individual human rights is something solely for the West to conceive and enjoy.

The current discussion concerning second and third generations of human rights, interesting as it is, cannot do without a thorough understanding of the way the classic first generation has developed, of the high and demanding mission which it assigns to contemporary national governments as well as to the international community, in a universalist view rather than the disparaging one of tepid cultural relativism.

If the United States is taken as a case that might help us to explore these more general issues, two points at least deserve further discussion, both to do precisely with the question as to why and how the classic civil rights have retained their monopoly hold on the American human rights scene, despite that country's important contribution to international human rights ideas. We shall have to ask ourselves why it is that the United States, a cosignatory to many international human rights treaties, has been slow to ratify them and make them into national law. We shall also have to see what equivalent law, if any, has developed in the United States in the absence of texts reflecting present-day international human rights views.

IV. International Human Rights Treaties and American Law

At best, the United States has been tardy ratifying international human rights treaties. Only in 1986 did the American Senate give its consent to the ratification of the Treaty concerning the prevention and punishment of Genocide, a full 35 years since it became international law. Obvious political reasons, such as the fear of finding itself in the dock on account of racial segregation in the South or, later, the Vietnam War, had kept America from ratification at an earlier date. But there seems to be a further, more general reason for America's tardiness in this respect. In the case of the Genocide Treaty as well as that of other recent cases which have reached the Senate floor, awaiting its consent, there has been a recurrent pattern of "reservations, declarations, understandings" being added to the treaty texts. Thus one of the main reservations added to the Genocide Treaty stipulates that the American Constitution as interpreted by the United States will be superordinate to the Treaty. A reservation of similar portent, preventing treaty articles which individual citizens could use as legal ground in litigation from becoming "self-executing", requires prior national legislation. A general reservation, finally, added to all treaty texts, stipulates that all obligations entered into under the treaty will be binding upon the Federal government only. Here's the rub, it seems. Irrespective of whether or not an international treaty in so many words extends its reach into the component parts of a federal state - and some do - the prevailing fear among the many political and legal opponents to the ratification of international human rights treaties seems to lie in their alleged breach of federal arrangements as codified in the Constitution.

Yet what legal ground do these people have for their opposition? The Constitution itself quite clearly vests the treaty-making powers in what has sometimes been called a fourth branch of government - the president plus two thirds of the Senate. Quite logically so, it seems, combining as it does the chief executive with the federal chamber, representing the separate states. For a while, though, it appeared as if the tenth amendment, reserving to the states those powers not granted to the federal government, could offer a way out. Through its ratification of treaties, some argued, the federal government could not gain powers over the states without their consent. As early as 1920, however, in Missouri v. Holland, the Supreme Court decided that "Valid treaties of course are as binding within the territorial limits of the states as they are elsewhere throughout the dominion of the United States". The treaty in this case concerned the protection of migratory birds, trekking across the international border with Canada, and threatened with extinction. If their protection was considered a matter of national interest, transcending the autonomy of the individual states, why then is the protection of human rights through international treaties still so much the object of trepidation?

Within the United States, in the area of the protection of rights and liberties, the whole drift has been toward an ever greater role for the federal government. Ever since the incorporation of the classic guarantees of "due process of law" into the Fourteenth

Amendment, the federal government has had a supervisory role, especially in such areas as penal law and criminal procedures, which before had been left to the sole authority of the single states. There was nothing automatic about this extension of reach, though. It has taken many Supreme Court decisions, especially during the 1960s and '70s, for the full implications of the Fourteenth Amendment to take effect.[4]

Arguably the single most important legal ground for the extension of the federal sway over the separate states, in widely varied areas including human rights, has been the Constitution's Interstate Commerce Clause - "The Congress shall have power ... to regulate commerce among several states". Thus the anti-discrimination sections of the Civil Rights Act of 1964 were upheld by the Supreme Court on the basis of the Commerce Clause. As Justice Clark, writing for the Court, put it,[5] federal law should be deemed duly applicable if the activity it meant to regulate "affected commerce which concerns more states than one and has a real and substantial relation to the national interest". A criterion as elastic as "affecting commerce" leaves few areas of state authority immune to federal intervention.

And yet, in 1978, when President Carter asked senatorial consent for four international Human Rights Treaties, he made the following reservation in his accompanying letter of transmittal: "The United States shall implement all the provisions of the convention over whose subject matter the Federal Government exercises legislative and judicial administration; with respect to the provisions over whose subject matter constituent units exercise jurisdiction, the Federal Government shall take appropriate measures, to the end that the component authorities of the constituent units may take appropriate measures for the fulfillment of the Convenant." Once again a "federal/state reservation" was made, despite the drastic changes which the federal/state relation had undergone. It is no longer conceivably a strong legal case. Apparently, then, it is still considered a strong political argument, meant to accommodate oppositional sentiment in the Senate and in the country at large.

V. Second Generation Rights - the American equivalent

Among the International Human Rights Treaties, still pending in the Senate, is one concerning "Economic, Cultural and Social Rights". It is not yet incorporated into the body of American Law, nor is any equivalent text. Unlike the Dutch Constitution, for example, which in its latest version enumerates social rights alongside the classic civil rights, the American Constitution is still squarely within the classic civil rights tradition. Yet, as we have shown, from the beginning this tradition has been informed by both individualist views of society and by corporatist conceptions. Following the Civil War a body of law and jurisprudence has grown which in a sense has merged the two. It has gradually extended civil rights views and ideas concerning equal protection as a government responsibility to apply to entrenched patterns of inequality in society. This trend has undergone a quantum leap since the 1950s, when following the watershed decision of the Supreme Court in *Brown v. Board of Education* a period of sustained judicial, legislative and executive activism set in in a massive onslaught on patterns of discrimination in society. Racial discrimination was the initial focus of attention. Later on, discrimination in general, in relations between the sexes, in relations between the sexes, became the overriding interest. Social inequality, seen as the outcome of a history of patterned discrimination, became the central yardstick for a government policy, sustained by the judicial branch, of socalled "affirmative action". Across a wide range of social areas, housing, education, employment, career patterns, government provided guidelines aimed at restoring a proper balance, or mix, of races, ethnicities, sexes. Government intervened in its own sphere as much as beyond, touching a great many areas of social activity. All this it did in its role as final guarantor of the "equal protection of the law".

If we look at this history of governmental remedial intervention in the area of group inequalities, it is clear that in fact, on the basis of time-hallowed ideas concerning liberties and equality, human rights policies in the United States have undergone a dramatic change. From their initial individualist mould they have evolved to apply to complex processes of group interaction and social inequality. The intricate balance of liberties and equality (or should we say: versus equality?) has shifted toward equality, at the price of restricting liberties. Through affirmative action it bindingly imposes courses of action which, in freedom, people might not have chosen to take.

The change, dramatic and drastic as it has been, roughly coinciding in time with America's somewhat belated introduction of large-scale welfare-state programmes, has not gone unnoticed. In fact, a highly vocal opposition has emerged which rejects the affirmative action approach precisely on account of its alleged infringement upon the time-hallowed individualist cast of egalitarian thought in the United States.[6] And, in fact, many of those who challenge affirmative-action decisions in court, base their case on precisely those equal protection clauses that have undergirded the affirmative action approach itself. It makes for an intriguing creative tension, within a shared universe of legal discourse, which continually affects the precise balance between liberty and equality.

184

But does all this mean that in America the classic human rights have evolved to function as an equivalent of what in other parts of the world goes by the name of social rights? Some people would say no, on purely formal grounds. Classic civil rights, according to them, are negative; they proscribe actions, especially on the part of government, rather than prescribing them. Social rights are positive, in the sense that government should act toward certain social and economic goals. There is some truth in this rejoinder. If discrimination is taken to be the key operative term in the American case of affirmative action, government in the final analysis is still acting to protect individual human rights, ordering people to desist and refrain from discriminating against individuals.

But the American government does more. As we have said before, its responsibility for the equal protection of the law has always assigned it a positive duty, but it can take it in several ways. The history of the last thirty years has shown it in positive pursuit of the social goal of eradicating the outcomes of a long history of discrimination, in a number of different areas of social life. It is acting in fact as any government should, once it has the positive goals of social rights assigned to it. The irony is that more often than not a Bill of Social Rights remains a dead letter, whereas, in the absence of such a Bill, the American government is in active pursuit of the high goal of social equality.

VI. America and the Welfare State

The foregoing analysis, looking at the way in which legal thought in the United States has developed in response to contemporary views of social problems and social policy, has in a sense been taking an inside view. It has borrowed the language and perspective of a society which more strongly than any European country is legalistic in its approach to problems of social policy. In that sense the analysis may have been overly formal, and insufficiently sociological. Yet, as a general point, it is my view that one cannot begin to grasp the world of historical experience of a country like the United States without playing the role of a vicarious insider.

Yet there are those who, on the basis of comparative views of contemporary welfare states, are inclined to disparage such trends in civil rights thinking as we have been exploring. To them, what is striking about America's record in the area of social policies, is its underdevelopment as a welfare state. There are many glaring cases of poverty and injustice outside the protective reach of welfare state programmes. On a number of indicators of social health and welfare the United States lags behind countries in Europe. Yet one should try to see this in perspective.

One way to conceive of the welfare state is by referring to government practices of allocating a certain percentage of the gross national product to welfare. The definition of welfare includes all public expenditures for health, education, income maintenance, deferred income and funds for community development, including housing allocations. In one area - education - the United States has long been leading Europe in the expansion and democratisation of its public education system. In other areas, though, on a comparative cross-national basis, the United States has expanded its welfare expenditures more slowly than major Western European nations. But the gap has been closing. By 1970, welfare expenditures in the Federal Republic of West Germany had reached 19.5 percent of the gross national product, in France, 20.9 percent, while the comparable figure for the United States was 15.3 percent, reaching 18.5 percent by 1979. By the latter year social welfare costs consumed 55.0 percent of the federal government's budget and 56.8 percent of outlays at all government levels.[7] A huge government bureaucracy has arisen to administer the various welfare programmes. Its cost is technically an overhead of the welfare system and should be taken into account if we want to assess the over-all share of the gross national product taken up by the system. Much of the growth of this area of government is fairly recent and can be dated back to the Kennedy-Johnson years. It is a development which coincides in time with the emergence of affirmative-action programmes. The latter can in fact be seen as a non-pecuniary variant of essentially the same interventionist conception of the contemporary state. The state, in this view, is the natural vehicle for collective action, expressing society's sense of solidarity in programmes meant to assist individuals in realising their personal goals, their dignity, and their self-esteem.

It is quite remarkable that such a view of the role of the state has sunk roots at all in the United States. Ever since the advent of the nation state in Europe, there the state has always been seen as the natural instrument for the realisation of collective aspirations, whatever their object, be it national aggrandisement through war, or the establishment of justice through social welfare. In the United States, on the other hand, the natural avenue for collective action has long been the voluntary association rather than the state. Not until the Progressive Era, and more particularly the mobilisation of collective energy by the state in World War I, did activists, reformers and intellectuals begin to consider the state as an instrument for positive collective action. Yet it took another fifteen years, under the impact of the Great Depression and Roosevelt's New Deal, for the

186

modern state to develop on American soil. Where, according to European standards, the state had virtually been non-existent as late as the nineteen twenties, a total transformation of the political stage had taken place by the end of thirties. The New Deal in fact is the first sustained manifestation of state activism in response to pressing social problems. Yet the change of mind implied here did not come overnight. The enactment of the Social Security Act of 1935, e.g., the first of its kind in the United States, had organised labour playing only a limited role, due mainly to labour's ambivalence about the benefits of a national welfare system.[8] Thus, interestingly, one of the organised interests in society that one normally would have expected among the main proponents and supporters of the idea of social security, stood aloof due to its entrenched aversion towards government interference.

The New Deal, then, followed by World War II, have made America safe for the welfare state idea. Both were crises that have formed the critical threshold periods for the idea to be adopted. Trends in intellectual life concerning the essential manipulability of the social system, like, e.g., the idea of social engineering among social scientists, or Keynesianism in economics, have further tended to confirm the newly-found role of the modern state.

During the seventies, at the time of its fastest expansion, the welfare state has come under attack, both in Europe and in the United States. Attempts at checking its growth, or even at curtailing its reach, have been relatively unsuccessful. Many of its entitlement programmes have proved politically sacrosanct. Much of the growth in expenditure is self-generating, due to indexing and the increase in the number of duly entitled recipients. The only retrenchment in the United States during the Reagan administration has been in the means-tested programmes for the most needy. The share of such programmes has gone down from 22 percent to 17 percent of all federal welfare expenditures.[9]

VII. The right to a cultural identity

So far we have been exploring human rights traditions in the United States. Compared to Europe, the United States offers a special variant in the way in which human rights conceptions have been operative throughout its history. We propose to explore one final area where again there are telling differences between Europe and the United States, the area of the rights of minorities to their own cultural identity. In a fairly recent development, in the West as much as elsewhere, regional and other cultural minorities have been trying to promote their case for cultural autonomy by presenting it as a human rights problem. In their view it is clearly a case of a collective right, adhering to groups rather than individuals, not unlike the right to self-determination. Generally speaking, theirs is only one specific instance of the wider problem of the tyranny of a majority, a topic equally urgent to Madison and Tocqueville. Yet the country of Madison has handled problems of cultural diversity differently than the European world that Tocqueville addressed.

Where Europe went the way of the independent nation state, each of them harbouring one or more national minorities in its midst, the United States, quintessentially an immigrant nation, can be seen as a multi-nation state. Its national minorities are the defining characteristic of its national identity. Seeking unity in diversity, it has always had to walk the tightrope between a narrow and oppressive Americanism and a more cosmopolitan and diverse sense of itself. Vigilant nativism has always served to keep a centrifugal cultural pluralism in check. Ironically, wave after wave of immigrants have willingly undergone this pressure towards their Americanisation. More often than not, they experienced it as a rite of passage, an emancipation if not a regeneration, in which they willingly traded in their ascribed cultural identity of their country of origin for the newly achieved status of Americans. In spite of the outside pressure exerted upon them, their Americanisation characteristically was an act of individual voluntarism. What pressure there was, was hardly ever of a totalitarian kind, working toward total assimilation in every sphere of life. On the whole, the same spirit that had informed the constitutional view of spheres of life beyond the reach of politics and public life, was evident here. If Americans should be free in their religious life or in their choice of voluntary associations to arrange their social life, they should be equally free in their homes, neighbourhoods, their press and social organisations, to use any national language or to keep any national cultural tradition alive. Only in those spheres which were commonly deemed to constitute the public life of the Republic, national standards were uncompromisingly enforced. In education and politics the language should be English, in politics the guiding ideas should be American, not "un-American". Over time the combined impact of these freedoms and pressures have produced a remarkable amalgam of a vigorous sense of nationhood and of ethnicity.

In recent years there have been some developments which are of particular interest to our discussion of the alleged collective rights to a cultural identity. In many quarters we have been witnessing a militant reassertion of ethnic identity, accompanied by a search for the recreation of separate cultural histories as distinct from the dominant history of "the American people". Various factors have been at work. For one thing the cultural revolution of the sixties, stressing the quest for cultural identity and self-fulfilment, has made for greater cultural relativism. It may have been a case of third-generation immigrant children reclaiming an ethnic heritage which their parents and grand-parents had neglected. Also the policy of affirmative action, aimed at bringing the victims of discrimination within the mainstream of American life, has caused the defensive rally of other groups in society around themes of ethnicity. There is a paradox involved here. For much as ethnic groups may have seen their entrenched collective positions in society threatened by the onslaught of positive discrimination, their defence was cast in the language of individual rights. What they protested against was the alleged "un-Americanism" of a government policy that seeks to establish equality among groups rather than among individuals. As one of the leading polemicists, Nathan Glazer, once put it: "Those who in the 1960s thought equality demanded that no person be required to give his race or ethnic group in applications for admission to schools and employment now think that it is essential, in order to achieve equality, that every person be required to do so. Troubling and difficult questions have been raised as government, to achieve a greater equality, begins itself to impose limits on the dreams and aspirations of individuals on the basis of their race or ethnic group."[10]

Clearly, the assertion of group cultural identities has posed dilemmas which are quintessentially American. Old debates about the defining characteristics of a common American nationhood have resurfaced. Most patently in the case of an ethnic group which may have proved most resistant to forces of Americanisation: the SpanishAmericans. Given the shift toward greater cultural relativism, given also the official affirmative support to the reassertion of group cultural identities, bilingualism has been on the march in public education as well as more generally in the area of public communication. But the trend has not remained unopposed. In 1984 California voted in favour of a proposition establishing English as the sole official language. Never before had the affirmation of the common core of a national political culture been sought through legal codification.[11]

Similar trends towards cultural relativism in intellectual life have occurred in academic curricula. If America is truly a nation of nations, some are of the opinion that there is little point in neglecting their varied contributions to world culture, universally conceived. Thus, at universities across the country, the Great Classics are no longer selected according to their contribution to Western culture, seen as a line of gestation culminating in America, but rather on the basis of a global catholicism. The dilemma this poses to a national culture like the American is evident. Cosmopolitanism as a value sees itself - as it has throughout American intellectual history - opposed once more to the value attached to a vibrant, vital core of a common national culture. The outcome is yet uncertain, and essentially for Americans to work out. Yet, to outside observers, the debate is of crucial relevance. If the United States, among contemporary nation states, is the one most truly representing a global melting pot, it is only the harbinger of trends which are in store for all of us in our global village.

REFERENCES

1.   John P. Diggins, *The Lost Soul of American Politics: Virtue, Self-Interest, and the Foundations of Liberalism.* New York: Basic Books, 1984. Jack R. Pole, "The Individualist Foundations of American Constitutionalism", (Unpublished Paper), 1987.

2.   The term propertarianism was coined by Marcus Cunliffe in a series of courses which he taught at George Washington University, Washington, D.C., in 1984/85. The gradual erosion of this initially corporate view of property, assuming more radically individualist contours over the years, is well documented by R. Jeffrey Lustig in his *Corporate Liberalism: The Origins of Modern American Political Theory, 1890-1920.* Berkeley: University of California Press, 1982.

3.   See, e.g. G.F. Kennan, *The Cloud of Danger: Current Realities of American Foreign Policy.* Boston, 1977, p. 43: "Those Americans who profess to know with such certainty what other people want and what is good for them in the way of political institutions, would do well to ask themselves whether they are not actually attempting to impose their own values, traditions, and habits of thought on peoples for whom these things have no validity and no usefulness." (Quoted in A.M. Schlesinger, Jr., *The Cycles of American History.* Boston: Houghton Mifflin Cy., 1986, p. 101).

4.   H.J. Abraham, *Freedom and the Court: Civil Rights and Liberties in the United States* (1967), New York: Oxford University Press, 1972; cf. Chapter IV.

5.   *Heart of Atlanta Motel, Inc., vs. U.S.,* 379 U.S. 241 (1964).

6.   The most vocal opponents are to be found in Jewish intellectual circles around *Commentary*. An early, angry blast is Nathan Glazer's *Affirmative Discrimination*. New York: Basic Books, 1976.

7.   For these figures, see A. Hacker, ed., *A Statistical Portrait of the American People*. New York: The Viking Press, 1983.

8.   J.S. Quadrango, "Welfare Capitalism and the Social Security Act of 1935", *American Sociological Review*, 49, 1984, pp. 632-647.

9.   Cf. J. Rivière, *Les Etats-Unis à l'horizon de la troisième révolution industrielle*. Nancy: Presses Universitaires de Nancy, 1986.

10. Nathan Glazer, "Individualism and equality in the United States", in: H.J. Gans, a.o., eds., *On the Making of Americans: Essays in Honor of David Riesman*. Philadelphia: University of Pennsylvania Press, 1979.

11. The initiative was sponsored by S.I. Hayakawa, socio-linguist and former U.S. Senator from California. Its adoption means the elimination of bilingual voting forms and bilingual education, among other things.